The School Choice Hoax

The School Choice Hoax

Fixing America's Schools

Ronald G. Corwin
E. Joseph Schneider

Foreword by James McPartland

Rowman & Littlefield Education
Lanham, Maryland • Toronto • Plymouth, UK
2007

Published in the United States of America
by Rowman & Littlefield Education
A Division of Rowman & Littlefield Publishers, Inc.
A wholly owned subsidiary of The Rowman & Littlefield Publishing Group, Inc.
4501 Forbes Boulevard, Suite 200, Lanham, Maryland 20706
www.rowmaneducation.com

Estover Road
Plymouth PL6 7PY
United Kingdom

British Library Cataloguing in Publication Information Available

Library of Congress Cataloging-in-Publication Data

Corwin, Ronald G.
  The school choice hoax : fixing America's schools / Ronald G. Corwin, E. Joseph Schneider ;
foreword by James McPartland. — 1st paperback ed.
    p. cm.
  Originally published : Westport, Conn. : Praeger. 2005.
  Includes bibliographical references and index.
  ISBN-13: 978-1-57886-586-4 (pbk. : alk. paper)
  ISBN-10: 1-57886-586-7 (pbk. : alk. paper)
  1. School choice—United States. 2. Charter schools—United States. 3. Educational vouchers—
United States. I. Schneider, Joe. II. Title.
  LB1027.9.C69 2007
  379.1'110973—dc22   2007006442

  ⊖™ The paper used in this publication meets the minimum requirements of
American National Standard for Information Sciences—Permanence of
Paper for Printed Library Materials, ANSI/NISO Z39.48-1992.
Manufactured in the United States of America.

Contents

Foreword

I was surprised to find this book, *The School Choice Hoax: Fixing America's Schools*, close to home for me. My own university group has recently opened, and is operating a new small high school of choice under a contract with the local Baltimore public school system. The school is called the Baltimore Talent Development High School. Our experience has turned out to be a practical application of some of the ideas advocated in this book. The district had invited external proposals with the intention of contracting for some new public high schools of choice in high-poverty city locations, where school boundaries were very large or overcrowded, and where the existing schools had very low academic achievement. The district chose the particular new school location to give parents—both those who live close by and others from throughout the city—another choice. However, we were allowed to select the principal and teachers and to implement a comprehensive reform model, including a career academy structure and a new catch-up curriculum.

We are now negotiating with the district for another new partnership to reorganize an existing small high school that is struggling to serve its high-poverty students. These negotiations are leading to a proposal similar to a vision that the authors, Ronald Corwin and Joseph Schneider, advance in this book. They propose in great detail a network of specialized smaller schools (including charter schools) operating throughout a district and open to parental choice from across the city. The authors believe that choice schools should be part of school districts, not independent of them, which is consistent with our situation. The Baltimore school district will set the priority needs and location, but it is also eager to install promising innovations from qualified outsiders, to give parents and students another real choice within the district. While more hard evidence of success is surely needed over time in our case, I feel that I am living with a very positive example of school choice under a public school district plan which addresses critical needs of the kind of low-achieving, high-poverty students the authors are concerned about in this book. My experience confirms the utility of this book's main policy recommendation, namely to create specialized charter schools and other schools designed to meet the special needs of all kinds of students.

Corwin and Schneider recommend that choice schools should not select out students who attend, and in the Baltimore Talent Development High School we do not screen students. At the same time, we must meet the demanding learning goals of the district. The staff we selected had already been employed by the district, but as we predicted, they are clearly turned on by the prospect of a new school where they can be involved with an innovative curriculum. The first class of 150 ninth graders who chose our school were mostly far below grade level in core subjects, but they now appear to be very positively engaged with their new school and their class work. Daily attendance is in the mid-ninety percent range. The same students had averaged ten or more points lower in middle grades, and there is a palpable school climate of academic seriousness and excitement.

My practical experience with school choice has helped me appreciate *The School Choice Hoax*. I believe that the book can be read with great profit on three different levels that together add up to a strong original proposal to revitalize school reform in this country. First, detailed policy analyses lead to a strongly argued new direction for school choice within public school systems. The views expressed reflect each co-author's own experiences, expertise, and style, and will appeal to different audiences who are thinking deeply about improving American education. Second, the reader will find up-to-date frameworks and theories needed to explain how schools now operate and their prospects for future reform. Third, there is a critical review of available school choices, which will help readers weigh existing evidence related to district reform.

The authors review population trends showing that racial segregation has been increasing in America and tackle the problem of highly segregated schools. As they observe, those schools which enroll the most poor and minority students usually have the greatest difficulty attracting well-qualified educators, and they also often have the least attractive facilities. They propose that school districts should operate these schools as charters, which provide more leeway to give good teachers incentives to work in them. The book's culminating proposal is to embed charter schools, and the best of other school choice options, within public school systems under a local plan of specialized schools addressing different student needs.

We are also invited to consider what social science has taught about the pros and cons of bureaucratic structures, especially concerning the forces for and against innovation and change, and to think about school size as an organizational feature for personalizing the learning environment. To really close learning gaps, say the authors, reforms must be comprehensive. Not only are structural and organizational changes needed for a safe and serious school climate, but support is also necessary for teachers who want to try out instructional innovations designed to close student academic skill gaps and to encourage good use of their minds.

The authors' basic goal—to explain exactly how different policies and practices lead to the intended change, or not—is pursued throughout, as they weigh evidence concerning alternative explanations related to a variety of different types of school choice. In particular, the heated advocacy debates about vouchers and charters are joined here, but with an effort to separate ideology from the evidence. Also, new attention is given to the exaggerated initial claims about what charters and vouchers were expected to accomplish, and to the often overlooked variation among schools within a particular choice category. To understand where gains have and have not occurred, the authors stress the importance of looking at changes in achievement distributions, rather than dwelling on averages (means), as most studies do.

In addition to vouchers and charter schools, the book also reviews other approaches to school choice, including: open enrollment, school-based management, Coalition of Essential Schools, magnet schools, and smaller innovative schools in specific cities. Many readers will be impressed, as I am, with the authors' efforts to come to reasonable conclusions about actual impacts of different types of school choice on school climates, student growth, teacher efficacy, and the reform process throughout a district.

Anyone interested in how the real potential of school choice can be captured to solve the most serious problems of American schools will gain much from this book's serious and thorough sociology, and its evaluation and policy analyses on this topic. The authors' proposals are bold enough to deal with the most challenging issues of American schools, and imaginative enough to encourage the various camps of school reformers to ponder how different ideas can come together in new ways for positive political and practical impacts.

James McPartland
Center for the Social Organization of Schools
Johns Hopkins University

Preface

We have been closely following the school choice movement since 1992, when, along with Marcella R. Dianda, we embarked on a study of the 1994 California voucher initiative, the results of which were published in the *Phi Delta Kappan* and in a monograph titled *What a Voucher Could Buy*.[1] Our findings—that there were not enough private schools or projected openings in them to accommodate the potential demand—caught the attention of several professional groups and some news outlets, including the *Los Angeles Times*, *Orange County Register*, and *Sacramento Bee*.[2] About that time, California was launching its charter schools. We were dubious about vouchers, but hopeful for charters. Working with Dianda, we designed one of the first charter school studies in the nation, based on a survey returned by twenty-one sponsors and thirty-four schools that had been issued charters by the state. The results were published in May 1994 under the title, *Vision and Reality: A First-Year Look at California's Charter Schools*.[3] That study was followed a year later by *Freedom and Innovation in California's Charter Schools*, authored by Corwin and John Flaherty. During those early years, we remained steadfastly neutral, but also cautiously optimistic about the potentials of charter schools for expanding parents' choices.

By 1995, Schneider had the audacity to suggest to a meeting of the American Association of School Administrators that school administrators ought to take control of the fledging charter-school movement and make it part of the reform movement within the regular school system. Districts, he said, should create and operate their own charter schools. His words fell on deaf ears, however, and it would be years before savvy superintendents saw the virtues of using charter legislation to address the challenges inherent in district bureaucracies. Schneider went on to write and speak out against the spread of "cowboy charters" that were popping up in states that allowed anyone with an interest to create and operate a school for children. Meanwhile, Corwin and colleagues were reanalyzing their own charter-school data on parent contracts; and they were beginning to have serious reservations about actions by unregulated, renegade charter schools. In 1997 Corwin collaborated with Henry Becker and Kathryn Nakagawa on a paper adapted from the *Freedom and Innovation* volume and published in *Teachers College Record*, titled "Parent Involvement Contracts in California's Charter Schools: Strategy for Educational Improvement or Method of Exclusion?"[4]

We concluded that some schools were abusing their freedom, forcing parents to donate time to schools as a formal or informal condition for admission. Shortly after that, Amy Stuart Wells published a paper asking the provocative question, do charter schools meet expectations?[5] We thought about that. They clearly were not. More important, we realized that they could not meet expectations, because too much was being promised. And worse, the only choice they were giving parents was to leave the public school system for risky, sometimes financially unstable schools with unknown curricula and unpredictable futures. The public was being duped.

For reasons explained throughout the following chapters, we have concluded that independence for choice schools has been an unproductive dead end. We arrived at that position not from self-interest or ideology, but from years of research and observation. However, we have not given up on school choice. Far from it. Our goal now is to redirect the nation's attention from the misleading hard sell for existing forms of charter schools and school vouchers to the realities—the things that need to be fixed to make choice viable for all parents. The title and subtitle of this book reflect this dual mission—exposing the fallacies behind the choice movement and offering suggestions for improving the choice model itself. The main title describes an all-out attack on the phony ideologies, misleading assertions, and false hopes that are now driving the choice movement. Whether the product of misplaced idealism or an ideological ruse, the torrents of irresponsible half-truths can only mislead and disappoint many parents, educators, politicians, and taxpayers.

Chapter 2 hammers away at the frail and contradictory evidence precariously propping up the movement's shaky tenants—from empty boasts about student achievement, to a convoluted argument that pins hope for improving schools on damaging opposition, to the lame complaint that phantom bureaucracies have conspired to prevent reform in public schools. Endless bickering among proponents and opponents to school choice over the evidence has been fruitless, largely because the evidence comes from seriously misguided research models based on statistical averages. Americans are paying for the free-market ideology, not only with hundreds of fraudulent, marginal, and inept schools, but also in loss of control over their local tax dollars. Other chapters underscore the point that charters are not as exceptional as advertised. Not only might they arguably be skimming off some good students and some creative teachers, but also most charter schools are not doing much that is exceptional. And in any case, their most outstanding features already exist as alternatives in many public school districts in the form of specialized schools, magnets, school-based management, small schools, and a variety of other special programs.

Notwithstanding all of that, the subtitle expresses optimism about the potentials within choice models themselves, and in particular the charter-school model, based on our firm conviction that they are worth fixing. And, we have proposals for how to go about it.

Chapter 3 reviews several other alternative school-choice models that are already operating within the public sector. The main purpose of this chapter is to identify features in these models that would improve charter schools. The alternatives reviewed include open enrollment, small high schools, Boston's Pilot Schools, school-based management, and the Coalition of Essential Schools. While we readily acknowledge that these models all have flaws, we believe some approaches they are taking should be transplanted to the charter-school model. The models reviewed operate within public school districts, not outside of them—a feat that choice advocates don't mention when they cry that public school bureaucracies are immune to innovation.

Chapters 4 and 5 spell out proposals to permit school districts to plan, monitor, and even start and operate their own charters. We maintain that all choice schools must give back to the public school system by participating in networks of schools that strategically address specific types of identified district needs and challenges. In other words, every choice school should specialize in handling a challenging problem area where public school districts need help. Specialized schools would have the advantage of building on existing specialized schools and magnet schools.

In Chapter 5, we tackle in greater detail the fundamental task of improving poverty schools through charter schools created and operated by school districts. They should be located in every poverty neighborhood within a district and funded through special federal grants. Charters would give districts the flexibility needed to give teachers in low-income schools combat pay and to use other incentives in connection with training and recruiting teachers to work in poverty schools. We maintain that charters can be more useful and focused if they are operated by school districts, rather than under the existing cloak of independence, which creates more problems than it solves. True, some districts do not seem to care about children at risk, and our recommendations probably won't work as well in those districts. But there are many districts striving to do better, and we think charters will be helpful to them.

The last chapter, Chapter 6, pulls it all together with a synopsis that cuts across the key issues addressed throughout the book. We venture to take a retrospective look back as a standpoint for speculating about where charter schools can go. Any consideration of the future must cope with the dilemmas buried within the ubiquitous No Child Left Behind legislation, which in only a few short years has become part of the culture of education in this country. While we are not especially happy about the overblown importance being placed on tests, we are resigned that testing has become a way of life. Therefore, we think it is important for parents to understand the advantages and disadvantages of testing.

Both charter schools and school vouchers are covered in this book. Our reasons for tackling such a broad scope are that the programs are historically intertwined, they share the same underlying free-market ideology and quest for independence, and both are touted as competitive options for parents seeking to escape public schools. These shared characteristics have enabled us to make some blanket statements germane to both approaches to school choice. However, the scope also complicates the task. Critical programmatic and political differences between vouchers and charters have at times forced us to zero in on one program at a time. Available research and space limitations have precluded making uniformily detailed comparisons of both programs on every topic.

When it was necessary to narrow our focus, we have usually chosen to pay more attention to charters than to vouchers. We chose this slant because we are convinced that, with some tweaking, charters have the potential to improve public education. Charters compete with other public schools only to the extent they demand independence, and we shall argue that independence is not essential. Operating under the direction of public school districts, charter schools not only could become compatible with public education, but they also could provide useful services that now overwhelm districts. Vouchers, on the other hand, are inherently competitive, and a drain on tax dollars. The very concept seems to require independence for the limited purpose of serving a few families at the expense of the public schools. While we have ventured to offer some suggestions that might enhance their usefulness to the public, we are not optimistic about vouchers as vehicles to improve education in either the public or private sectors. Therefore, if our treatment of vouchers seems uneven in places, we believe the trade-off is justifiable.

Our disappointment with the direction the choice movement has taken does not take anything away from the dedicated and creative teachers and administrators who are now working in choice schools. We have met some of them and know firsthand that many are doing an exceptional job, often under difficult circumstances. We admire their optimism, hard work, and tenacity. However, this book is not about individuals. It is about irresponsible promises and windy boasting, which suggests charter and voucher schools work better than they do. It is about the fiction that making some schools independent of school districts will somehow be helpful to parents and to public education. It is about a smug head-in-the sand approach to school reform, which only distracts from the need to overhaul what is going on. It is about calloused free-market advocates who, rather than working to repair the public schools that our children attend, have turned their backs on them. It is about the absurd policies that require parents to abandon the public schools in order to exercise choices. And, it is also about some promising models of choice that are now in play, what they can tell us about reforming the reforms, and why they should be merged with the charter-school model. Most of all, this book is about what needs to be done to fix America's schools, especially troubled schools badly serving impoverished minority children.

In sum, we think school choice as it stands is a hoax. Independence is a blind alley, and charter schools need to be reined in to make them work for the school districts that most children attend. We are going to explain why we have reached these conclusions in the following pages. We will go beyond that and propose ways to make choice work for parents and for public education.

Ronald G. Corwin
E. Joseph Schneider

NOTES

1. Marcella R. Dianda and Ronald G. Corwin, *What a Voucher Could Buy: A Survey of California's Private Schools* (Los Alamitos, CA: Southwest Regional Laboratory, February 1993); Ronald G. Corwin and Marcella R. Dianda, "What Can We Really Expect from Large-Scale Voucher Programs?" *Phi Delta Kappan* 75, 1 (September 1993): 68–74.

2. See, for example, Catherine Gewertz, "Voucher Plan's School Impact Seen as Limited," *Los Angeles Times*, 10 February 1993: B–1; Carlos Alcala, "No Big Exodus from Public Schools Seen," *Sacramento Bee*, 11 February 1993: A–1; Denise Rios, "Study: Little Room at Private Schools," *Orange County Register*, 11 February 1993: B–8.

3. Marcella R. Dianda and Ronald G. Corwin, *Vision and Reality: A First-Year Look at California's Charter Schools* (Los Alamitos, CA: Southwest Regional Laboratory, 1994); Ronald G. Corwin and John F. Flaherty, eds., *Freedom and Innovation in California's Charter Schools* (Los Alamitos, CA: Southwest Regional Laboratory/WestEd, 1995).

4. Henry J. Becker, Kathryn Nakagawa, and Ronald G. Corwin, "Parent Involvement Contracts in California's Charter Schools: Strategy for Educational Improvement or Method of Exculsion?" *Teachers College Record* 98 (Spring 1997): 511–536.

5. Amy Stuart Wells, "Charter School Reform in California: Does It Meet Expectations?" *Phi Delta Kappan* 80 (1998). Available at www.pdkintl.org/kappan/kartide.htm.

1

The School Choice Quagmire: Anomalies within the Movement and the Models

This book is about school choice. But that doesn't tell you much. That word, choice, is so slippery it can refer to anything from the innocuous practice of allowing secondary students to concurrently enroll in college to fishy uses of taxpayer's money to pay tuition at private schools. It includes magnet schools, specialized alternative schools, vocational schools, and minischools. It covers change of residence, open enrollment plans allowing parents to choose almost any school within a district's boundaries, student transfers across districts, tax credits to reimburse parents for the cost of private schools, publicly funded vouchers to pay for private schooling, and independent charter schools precariously straddling the public and private sectors. These are only a few of the options riding myriad reforms today. Pitirim A. Sorokin, a major figure in social thought in the previous century, wrote a book with the catchy title, *Fads and Foibles in Modern Sociology and Related Sciences.*[1] He picked on the social sciences, but to find fads, he needed look no further than the reforms that have been coursing through public education over the past half century. Every decade or so educators and journalists become enthralled with another craze designed to revolutionize schools—including preschools, new math, sex education, mandatory bussing, alternative schools, magnet schools, open education, deschooling and home schooling, small schools, and work-study programs. Fortunately we do not have to cope with all of those here.

Our focus is on two reforms that are hot today: government-sponsored charter schools and school vouchers. Both give tax money to parents so they can send their children to self-governing, independent schools beyond the customary purview of traditional school boards. Such unregulated schools give most local taxpayers no say in what happens in them. They are the forms of choice we will be concerned with here. For simplicity, we can say that school vouchers set aside a specified amount of public money that parents may use to pay their child's tuition to a receptive private (or public) school. In most cases, vouchers must be used for schools within defined geographical boundaries, such as a city or school district. We shall refer to them as voucher schools. Charter schools are publicly funded, tuition-free, nonsectarian public schools that have been released from many of the laws and rules that govern school districts, including for example, rules pertaining to teacher qualifications, curriculum, and calendar. At a minimum, 72 percent of charters nationwide are new start-up schools; most of the others are existing public schools that have converted to charter status.

As we shall be using the term, school choice applies to both a wide assortment of charter schools and to voucher schools. There are, of course, obvious differences between the two types, but they also share three vital features: most operate independently from school districts; both are being rationalized with free-market ideologies premised on unsupportable claims that market-driven organizations outperform traditional public school monopolies; and, perhaps most important: not all students can participate in either type. It is the overlap between charters and vouchers that we are concerned about.

CONCEPTUAL FLAWS

Although we have narrowed the focus to only two types of choice, our task will not be easy. School choice is a product of political compromise and some muddled thinking. The choice movement, as we shall see, defies simple generalizations, because it is riddled with contentious anomalies and dilemmas, and set apart by nearly incomprehensible diversity. Consequently, the straightforward definitions just cited mask underlying defects that pervade the concept itself. Some of the problems are limited to programmatic elements associated with charter schools, while others pertain to both types of programs. Since conceptual flaws seem to us most evident in charter school legislation, we will focus on them in this section. But the following sections include vouchers as well.

Inconsistencies in the Legal Status of Charter Schools

Most charter schools, managed by their own governing boards, are legally independent. Eleven states grant them independence outright and eight others permit them to be independent. The thirteen states that curiously require their charters to operate as part of a school district account for only about 12 percent of the nation's 3,400 charters schools. Their legal status notwithstanding, charter schools as conceived, are supposed to operate autonomously, although their actual freedom varies widely in practice.

Accountability Loopholes

Depending on the state, charters can be launched by parents, educators, community members, state universities, private firms, or by any entity designated by the state. Notwithstanding their creators, under the definition, in exchange for being released from most rules, charter schools are supposed to be more accountable than other schools, a provision that supposedly includes closing schools that fail to perform adequately. There are two types of accountability criteria: market accountability and contractual accountability. Market accountability means that they must sustain adequate levels of enrollment. Contractual accountability means that they must fulfill terms of their contract with sponsors under terms set by state legislation, which can include stipulations about meeting student achievement goals. In practice, both forms of accountability are problematic. Market accountability provides no assurance that a school is providing a sound education and operating legally. Contractual obligations, especially those pertaining to student achievement, are difficult to monitor or measure. Consequently, few schools have been closed for failure to produce good results.

Ambiguous Relationships with Sponsors

Authorized by state statutes, charter schools operate under a contract with an overseeing chartering agency, which for most is a local, county, or intermediate school board. In addition, state boards of education, state education agencies, universities, and colleges also sometimes act as sponsors. However, over three-fourths of all charter schools are sponsored by local school boards. Sponsors approve contracts and, theoretically, can revoke or refuse to renew them. However, a sponsor's actual control over schools varies enormously. Many schools seem to be operating almost like any other public school, while some are runaway mavericks. Adding to the confusion, several states require each school to negotiate with the sponsor over which decisions it is permitted to control, and the outcomes of these negotiations are not always clear. It does seem clear though, that many charter schools are precariously straddling a bewildering status: while they operate inside school districts that are responsible for them, the districts are not permitted or inclined to interfere with them.

Selective Enrollment

Legally, charter schools must accept students who apply, provided there is space and provided the child meets criteria that may be mandated by the states. Most charter schools say they are oversubscribed, in which case they are allowed to select students randomly or from first-served waiting lists. In practice, at least some charters select students, both by mandate and through informal practices. At least one in four admit to imposing admission requirements, which in many cases include academic records, tests, or aptitudes.[2] Some states limit enrollment to low-income or low-achieving students. And, often charter schools give priority to local neighborhood children, either by mandate or by policy.

They also use a variety of informal techniques to select particular students, for example, by targeting recruiting practices to preferred types of families, by counseling out unpreferred individuals, and by expelling difficult students. Just how frequently charters use such informal practices is difficult to document. Most schools deny having any special admission requirements. At the same time, as just noted, many do require applications and interviews, and some admit to considering factors such as academic records, admissions tests, recommendations, and other personal criteria. Moreover, a large percentage of charters require or expect parents to work on behalf of the school, including fund raising activities—which conveniently excludes families who choose not to participate. Therefore, voucher and charter schools are not as divergent with respect to selective admission policies as appears on the surface.

THE PARENT CHOICE DILEMMA

There are two parts to school choice: the options and the parents who choose them. A potpourri of reforms offers parents a wide array of options. But what do they really want? Critics charge that choice has more to do with escaping neighbors than with school programs. Unfortunately, it is true that as currently structured, school choice can promote white flight and other forms of segregation. As we show in Chapter 5, the fact is that this nation is still struggling with what a half century ago Myrdal called "the American dilemma."[3] Like it or not, choice schools are central players in that struggle.

Winners and Losers

When Meier and Smith analyzed enrollment shifts in Florida's private schools for the latter half of the 1980s, they found that public school quality, as measured by achievement test scores, had no impact on changes in enrollments in private schools. Most of the enrollment increases were explained by the percentage of Catholics in a district, and by the number of new black students entering a district.[4] The authors contend that parents turn to private schools in order to get their children into white schools, and into religious schools. There is more to it, of course. But no matter how you look at it, an element of privilege and selectivity seems inherent in all forms of choice. Not everyone can play and not everyone gets their choice. The children who leave, and the children in schools that accept them, often have exceptional advantages.

So, the policy question becomes this: should this society spend public money to give a few select kids a better education, knowing it could contribute to already segregated schools? Probably not. And yet, should parents be deprived of the right to choose their children's schools? We see only two fair ways around this dilemma. One is to require choice schools using public money to give back by participating in larger, more far-reaching programs devoted to serving public school districts where they need help—whether that requires special programs for slow or for gifted learners; for children learning English; for those who elect music and the performing arts; for students at risk; or for those preparing for college. The other is to create more choice schools specifically for low-achieving, poor minority children, as Coons and Sugarman advocated long ago.[5] Chapters 4 and 5 lay out our suggestions for both tacks. But we do not believe for a moment that sending kids outside school districts is a solution.

Mixed Motives Driving Parents from Public Schools

Is escaping poor and minority students the only thing pushing parents out of public schools? Terry Moe's 2001 book, reporting a Brookings survey of parent attitudes toward private schools, sheds some light on this subject. His data confirm critics' charges that race is sometimes a major reason whites want out of the public schools. However, he concludes that race is a motivating factor only for whites who live in inner cities.[6] Outside the inner cities, even parents who generally oppose diversity are no more interested in going private than those who support it. The study also reveals a perplexing anomaly. On the one hand, most parents—including people with low education and low expectations—like the public education system. And yet, most people think private schools are superior to public schools and would consider sending their kids to private schools if money were not a problem. For most parents interested in going private, what matters is their belief that the public school system is inequitable; this concern is especially salient for low-income parents, who are most likely to suffer from it. They are also attracted by the small size of schools in the private sector, which allows them to have more personal contact with each child. And, they like the values private schools instill, along with the opportunities they provide for children to pray in school. Parents who are attracted to private schools also tend to firmly believe in a market ideology.

So, there is much more to choice than race and class. White flight may be alive and well and riding on the backs of vouchers and charters, but it doesn't exhaust the reasons parents are demanding more choices. Often, they are simply looking for better education—which usually boils down to small schools with involved parents and good teachers. Sometimes parents have more pragmatic objectives. For example, they may be looking for a school that is closer to home, or to work, or to babysitters. Sometimes choice has been used by aggressive coaches to recruit winning sports teams. Let's be frank. Often parents, of all races, and in various states of poverty, are desperately seeking to escape a crime-ridden, violent, drug-infested school, or one staffed with unqualified, inexperienced teachers. In big cities, such schools are typically located in poor and minority neighborhoods. That doesn't necessarily mean that race is the motive for wanting out. Large numbers of minorities, especially well-educated black parents, are dissatisfied with their schools and want more choices. In fact, more black children than white children have left their assigned public schools behind to take advantage of the numerous public school open enrollment plans available in many cities.[7] These parents, along with many white parents, are looking for better educational and social climates.

SCHOOL CHOICE AS PRODUCT OF SOCIAL CHANGES AND IDEOLOGY

What accounts for all the dissatisfaction? Critics like the simple answer. Invariably that answer hinges on an inflexible and indifferent "education bureaucracy." School choice, the story goes, surfaced in the early 1990s because frustrated parents realized that school districts were incapable of meeting their needs.[8] Critics are quick to cite low test scores, high dropout rates, overcrowding, and other negative statistics as evidence that traditional schools are failing to prepare the skilled and culturally rounded workers needed in a specialized, technological world marketplace. Therefore, they contend, frustrated parents started looking for options, and charter schools emerged to do the job.

However, while it is true that school districts have not kept up with the challenge of educating ever-growing numbers of at risk students, that failure does not explain the choice movement. Pinning choice on bad bureaucracy falls short in two respects. First, it ignores the role of awesome societal forces beyond the control of school districts. It would be more accurate to blame society for failing to provide the resources and leadership districts needed to cope with the drastic social changes that swept over them. And second, frustration with bureaucracy does not account for why choice admirers pushed to make charter schools independent from public school districts. They say independence was, and remains, necessary because public educators are incapable of changing, and too often are uninterested in doing so. Yet, in the early 1990s, as charters and vouchers were being so vigorously promoted, social conditions were already forcing school districts to adapt. They were ripe for sweeping internal reforms. Charter advocates could have chosen to use their clout to push for choices within school districts. They chose instead to press for independent schools operating outside public school districts. How can we explain that?

School Choice Was a Response to the Same Social Forces That Overwhelmed Public Schools

Most social changes result from a convergence of societal forces, and the school choice movement is no exception. Over the last century, public schools have been battered by an onslaught of powerful social forces, which also are responsible for grave anomalies in choice schools. One of these forces is the ferocious pace of urbanization that has been occurring over the past century, accompanied by higher school retention rates and more immigration in many parts of the country. Not only were cities growing larger and denser, but they were spreading out across vast metropolitan areas and breaking through middle-class suburban walls. Compared to the first part of the 1900s, more students were staying in school longer. Immigrants were pouring into some states from Latin America, Asia, the Caribbean, and Eastern Europe. Combined, these factors produced mammoth schools unable to cater to individual needs. And these needs were compounded by growing diversity that required specialized types of educational settings. School districts were enrolling more low-income students, racial and ethnic minorities, and immigrant children needing special help with language.

Also, they were slowly learning to accommodate special education students, being protected for the first time by laws passed in the 1980s and 1990s. Of course, the critical importance of credentials cannot be overlooked in this emerging picture. As more students graduated from high school, preparation for college became more important, prompting many parents to seek schools designed to help their children compete, while at the same time segregating them from the low-income ethnic minorities they were unaccustomed to. Then too, a segmented labor market was forcing schools to prepare students for a wide range of skill levels.

All considered, these forces were producing crushing pressures on school districts to accommodate the diverse needs of the students swarming into schools. Most districts did respond by adding more specialists, facilities, courses, programs, and services. The critics who complain today about the slow pace of change are the same ones who denounce the added staff required to mount the adaptations the districts were attempting to make. No one knew exactly what to do. As an example of the hard choices, Prince cites this case in point: after teachers agreed to extend their work schedules 100 minutes per week, they couldn't agree whether to add the extra time to instruction or to training workshops, and whether to target low-income schools or to spread the effort equally across all schools.[9] The incapacitating indeciveness has been compounded by the lack of resources needed to implement promising options. Seldom did districts have adequate resources to meet the severe challenges they were facing, especially given growing student enrollments and unfavorable economic cycles. The public was not inclined to pay much more for its overflowing schools.

On the one hand then, we have to remember that districts cannot control conditions such as overcrowding, voter resistance to tax increases, and vested interests opposed to particular types of changes, which undermine their capacity to improve. On the other hand, we should acknowledge the fact that many school districts were indeed struggling to adapt, through a succession of school improvement reforms starting in the 1960s and proceeding through today. It is naïve to blame the "bureaucracy" for this complex chain of events. The real story is that school districts were being challenged by devastating changes and they needed more resources, and just as important, effective leaders—leaders such as the school choice devotees who turned their backs on public schools.

The Laissez-Faire Movement Provided the Ideological Basis of Independent Schools

While the forces we mentioned may help explain why many parents were demanding the right to choose their own schools, they cannot explain the overzealous proponents' tenacious resolve to create independent schools operating outside conventional school districts. That answer is buried in a nationwide ideological movement, which took hold and gained momentum starting in the 1950s. This so-called laissez-faire movement called for the privatization of almost every commodity and service in the public sector. Public education was one of these services, along with utilities, the postal service, and other enterprises once controlled by government. School choice fans hitched their ideological wagon to a preposterous free-market dream that promises a world where all goods and services are produced for boundless profits unhampered by government oversight and interference.

School Choice Is a Creation of the Free-Market Fantasy

Charter schools might have been inevitable. Independent charter schools were not inevitable. Parents can have the right to choose schools without forcing them to leave school districts. Independence was an unnecessary add-on—an artifact of the free-market fantasy. If frustration with bureaucracy had been the only motive, charter proponents could have seized upon the existing foundation of precursor choice experiments within the public sector—such as specialized alternative schools, magnets, and decentralized, site-based schools. The existing choice models could have served as strategic bases for launching still more robust approaches. But, preoccupied with winning independence, voucher and charter enthusiasts deliberately shunted them aside. No, it was not frustration with bureaucracy, but ideology that accounts for the course that charters took. Had the energy and fervor driving the charter schools movement been channeled into school districts, public education today probably would be much farther along the road to reform. Charter schools could have, and should have, been created within school districts where they could have made a real difference.

The Argument for Independence Is Based on Ideological Fallacies

The argument that schools must be independent to engage in reform simply does not hold up. In recent years school districts have experimented with preschool programs, middle schools, year-round calendars, magnet schools, alternative education, school-based management, individual instruction, before- and after-school interventions, nongraded instruction, team teaching, smaller schools, and work-study programs—to mention only a few of the countless reforms. The bizarre idea that they are unreceptive to new forms of schooling exploits a false sense of hopelessness. While it is probably true that most school reforms haven't lasted for long, the same can be said of reforms adopted by businesses. Reform is a trial and error process. However, that doesn't mean that school districts are impervious to change. It means that most reforms require structural modifications and other institutional supports, which they usually do not get. This failure of institutional follow-through is partly, if not largely, because most reforms are imposed by outsiders who have little day-to-day stake in schools—college professors, politicians, and government officials.

Historians have identified some features that help reforms survive, such as simplicity and a supportive constituency. However, it seems to us that there are two other essential elements. First, the people who will be responsible for the implementation must participate from the beginning, since they will be acutely aware of the practical constraints (for example, schedules, work loads, and other contingencies that must be adapted). Second, the reform should capitalize on forces already producing natural adaptation. All organizations must adapt or die. They are continually adapting. We have already recounted above a confluence of societal forces preparing school districts to meet irresistible demands to create more options. Given their political appeal, had charter schools been formed within school districts, these schools could have ridden a tidal wave of reform that had already warmed up school districts to new approaches. And voucher advocates would not have had a loyal audience.

Instead, charters were created as independent schools, peculiar creatures often operating within the physical boundaries of school districts and accountable to them—but legally independent of them. And what has this superlative approach accomplished? As we shall describe in detail in other chapters, independence has accomplished this: (1) too many anemic charter schools without adequate funding, experiencing low enrollments or a substantial loss of students, and unable to provide even the basic services and extracurricular activities that most other students enjoy; (2) a host of wayward schools reeling under accusations of wrongdoing, festering financial difficulties, discipline issues, and infighting among staff, parents, and board members; (3) many overworked and poorly trained teachers; and (4) traditional programs yielding average test scores that are about the same as those being produced by most other schools. Beyond all of that, because charters are independent schools, they have had little impact on school districts. Most teachers and parents have never heard of them, and those who have regard them as irrelevant to their situations.

A HARD LOOK AT THE CHOICE MOVEMENT AND MODELS

Choice enthusiasts portray all forms of school choice as reforms. That is another tricky term—reform. Sometimes it is downright manipulative. Robert Samuelson, columnist for the *Washington Post* and *Newsweek*, calls it the worst word in our political vocabulary.[10] By casting their agendas as reforms, Samuelson argues, political advocates aim to suppress debate and discussion, not stimulate it. But we need the debates, especially when reforms make matters worse. The truth is that reforms of all kinds—not just those devoted to education—often do not live up to their promise. Samuelson quotes Richard Hofstadter, a respected historian, who once said of the reformist impulse that it "often wanders over the border between reality and impossibility." Unless school choice proponents dedicate themselves to improving choices within school districts, Hofstadter's observation may become the epitaph for today's hot school choice reforms. This society can no longer afford to be intimidated by the torrent of misinformation glossing over the fundamental flaws in the school choice model as it currently exits. This book is dedicated to the task of identifying the defects and finding ways to fix them.

Distorted Hype Driving the Choice Movement: An Example

Throughout the book we shall advance several criticisms of both the school choice movement and the choice models themselves. They are worth mentioning here. Our most fundamental objection to the movement is that school choice, in the forms of vouchers and charters, has been oversold by spokespersons who have exaggerated the benefits to the point that parents and politicians who believe the claims will necessarily be disappointed, if not defrauded. Charters and vouchers can't possibly deliver what has been promised. It isn't just the hype that bothers us. It is the distortions of truth that run through the believers' litany of reasons to abandon public schools. You want proof? Take a letter written to the *Orange County Register* by the President of California Parents for Educational Choice. He cited the success of the GI Bill enacted in 1944 during World War II as proof that school vouchers work, saying, ". . . the whole of America's educators voiced their praise for this historic legislation. . . . The GI Bill was and is, after all, a voucher system allowing full freedom of school choice."[11] He goes on to equate that legislation with the Milwaukee K–12 voucher program and similar programs around the nation, concluding, ". . . will the public education establishment figure out that the GI Bill that it so recently praised to the heavens is precisely the kind of voucher system it vehemently opposes?" Whoa! Hold up! The proposition that the GI Bill serves as a model for current school-choice programs is absurd. Only two lessons applicable to public schools have come from that legislation: (1) vouchers are administratively feasible, and (2) they must be regulated. The second lesson came the hard way after thousands of GIs were defrauded by "fly-by-night" schools.

Here are a few features of the GI Bill. What do they have to do with public schools?

• The GI Bill expanded the education market by supporting people who otherwise might not have attended college; choice schools compete for an existing market of students.

- It is fully funded and does not compete for allocated funds; choice takes tax dollars from public schools already coping with awesome responsibilities, contributing to their debilitation.

- Its purpose is to assist people who want to go to college; choice is designed to give select families tax dollars so they can escape from an available system of education.

- It uses federal tax dollars; choice takes local tax dollars intended to support public schools and gives them to schools in which local taxpayers have no voice.

- It supports adults; choice schools are responsible for the welfare of children, and so require close oversight.

- It is not restrictive, provided only that the eligible applicant has the necessary academic ability; many choice schools select out students on nonacademic criteria, including past behavior, physical and language disabilities, and personal beliefs.

Defects in the Choice School Models

Our biggest concern with school-choice models is that they provide only one choice: the choice to leave the regular public schools. Why is that? Not because it is impossible to create effective choice programs within the public school system. There are hundreds, probably thousands, of good schools within the public sector; many of them have been given the flexibility enjoyed by some charter schools. Some of these approaches will be discussed in following chapters. The demands from choice backers for freedom and autonomy have more to do with their free-market ideology than with creating choices that will be available to most parents. If choice fans were really concerned about the welfare of children, they would spend less time and money churning out misleading allegations that promote one-sided choices requiring taxpayers to support schools over which they have no say and that can only undermine public schools, and devote more energy to the task of fixing the public schools that most children attend.

There is no hope for public education without improving the school districts that most students attend. Independent charters and vouchers are designed to do the opposite. Both reforms create autonomous sanctuaries for a few families ready to give up on regular public schools. These safe harbors will have no positive effect on public education. If you believe, as we do, that all parents deserve more options, then the solution is to incorporate charter schools within networks of schools that serve public school districts. That need is especially critical in large urban districts. Moreover, even private schools that accept public money should be required to participate in such service networks. We will elaborate in Chapter 4. We are not advocating that either type of reform should be abolished, because we believe there is much at the core of both worth preserving when incorporated as part of school districts.

Another problem with choice models is that the schools are able to skim off some of the best, most creative and dedicated students and teachers, both of whom would probably do just fine in upgraded public schools. And finally, we should note that both private schools and charter schools are typically smaller than regular public schools. A growing body of research indicates that small schools of all kinds—not just charter schools or voucher schools—do better than other schools. So, it seems likely that charter schools are being given credit for outcomes that have more to do with their size than anything else. In Chapters 4 and 5, we propose another model based on district-planned and district-operated specialized schools, which we are convinced would vastly improve the impact of charter schools. Chapter 3, where we discuss several other approaches to choice, is also devoted to the task of fixing and improving the charter-school model.

CONCLUSIONS

When we read the implausible claims and boasts being asserted by rabid choice proponents, we always wonder who is speaking, and who is listening. We know there is more than one voice, more than one audience. Some of the fans of choice are idealistic educational reformers who honestly believe that choice will improve public education and are eagerly searching for ways to prove it. They should welcome new proposals such as the ones we will offer later, proposals designed to support and refine existing approaches to choice. Others are cunning disciples of free markets who, under the guise of bogus pledges and unfounded allegations, have succeeded in creating publicly funded safe havens. Their rants against bureaucracy, and their impossible promises, were from the start devious ploys to justify what amounts to a special status for select groups. Still others in the audience include concerned parents desperately looking for higher quality education and better environments for their children. They are the ones who most need more choices, and the information and viewpoints we offer in this volume. It is that group, in particular— and especially the undecided among them—we hope to reach.

We don't mean to belittle the choice movement. Far from it. Parents do need better choices, especially the parents looking for higher quality education and good environments for their children. No doubt about it. But they should not have to abandon regular public schools to exercise their choices. Parents need both better schools and better choices *within* the public education system. Of course, most parents are not dissatisfied. But too many are. Some are seeking a better education for their children and aren't sure where to turn. Some are trying to escape a school riddled with drugs, gangs, and violence. Let's admit it; perhaps some are not comfortable with the race, ethnicity, income, or education level of their neighbors. Notwithstanding the motive, any parent thinking about taking a child out of the public schools deserves better choices, and just as important, better information. That is the purpose of this volume.

In his landmark book, *Exit, Voice, and Loyalty*, Albert O. Hirschman identifies three groups that populate a market for goods and services: (1) those who have given up and want out; (2) those who are dissatisfied but intend to stay and work to change the system; and (3) those who are content and plan to stay. This last category, we should remember, probably includes the majority of parents—especially in the suburbs where polls indicate parents usually express high levels of satisfaction with their schools.[12] Hirschman's three categories are provocative. However, for practical purposes, they capture only part of the story. Each of his groups contains two subgroups: (a) a hard core whose mind is made up, and (b) marginal hangers-on who still have an open mind and are considering the alternatives. It is those people, the ones still searching for truthful answers, to whom we are speaking. Nothing we say will change the hard core supporters of choice as it currently exists, who simply want to get out of the regular public schools. They probably already recognize the idle promises, distortions and falsehoods for what they are, namely thinly veiled excuses for parents to abandon the schools their children are assigned to attend. Wanting out is okay. The deception is not, because the puffy rhetoric and all the hyperbole may fool some people who are sincerely trying to weigh the evidence. These people should not be victimized by zealots pushing choice on false pretenses. We hope what we have to say will help them make up their minds, and more generally that it will get the attention of decision makers and stakeholders who are looking for fair reform within public education.

NOTES

1. Pitirim A. Sorokin, *Fads and Foibles in Modern Sociology and Related Sciences* (Chicago: H. Regnery Co., 1956).

2. L. Anderson, N. Adelman, K. Finnigan, L. Cotton, M. B. Donnelly, and T. Price, *A Decade of Public Charter Schools: Evaluation of the Public Charter Schools Program, 2000–2001* (Stanford, CA: SRI International, 2002), 18.

3. Gunnar Myrdal, with Richard Sternet and Arnold Rose, *The American Dilemma: The Negro Problem and Modern Democracy* (Somerset, NJ: Transaction Publishers, 1996 [1944]).

4. Kenneth J. Meier and Kevin B. Smith, "School Choice: Panacea or Pandora's Box?" *Phi Delta Kappan* 77 (1995). Available at www.pdkintl.org/kappan/karticle.htm.

5. J. E. Coons and S. D. Sugarman, *Education by Choice: The Case for Family Control* (Berkeley, CA: Berkeley University Press, 1978).

6. Terry M. Moe, *Schools, Vouchers, and the American Public* (Washington, DC: Brookings Institution Press, 2001).

7. National Center for Education Statistics, *Trends in the Use of School Choice: 1993 to 1999* (Washington, DC: U.S. Department of Education, 2000).

8. See Anne T. Lockwood, *The Charter School Decade* (Latham, MD: Scarecrow Education, 2004), 21–51. Lockwood believes that charter schools were not a historical accident, but were an inevitable response to the public's growing frustration with perceived lack of progress, for example as reflected in students' achievement scores.

9. Cynthia D. Prince, *Changing Policies to Close the Achievement Gap* (Lanham, MD: Scarecrow Press, 2004), 84.

10. Robert J. Samuelson, "It's Time for 'Reform' Reform," *Orange County Register*, 6 June 2004.

11. Alan Bonsteel, "The Original School Voucher Plan: Success of GI Bill of Rights Offers Lesson in Debate Over Educational Choice," *Orange County Register*, 18 June 2004; and Ronald G. Corwin, "Likening the GI Bill to School Choice Is Absurd," *Orange County Register*, 27 June 2004.

12. Albert O. Hirschman, *Exit, Voice, and Loyalty: Responses to Decline in Firms, Organizations, and States* (Cambridge, MA: Harvard University Press, 1970).

Claims for Charter Schools and School Vouchers: An Assessment

Americans are being duped by incessant propaganda peddling charter schools and school vouchers. The inflated claims are probably fraudulent enough to bring jail time. Chester E. Finn, Jr., and his colleagues proudly quote Connecticut Democratic Senator Joseph Lieberman who wrote: "Competition from charter schools is the best way to motivate the ossified bureaucracies governing too many public schools. This grass-roots revolution seeks to reconnect public education with our most basic values: ingenuity, responsibility, and accountability."[1] The authors go on to cite an Arizona official who calls charter schools "the most important thing happening in public education." And, as already mentioned in the first chapter, proponents have likened vouchers to the exalted GI Bill. Both reforms are described as alternatives for parents—alternatives that obviously require a child to leave a regular public schools. They are supposed to force public schools to reform to keep their students from defecting. The charter school bargain—implicitly extending to school vouchers as well—is freedom in exchange for better student outcomes.

None of this is happening, and it won't. We have arrived at this conclusion after more than a decade of research and observation. The claim that choice schools are producing superior education through innovative approaches is insupportable because the research findings are uneven, because the analysis techniques being used mask more than they reveal, and because there is too much variation in programs and students to make meaningful generalizations. But, are choice activists giving up? No way. The number of charter schools grows yearly, the rhetorical and legislative push for vouchers remains vigorous, and the Federal government continues to pour over 250 million dollars into the charter school pot. By January 2005, forty states and Washington, DC had laws that provide for about 3,400 charter schools serving close to one million students nation-wide, and six states plus Washington, DC have publicly funded voucher programs. The No Child Left Behind Act of 2001 encourages parents with children enrolled in persistently low-performing schools to transfer them to better public or choice schools, although few spaces are actually avail-able in some urban schools.[2] It is time to call a halt to the misleading hy-perbole driving the choice movement.

Proponents of charters and vouchers believe that some parents should be able to use public money to pay for autonomous schools that operate outside conventional school districts. Unless your child is in one of those schools, your local tax dollars are paying for schools over which you have no say. Why? Proponents will tell you that education bureaucracies are ineffective, lethargic and unresponsive, that schools need a strong shot of competition to force them to reform in directions that will result in bet-ter student performance, and that school vouchers and charter schools allow teachers and parents to take back their schools and control the re-form process.[3] They have promised that students will do better when schools can operate autonomously and out from under stifling rules. They even made a deal: freedom in exchange for results. While all of this may sound good, most of it is not happening, and it won't. In the pages that follow we are going to explain why.

In 2004, The California's Legislative Analyst's Office (LAO) issued a statement concluding that ". . . charter schools are a viable reform strategy—expanding families' choices, encouraging parental involve-ment, increasing teacher satisfaction, enhancing principals' control over school-site decision making, and broadening the curriculum without sac-rificing time spent on core subjects. The most recent evaluation deemed charter schools cost-effective—finding that charter schools achieve aca-demic results similar to those of traditional public schools even though they obtain significantly less state and federal categorical funding."[4]

Now, wait a minute. What about the promise . . . the one about freedom for results? Former California state senator Gary K. Hart, the original sponsor of the California charter schools program, put it this way: ". . . the tradeoff has always been outcomes versus deregulation. And if we can't demonstrate the outcomes, we're not entitled to the deregulation."[5] But, you might point out, that statement was made a decade ago. And that is our point. A decade ago, as charters were just getting started, choice pro-moters were selling them to a skeptical public as a way to improve stu-dent achievement and, they said, schools would be shut down if they didn't measure up. Gary Hart was only repeating the basic theory under-lying charter schools in most states, namely that schools are expected to offer an exceptional educational program that leads to significantly im-proved student achievement. On the premise that authorizers have the ability to revoke charter contracts, they were to be more accountable for educational performance than traditional schools.[6] The idea was that greater autonomy could be traded for the right to make more stringent demands of the schools to demonstrate improved educational performance. Many people bought it. But now, a decade and a half after Koldrie's influential book on the topic, it is time to face the fact that some of their most attractive features have become tarnished beyond recognition.[7]

The generous trade-off—results for autonomy—has itself been traded off, by the California LAO and others, for a modest disclaimer that charter students are no worse off than their public school counterparts. Now it's about cheaper schools and making some groups happy, and hey, it's a buyer's market and if the parents are not satisfied with their children's charter school, they can enroll them someplace else. Now the California LAO is talking about cost effectiveness. But why do some charters cost less? Not efficiency. True, charter schools can hire nonunion, noncertified teachers, and often the teachers work longer days for less money. But the lower cost is also because charters are half as likely to offer bilingual programs and several times more likely to mainstream special education students rather than targeting special services, and because one-third of the charters do not have standard classrooms. Costs are lower also because most charters do not offer extracurricular programs, courses in theater, the arts and music, or employ specialists in areas like speech therapy. Ironically, charter schools receive more private funding than most public schools.

The rhetoric has shifted from improving student achievement to expanding choices. What choices are those? True, some charters have taken esoteric twists like Waldorf programs, Internet-based instruction, and home schooling, but the truth is that in most classroom-based schools, approaches to the curriculum have not expanded much beyond what some schools were already doing. As we will document later, there are few models of education carried out in charter schools and private schools that are not also being used in many public schools and without all the fanfare and uproar over school autonomy. While many charters, and perhaps many private schools, offer exceptional teachers a chance to teach the way they think best, many do not. Moreover, thousands of the 91,000 schools in this country provide the same opportunities for good teaching without elaborate choice programs.

What about the vast differences in how choice schools function and perform? Not a word from the California LAO cited above, or from some other choice activists for that matter. Choice apologists like to boast about average test scores in the few instances when they make charter schools look good. But unless it suits their purpose, they don't tell us about the wide variation in how charter schools actually perform. The truth is that many charter schools do not measure up even to the average public school. Existing studies are preoccupied with averages, which only obscure the wide variations in performance among the schools being compared. For every success story there is a lollapalooza. Bottom line: there is no convincing evidence to support claims that most choice schools produce superior levels of student achievement. Worse: it is not even possible to prove such claims, because choice schools are not comparable—either in programs or in students' qualifications. Therefore, they cannot be held accountable to common measures. The only way around this hitch is to limit studies to the choice schools that function just like most regular schools. Some researchers have tried to do that, but most studies are not designed to account for the extreme differences among these schools. Even when samples include comparable types of schools, selective enrollments in choice schools cast doubt on the validity of the conclusions.

Don't be fooled by the misleading hype about high rates of parent participation in charter schools. It is not quite as it seems. In the first place, while charter schools do give parents more opportunity to participate in various ways, relatively few parents actually participate. For example, Corwin and Becker, and Becker, Nakagawa, and Corwin found, in studies reported in 1995 and 1997, that although charters had higher rates of participation than regular schools, only a small minority of the sixty-six California charter schools studied could count on even 25 percent of their parents helping at school, and only 10 percent helping to raise funds.[8] Most parents didn't even vote in their school board's elections. Secondly, as a condition for admission, charter schools often require parents to sign contracts promising to donate their time, which is a not-so-subtle way to keep out those unwanted students saddled with busy or obstinate parents who can't or won't commit. Remember, charter schools—not parents—dictate the terms of these contracts. One quarter of the twenty-seven schools we studied on this topic thought it essential for parents to participate in prescribed ways, and half admitted that they took a parent's willingness to do so into consideration when deciding who to admit. Nearly half the schools with parent contracts in our study reported having formally or informally excluded families who did not meet the school's commitment expectations. If charter schools were sincere about their professed commitment to parents, they would promote contracts empowering parents to hold the schools accountable.

Although steps have been taken to curtail using parent participation as a selection criterion, the truth is, participation agreements continue to be an intimidating force. For example, in a heavy-handed move to circumvent the law prohibiting charter schools from charging fees, one California school issued contracts requesting parents to pledge a hefty $2,500. Although needy parents were permitted to fulfill the "commitment" in other ways, such as persuading someone else to meet the obligation, parents had good reason to wonder what might happen to their child if they could not meet their assigned obligations. The so-called pledge was little more than a thinly disguised extortion scheme, but the school operated with impunity under the mantle of independence until it finally went down for lack of money.

With this background we are ready to evaluate in more detail the major arguments for choice and the evidence for them.

THE STUDENT ACHIEVEMENT SCAM

The claim that choice schools improve student achievement cannot be proven. One reason is that standardized tests are not suitable for the task. Another is because the wrong statistics are being used. And still another is that choice schools are not comparable either in programs or in students' qualifications and therefore cannot be held accountable to common measures. Consider first the last point. Zimmer and his colleagues said it best: ". . . there is no single charter school approach and therefore no single charter school effect."[9] The only thing charter schools have in common is their legal form—which is to say, the charter that authorizes someone to start a school. The same can be said of the more than 7,000 private schools. The only thing they share is their nonpublic standing. All of these schools, whether public or private, differ from one another as much as they differ from regular public schools. In Los Angeles, there is an exemplary charter school, headed by an award-winning administrator backed by dedicated teachers, which has sometimes demonstrated student gains in basic subjects. And, in San Diego, Corwin and colleagues studied a charter school teaching fairy tales, chants, and Bible stories, which in the first year lost its key leaders and its principal, and became the topic of controversial editorials in the local papers. Its students scored very low on the district's standardized test.[10] Will the "typical charter school" please stand up? How can anyone believe that such extremely different types of schools can be meaningfully compared with almost equally diverse public schools?

The private sector is also far from being homogeneous. The Catholic church enrolls almost half of all private school students. But one-in-three of these students is in a school affiliated with a wide array of religious organizations and sects, and the other 16 percent are in nonsectarian schools.[11] Most private schools are for elementary students, but 10 percent of them are high schools, and an exceptionally large number are combined K–12. Private schools are also widely dispersed throughout central cities (42 percent), the urban fringe or large towns (40 percent), and rural areas (18 percent). One-fourth of the private schools are small (under fifty), but one in five is large (300 or more). Few Catholic schools are small (1 percent), while 38 percent are large; this pattern is reversed for nonsectarian schools, 36 percent of which are large. Over 60 percent of nonsectarian schools, but only 7 percent of Catholic schools, use a specific instructional approach, such as Montessori. By a ratio of over two-to-one, more Catholic high schools than other religious schools offer advanced placement courses.

Many private schools serve wealthy, elite families; one in four families with children in private schools earns over $75,000 per year, and the percentage of private schools with poverty students is half that of public schools. Three-fourths of all private school students are white, but a large percentage of Catholic elementary schools are located in central cities, and some of these schools have racially mixed classrooms. In one out of five Catholic schools, over 50 percent the students come from minority backgrounds. About 70 percent of the Catholic schools have some students who qualify for subsidized meals, but other private schools are much less likely to have such students. Private schools are far less likely than public schools to enroll students with limited English proficiency.

Diversity among 3,400 charter schools is rampant. About three-fourths of the charters are new schools. Most of the others have converted from existing schools, and in sixteen states conversion from private schools is permitted. There are charters featuring Montessori, "back-to-basics," and Waldorf approaches. Others are indistinguishable from neighboring regular public schools. Many charters are legally independent, but others are members of traditional school districts, and still others are part of large networks operated by private corporations. Many are not even schools in the usual sense. Thirty-one percent are not classroom based. Eight percent operate as home schools, still others are classified as independent-study schools, and there are several dozen "online" cyber charters having no discernible physical boundaries or school buildings.[12] And then, there are those odd charter districts that have converted all of their schools to charters. Through a curious logic, these districts decided that if charters would free innovative schools from the clutches of repressive school districts, it would work for districts wanting to escape higher levels of bureaucracy. However, after studying some of the eight charter districts nationwide, Lockwood reports that their administrators admit that the charter is symbolic and that most improvements could have been made without it.[13]

Schneider has boiled down charters to the following five types:

- *Converted regular public schools*: mavericks that remain affiliated with their districts, but which tend to be neglected and ostracized by district officials and other educators;

- *Do-gooder charters*: new schools offering safe environments and a basic curriculum for at risk minority and disabled children;

- *Ethnic charters*: newly created, academically lagging schools for minorities, in which good behavior, multicultural courses, and language support eclipse the goal of academic achievement;

- *For-profit charters*: an unknown but large number of private firms typically serving at risk students in low-performing schools and gambling that self-proclaimed successes, low-cost staffing and glitzy curriculum will garner contracts;

- *Disgruntled parents' charters*: schools started for parents with children who have been harassed in regular schools, or whose children do not fit in because they lack self-esteem, are struggling with homosexuality, or for some other reason.[14]

Student achievement for this miscellaneous lot cannot be reasonably compared on the basis of multiple-choice standardized tests. Still, test scores are all we hear about. According to a 2001 SRI study, most charter schools report having measurable goals in the areas of academic achievement, and nearly all administer standardized tests as, in most cases, they are required to do.[15] Nearly all charters also administer performance-based tests, and most use student portfolios and student presentations. However, that hasn't helped matters. For, notwithstanding the array of assessments, or perhaps because of it, nearly half the authorizers have indicated difficulty in measuring charter school progress. They have revoked or failed to renew 12 percent of the charter schools, but student achievement, though a factor, was not the dominant reason given in those cases.

It would make good educational sense to assess performance through essays, music compositions, portfolios, or orations, especially since charter schools are supposed to take unconventional approaches.[16] But such methods do not provide the kind of comparative data needed to show whether or not charters are better than public schools. Notwithstanding which test is used, interpretations of results are often plagued by variability in criteria for including and excluding students from the tests and by student turnover from year to year. For all these reasons, it is misleading to talk as though student outcomes in charter schools and schools that accept vouchers can be meaningfully compared to regular schools with a single type of measure. Some may be comparable. Many are not. That could be one reason why studies of choice schools have not shown dramatic improvements in student achievement scores.

The Evidence for Private Schools

Consider the more than two decades of controversial research on achievement differences between public and private schools, which has failed to conclusively document private education's superiority. A seductive myth that private schools are superior swept the nation in the 1980s astride James Coleman's studies based on a handful of Catholic schools (eighty-four to be exact).[17] But that myth was refuted years ago when reanalyses of this body of work demonstrated that the small reported differences were primarily attributable to student backgrounds and in any case were trivial.[18] For example, sophomores in the Coleman study averaged 61.32 correct answers on one test battery containing 115 items, and as seniors they averaged 61.72 correct answers. The researchers applied elaborate regression analyses to explain this so-called "difference." The data used by Chubb and Moe were shown to be even more questionable.[19] According to Rosenberg's estimates, all of their private school variables taken together do not explain more than 5 percent of the variation in student achievement; taking account of the organization variables would close the achievement advantage for private school students to about half a year.[20]

Currently, voucher proponents are claiming to have demonstrated gains among students using publicly funded vouchers to attend private schools in several cities.[21] Greene observes that in the last few years there have been seven random-assignment and three non-random-assignment studies of school choice experiments from eight different programs, conducted by several different researchers.[22] He says that though they disagree on the magnitude, the authors of all ten voucher studies find at least some academic benefits to students enrolled in the voucher programs. That's what Greene thinks! In a fit of euphoria, he titled the article, "The Surprising Consensus on School Choice." Surprising, yes. Consensus? No! After all, the magnitude of some of the differences is negligible, and there are other studies that Greene didn't mention, in some of the same cities, which found no achievement benefit for choice schools over public schools.[23] In Cleveland, independent researchers hired by the state of Ohio found little difference in academic achievement between students who received vouchers and students who attended Cleveland public schools.[24] In February 2000, Wisconsin's nonpartisan Legislative Audit Bureau pointedly noted: "Some hopes for the [voucher] program—most notably, that it would increase participating pupils' academic achievement—cannot be documented."[25] Since that time, at least one reanalysis of the Wisconsin data suggests perhaps there were improvements, but they were minor and confined to only one or two subject areas.

One study included only students who applied to schools that were cooperating in a privately funded voucher program.[26] Some students were randomly selected from the applicant pool for admission into private schools. When their test scores were compared with applicants who were not randomly selected, it was found that the selected African-American students out-performed unselected applicants. But notice that the study failed to demonstrate progress for most other students, and more important, it included only a self-selected group of students who were motivated to apply to a private school. Therefore, it provides no information about whether private schools can help the general population of students.

And that is the key point. When differences have been found, they usually can be attributed to the kind of students who wind up in voucher programs. Parents of private school students not only tend to be wealthier than public school parents, but they also have much higher levels of formal education, a strong predictor of student academic success. More importantly, private schools screen on the basis of personal interviews, grades, and analysis of behavior.[27] Nearly half of all elementary private schools and nearly three-quarters of secondary private schools use at least one of the following admission requirements: an admission or achievement test, an interview, the student's academic record, special needs, special aptitudes, or recommendations.[28] In addition, nearly all Catholic schools in California require successful completion of the previous school year and recommendations of elementary school principals.[29]

Some voucher programs are now targeting low-income and minority families, and in particular African-Americans, who polls suggest, often support the idea of vouchers. The majority of students participating in privately funded voucher programs in Dayton, New York, Milwaukee, San Antonio, and Washington, DC, were from minority families. In Cleveland and Milwaukee, students taking advantage of the voucher program had been in the bottom third academically, and the majority was from single-mother households. However, we probably won't be able to tell whether the outcomes of these programs were due to the school or to the proficiency of private schools at picking well-behaved students—those with substantially lower rates of absenteeism, class cutting, drug use, vandalism, and verbal abuse of teachers.[30] Nor can we know how personal motivation and self-selection affects outcomes. After all, the family making the financial and other sacrifices necessary to send its children to private schools has, in Witte's words, an exceptional "taste for education."[31]

In the final analysis, private schools probably do not teach more effectively than public schools. But they do perform a function. They provide alternatives for a select few families who want out of the public schools—which underscores the need for better alternatives within the public sector.

The Evidence for Charter Schools

Nor is there convincing evidence from the test score results being published that charter schools improve student achievement. The safest conclusion is that, overall, they are equivalent to other schools in this respect. At best, the evidence on behalf of charters is mixed. At worst, some of it is outright negative.

Controversies. Moreover, many of the differences are trivial and much of the research has been controversial. There has been endless and largely fruitless contention over the validity and meaning of the published data. The strife is illustrated in squabbling that flared up in the fall of 2004 over a national comparison of test scores among children in charter schools and regular public schools that the Department of Education failed to publicize.[32] The data came from the National Assessment of Educational

Progress, which sampled only 3 percent of the relevant schools, and only a neglible number of charter schools that happened to fall into the sampling frame.

According to analysts from the American Federation of Teachers (AFT) who discovered the data on a website, the results, showed charter-school students often doing worse than other comparable students, by as much as one-half year. Charters located in low-income neighborhoods in big cities fared worse than their counterparts in the same areas. Researchers on both sides immediately began to duel over the results and interpretations. The Department of Education, a big supporter of charter schools, was criticized because it did not go out of its way to make the results known, while charter proponents contended that the study did not give a fair picture, because it provided only a crude snapshot of one grade level in a few schools at one point in time. Most charters, they contended, have been in existence only a few years, and could be attracting students who were already behind in public schools.

Later, the Department of Education released its own analysis, which concluded that fourth graders in charter schools do as well in reading but worse in math than their peers attending a traditional public school. When racial background was taken into account, there were no differences, but poor children attending charters performed worse in both subjects than their counterparts in other public schools. Of course the critics of charters leaped on that finding, while the supporters bragged that black children do okay in charter schools.

Occasionally a study will report positive results. The publicly traded company, Edison Schools, issued a glowing press release in May 2003, reporting that its students outperformed other students in their host districts by wide margins.[33] However, the press release did not indicate whether the background composition of Edison students exactly matched district enrollments with respect to percentage of English learners, disabled students, and other characteristics.

Hoxby's Study. In December 2004, Caroline Hoxby reported still another test score study. This one concluded that, compared to students in nearby regular schools, fourth grade charter-school students are 5.2 percent more likely to be proficient in reading and 2.3 percent more likely to be more proficient in math.[34] Hoxby, a Harvard economist, champions free-market education, and we have not come across any research she has published that would challenge her beliefs. While the study makes some notable contributions, it has shortcomings.

First, although Hoxby considers this study to be comprehensive because it includes 99 percent of fourth graders in the United States, it should be noted that this population accounts for fewer than 12 percent of all charter-school students. Junior high and high schools were not involved and schools that were too new to be included in statewide tests in 2002–03, and those with fewer than ten students did not participate. Overall, the approximately 1,050 schools in the study represent only about one-third of existing charter schools.

Second, the author managed to inflate the differences by excluding ninety-one of the lowest performing charters (8 percent of the total). Her dubious reasoning is that these ninety-one charter schools claim to serve "at risk" students (that is students who are not doing well in school), and so are not comparable to the nearby regular public schools that were used as matched comparisons. That is unreasonable. After all, at risk students are concentrated in a substantial proportion of regular public schools (far more than 8 percent), but the author made no effort to identify and exclude *them*. The logical design alternative would have been to include public schools anywhere within the region that are known to serve the same population of students.

Third, the un-inflated differences between charter and regular public school students in reading and math were, respectively, an unimposing 4.6 percent and 2.3 percent. As we have noted, other studies have reported equally diminutive percentage spreads, often in favor of noncharters. No study has demonstrated huge differences on either side. There is no justification for making decisions about the future of charter schools based on the slim margins being reported in the parade of studies focused on test results.

Fourth, all charter schools were treated as members of a single category, notwithstanding momentous differences among them—ranging from home schools to Internet-based programs. Parents faced with the prospect of sending their child to, for example, a Montessori, Waldorf, or Back-to-Basics school will find no help here.

Fifth, despite the author's statements to the contrary, the data say nothing about whether a charter school's autonomy contributes to favorable test results. This is because, as the author notes, autonomy is intertwined with (a) funding, and (b) number of years a state has had charter legislation. True, the data show that funding is correlated with performance, but that says nothing about autonomy, because an independent measure of autonomy was not included in the study. The author's attempt to use funding as a proxy for autonomy is not warranted.

Finally, as with most of these studies, the variance among schools was not reported. The state-by-state comparisons provide a clue about how much charter schools differ from one another. For example, in Alaska, fourth-grade charter students outperform their counterparts by 20 percent, whereas in North Carolina they confront a 4.3 percent disadvantage. In California, the differences are 9 and 5 percent respectively for reading and math. No doubt comparable variance also exists among the charter schools in California as well as in other states.

Lack of details about the full distribution handicaps a parent, who can be easily misled by information limited to averages. For example, let's say that there are fifty charter schools in a state, and that on average they have a 20 percent advantage over neighboring regular schools. That statistic does not tell you whether all fifty are doing better, or whether, for example, five outstanding schools are pulling up the average while the other forty-five are no better, or maybe a little or a lot worse. When the difference is small, it can be easily distorted by few schools. Hoxby's practice of weighting the regression equations by the number of students in the school increases the likelihood that a few big schools are having a disproportionate effect. Since the author says that she designed the study to reflect the way parents make choices—for example, whether to send a child to a charter school or a nearby regular public school—it is disappointing that she did not follow through with details about the sample variance that would actually help them make decisions.

In several respects, this study resembles many others of this genre: (a) individuals' test results being aggregated to state and national levels that have nothing to do with the individuals who take the tests; (b) authors gleefully celebrating relatively marginal statistical differences; and (c) overlooking within-sample and within-state variances. At the same time, this research does also make several contributions, including:

- Charter school students were compared to students in the nearest public school with a similar racial composition—presumably the school they otherwise would have attended. Corwin and Flaherty (1995) used the same type of matching approach in one of the first studies of charter schools, and with satisfactory results.

- The study examines the effects of a charter school's longevity, and finds that the charter advantage increases substantially the longer a school survives. The advantage reaches 10 percent for schools that have been operating nine or more years. This discovery fits with Hoxby's survival-of-the-fittest model, but it should be noted that the data do not reveal whether it is bad managers or bad students that get "weeded out."

- The findings suggest that schools with better funding do better. A charter school's proficiency advantage is 6.4 percent greater in reading and 11.7 percent greater in math if its funding is at least 40 percent of that available to regular schools in the same state. This is a reasonable, important finding, and consistent with our plea in Chapter 6 for increased funding for charters serving poverty students.

- The data show that positive effects on reading and math nearly double when charter schools operate in areas that are highly Hispanic. The reading proficiency advantage in high poverty areas also increases from 2.6 percent to 6.5 percent. These are schools that typically do much worse on tests.

These last findings, in particular, warrant more attention. We also see charters as an effective way to serve low-income, minority populations, and therefore in Chapter 5 we recommend that school districts should start up and operate special purpose charter schools specifically for students in poverty schools. Poverty schools typically have difficulty recruiting highly qualified teachers. However, if a poverty school is operating under a charter, it can pay above union scale in order to attract good teachers. Moreover, it is not subject to teacher union transfer policies, which usually encourage experienced teachers to transfer to other schools. If charters could demonstrate that they are helping under-served schools, and doing it with well prepared, experienced teachers, they would not be under the unreasonable mandate to continually prove themselves with heroic test results. That kind of proof is not likely to occur. We shall say more about this in Chapter 5.

A Mixed Picture. Since social research is seldom perfect, don't expect the wrangling to end any time soon. However, we think all the debate over often inconsistent and trivial differences has been fruitless. A few favorable reports notwithstanding, overall the research is plagued with small and inconsistent differences and suspect conclusions. Authors who have reviewed the existing body of research conclude that it ". . . reveals a mixed picture, with studies from some states suggesting a positive impact, studies from other states suggesting negative impact, and some providing evidence of positive and negative impacts. Overall, the charter impact on student achievement appears to be mixed or very slightly positive."[35] The authors of a study of student achievement in Michigan's charter schools concluded that charters schools ". . . will need to make up considerable ground as they become more established in order to overtake the test score levels and gains of students in traditional public schools."[36]

In 2002, the AFT looked at a batch of charter school studies that persuaded its authors that the majority of charter schools have failed to raise, and sometimes have lowered, student achievement compared to traditional public schools in the same area.[37] A 1999 study of Minnesota charter schools, for example, found that the percentage of charter students who met the state's graduation requirement for math was substantially below the state average (40 percent vs. 71 percent).[38] WestEd's study of test gains in five Los Angeles charter schools reflects a pattern of results characteristic of other studies.[39] In two low-performing charter schools, the students were more likely to move above the 50th percentile than students in comparison public schools, without hurting students who started above it. However, evidence for the other charter schools indicated only modest differences. The authors concluded that overall students either maintained or slightly improved their performance over time with respect to a comparison group of conventional schools. But perhaps more to the point, although some schools improved their rank in the district, others declined. For a Los Angeles parent thinking about enrolling a child, the likelihood of getting a better than average charter school is not much better than chance.

The AFT also found mixed results from their review of state assessment systems.[40] For example, in Michigan and North Carolina charter-school students scored lower on state standardized tests than their host districts, while studies of Pennsylvania, Arizona, and California concluded that charter students were making steady test score gains. Even so, Arizona's state assessments showed that gains by charter students were no better than those attending regular public schools. According to the Goldwater Institute, thirty-five charter sites made gains in reading, math, and language, while twenty declined in these subjects.[41] Some positive signs have been found in only a few states, while results have been mixed in several others. The Connecticut Department of Education studied changes in scores at the school level only, with mixed results. Six states that compared charter school performance with other schools reported negative results for charters; in three other states they were mixed to negative.

In 1999–2000, children in the Texas public schools passed the state academic achievement test at twice the rate recorded for those in charter schools.[42] According to a five-year study, the test scores of Texas charters increased, but the schools remained substantially below state levels, no matter which populations were served. The number of low-performing charter schools actually increased, while the number of high-performing schools declined. Texas charters also had lower attendance rates and higher percentages of dropouts.

Another state, California, ranks the academic performance of large schools serving similar populations. During one year, of the ninety-seven qualifying large charter schools that were included, fifty-four ranked below average when compared to similar schools; twenty-four ranked in the lowest-achievement decile, while ten ranked in the top decile.[43] In 2004, the spread in achievement gains between California charters and public schools was only about 3 percent, although the magnitude of increase favored charters schools—a pattern also, reported by a 2003 Brookings study.[44] The Brookings study, though, found that charter school students were anywhere from a half year to a full year behind their public school peers. That study was based on a review of 1999–2000 reading and math achievement test scores of 376 charter schools in ten states.[45] Fifty-nine percent of students at traditional public schools scored better than charter school students during the period studied. Scores of urban charter school students were no worse than others, but suburban and rural charter schools had much lower scores.

In general, studies have not substantiated the promise that charter schools would have a dramatic effect on student achievement. Good and Braden concluded in 2000 that "... student achievement, in general, has not been positively enhanced in charter schools."[46] In 2002, the New York affiliate of the National Education Association called for a moratorium on charter schools after analyzing twenty-three of the state's fifty-one charter schools, because the data provided no conclusive evidence they were improving student achievement.[47] Nevertheless, following the private school studies, authors have often leaped on negligible differences between charter schools and regular public schools to justify overblown conclusions.

Take for example an eleven-state study that selected only charters serving a general population and compared them with nearby public schools. That the authors attempted to narrow the comparisons to comparable types of schools is laudable, but their conclusions are suspicious. They found only 2 or 3 percent difference in favor of charters, but for some reason they considered the differences important.[48] Changes of this magnitude can easily be attributed to the types of students attracted to charter schools. Already murky results are further confounded by researchers acting as advocates or opponents of choice. No wonder that Good and Braden concluded, "Despite their growing popularity, charter schools have produced no convincing data to illustrate that, on the whole, they are prudent or productive investments."[49]

Defects in Current Testing Models

Inconsistent, trivial findings and diversity among choice schools are only two of the many problems plaguing testing research. Other problems are inherent in the statistical models being used and even more fundamentally, in the tests themselves. The idea that the success of a national program can be measured with standardized tests comes from an obsolete industrial model that treats schools as factories processing students as raw materials—with test scores reflecting the quality of the product. Of course, that is sheer nonsense, because in the first place, a school does not control most of the so-called production process. The way students perform on tests depends on many extraneous forces, such as parental guidance, peer group influences, job and travel experiences, and the like. And, in the second place, due to the way standardized tests are constructed (to maximize differences among individuals), they are inappropriate measures of higher-level organizational units like schools, school districts, and programs.[50] They simply were not constructed for this purpose, and consequently do not represent the range of diverse schools. The original purpose of standardized tests was to identify individuals who need special instruction. Therefore, test items are usually selected to maximize variance among individual test takers, not to measure differences between schools or to assess national programs. In fact, because of a statistical artifact, when variance increases within classrooms, it declines among schools, districts, and programs. The scores of individuals within classrooms are spread out so much that when they are averaged for each school or program, they tend to be similar for the aggregated units. There is little difference left to explain, as Alexander and Griffin have demonstrated.[51] Aggregating individual test scores to the level of schools, programs, or states inadvertently masks real differences among the units being compared. Researchers have been fussing over inconsequential differences derived from unjustifiable uses of standardized test scores.

These testing flaws are compounded by the fact that attention has been riveted to average (mean) differences between large pools of schools. Measures of central tendency mask the enormous variance among schools.[52] Most studies combine average test scores across all schools in a sample without breaking out important differences among various types of schools and without taking into account the range of schools included and how they differ from the average. A typical study, for example, will lump together all charter schools in the sample—across all districts and states represented—and then pretend the calculated average represents the population of charter schools. It doesn't. It only obscures differences within schools, within districts, and within each program or comparison group. A rare analysis based on distributions was reported by WestEd.[53] Test scores were divided at the 50th percentile. Schools were then classified based on the percentage of students below that mark. The analysis examined the percentage of students within each school who were originally on the low side and crossed over to the high side, as well as those who changed in the reverse direction. WestEd's approach makes more sense than comparing school means.

Statistical means do not reveal the fact that many public schools are as good as private schools, and that students who attend the best public schools outperform most private school students. Reporting averages that compare schools, programs, or states doesn't help parents who are trying to find a suitable school for their children. Everyone might want to believe that an increase in a school's mean scores implies that all students in that school are benefiting. But, the reality is that a school can increase its average score even if it is only the students in the upper part of the distribution who improve; this pattern would increase the gap between the top and bottom while still reflecting well on the school. Rosenberg observed that sophomores in the High School and Beyond survey answered 6.6 more questions correctly by their senior year, which is a small gain.[54] However, the lowest quartile of students answered, on average, 4.66 fewer questions correctly. By his calculations, the top quartile answered 18.13 more questions correctly, which had the effect of widening the achievement gap between the bottom and top groups by 22.79 questions, or 6.33 years.

Now extend this principle to a range of charter schools. Suppose that charter schools within a state have higher mean scores than regular schools. Shall we infer that all charter schools are better? Of course not.

Some are better, and some are worse. The question is how many are better. It is always possible that a few schools are pulling up the average, masking the poor performance of most other schools. Given the enormous differences among choice schools, averages and other measures of central tendency are not only meaningless, but also deceptive. What we need to know is the percentage of schools in the top, middle, and bottom of the distribution of charter schools, and how those percentages compare with the distribution of public schools. Knowing the percentages of schools with rising and falling test scores would help parents assess the risks and benefits of sending their child to a choice school.

Given the promise that choice would improve student achievement, one might expect that states would be insisting on proof of progress in student achievement. However, at least in part for the reasons being discussed, few states have reliable evaluation systems in place. Most of the forced closures that have occurred have been for financial mismanagement or fraud, not low-test performance.[55] How can we expect sponsors to hold charter schools accountable for producing superior academic achievement with a flimsy and inappropriate testing technology that conceals more than it reveals?

Implications

Choice supporters made a bargain that was impossible to keep, and it is therefore not surprising that not only is the evidence mixed, but also much of it is unflattering to choice schools—especially unflattering in view of the dramatic effects proponents had promised. Choice schools take too many different forms to be treated as meaningful units that can be sensibly compared to conventional public schools—which, of course, also differ among themselves. Notice that we have not said that most charters are inadequate. We said that it is not possible to make such an assessment from the data being reported. We do know that there is variation around any average figure, which suggests to us that many of them must be doing well. As we shall say in Chapter 5, we are counting on it. But the variation also suggests that others could be among the worst schools in the nation. There are also good and bad public schools.

Much of the dispute over test results has been senseless. Using antiquated factory models, driven advocates like to pound their chests over inflated statistics, while the other side natters on about trifling differences. Putting aside the embroidered claims on both sides, the only reasonable conclusion that can be justified by the evidence so far is that even if some charter students could be considered somewhat better off than most, the difference does not make much difference—certainly not enough to justify a federal program. The fact that some schools may be okay, even exceptional, is little comfort for parents who must make decisions about whether to risk sending their children to a particular school. Given the wide differences among schools, the risk is high. For parents, average scores amount to a crap shoot. They need better information. However, rather than sorting it out, researchers remain obsessed with meaningless averages, and then compound the ignorance by aggregating data collected from individuals in classrooms to the lofty levels of districts, states, and programs. Standardized test scores were not constructed for the purpose of comparing types of schools and other macro units. It is that simple!

But none of this seems to faze the allies of choice. Or, does it? At least some of them are getting the message that it is impossible to demonstrate whether or not charter schools and school vouchers are producing superior students across the board. But instead of backing down, they are looking for other ways to justify their shaky ideology.

THE COMPETITION FANTASY

Since school choice was peddled on the basis of the impossible promise that schools would be able to show improved student achievement, choice fans are scrambling to find other ways to justify charters and vouchers—especially the unsustainable claim that they are forcing regular schools to improve. They are not. Are they causing some regular schools to reevaluate their programs and practices? It's plausible. Are they giving exceptional teachers working in some choice schools an opportunity to teach differently? Yes, in some schools. Are they serving as models and implementing innovations that regular schools are adopting? In a word, no. They are not leading reform in that sense.

The Nobel laureate, economist Milton Friedman, proposed many years ago that if parents were given vouchers to purchase education for their own children, different types of high quality schools would form to meet their diverse demands.[56] He acknowledged that because education is a public good, the government is responsible for assuring that someone provides it. But he maintained the government does not itself need to operate schools. His plan would replace all public schools with a universal voucher plan. His was a far more radical idea than the current voucher programs, which flaunt a few voucher schools here and there as a fundamental reform.[57] In 1970, a sociologist, Christopher Jencks, proposed a voucher program along the lines Friedman had suggested, which the federal Office of Economic Opportunity unsuccessfully tried to implement at one site on an experimental basis.[58] Charter schools entered the picture in the early 1990s as derivatives of the voucher concept, and just as important, as a competitive alternative to school vouchers. For example, in 1993 California voucher activists placed a public initiative on the ballot to assess the voters' interest in school vouchers. Their opponents felt compelled to give the public another way to regain control over the way their children were taught. The compromise was legislation authorizing charter schools to form. There seems little doubt that the promise of charter schools helped defeat the 1994 California voucher-initiative. So, charters have become the premier competitors in the public education arena—not only competing with regular schools, but also out-competing voucher approaches.

The ideology of competition behind the choice movement is the same line being used to justify the privatization of all public institutions. The creed is derived from laissez-faire economics. But the problem is, public education is not a laissez-faire environment. There is no free market. Compulsory education laws guarantee a market for the providers no matter what they may do, and choice schools are underwritten by a vast public system obligated to finish whatever other providers prefer not to do. This includes taking care of the most difficult students needing the most costly services. Moreover, the government, not the market, regulates the competition, because by setting the size of the subsidy, politicians pick the schools that will benefit. But none of this deters school choice advocates. Charters and vouchers, they say, create competitive choices that will force public schools to change. Levin once said, ". . . it will be the threat of tuition tax credits and vouchers that will create the greatest stimulus for developing a system that increases meaningful public choices. . . ."[59] A 1990 U.S. Department of Education document was jubilant about the prospect, and credited school choice with injecting vitality into the education system, unleashing pent-up creativity, and ultimately providing the catalyst that drives other social reforms.[60]

Huh? The proposition that competition will force broadscale reform is couched in language so flabby it is unverifiable. Competition might merely sap the strength of public schools without killing them off. And, what will change, in which directions, and in which schools? How long will it take? Without a time frame, how shall we know whether a flailing school has failed, or is valiantly hanging on, or perhaps is about to be reborn? And, what happens to students left behind in a school coping with even less money because some of its students have defected?

One writer compares competition among schools to the U.S. Postal Service, which was forced to become more efficient by competition from private sector carriers.[61] Wait a minute. The analogy does not fit. Schools do not simply carry mail. They have many responsibilities, ranging from math to vocational education, from character training to the arts, from sex education to driver training. Test scores reflect only part of what public schools are expected to do. Consequently, a school is not merely good or bad. It can survive by doing one thing well, or several things in a mediocre way, even while failing in other respects. It could survive only because the district supports it and because it is a convenient place to send children.

How Much Competition Is Enough?

Choice supporters claim that rivalry causes achievement in regular public schools to rise. They need to explain how that occurs. That a little competition from the few existing choice schools will reform the vast enterprise of public education is sheer whimsy. There are only about 3,400 charter schools, and the entire private sector accounts for merely 11 percent of school enrollments (and few of those schools will be participating in voucher programs). These few schools are no match for 91,000 existing public schools. Besides, school districts have slack resources and can prop up schools that have lost a few students, thus minimizing the threat.

Still, these facts don't faze some writers. Hoxby maintains that it takes no more than 6 percent of a district's students transferring to choice schools to scare regular schools enough to somehow produce higher test scores.[62] Others are convinced that many more choice schools will be created soon. In a bizarre article, Danner and Bowman predict that 10,000 charter schools will become established, which a peculiar calculus leads them to conclude is the unique threshold that will force the education establishment to turn around.[63] It is unclear why 10,000 schools are a magic threshold, especially since the number of public schools continues to grow by that same number every couple of years. But no matter. That growth projection is pure conjecture. Marcella Dianda and Ronald Corwin found in 1993 that few private schools in California seemed willing to jump at the voucher program being proposed at that time.[64] While that could be changing, it is also plausible there will be few entrepreneurs ready and able to start viable charters, some low-quality start-up schools, and many failures—the latter a consequence of the financial instability associated with any new enterprise, along with the absence of experience.

Is Competition Reforming Public Schools?

But, all right, for the sake of the argument, let's suppose that competition does increase, and that struggle can be a motivating force. Is motivation enough to force public schools to improve? Why should we believe that competition, by itself, can produce reform? That is a stretch, because it does not assure there will be the leadership, skills, and resources required to implement reform. It is not exactly clear how lagging schools being threatened by rivals are supposed to suddenly come up with more effective practices and the resources that may be needed. A study of the impact of charter schools in three states indicated that school principals who felt threatened by the potential loss of students were attempting to introduce more reforms, but they also said that they often lacked the necessary autonomy.[65] Maybe even more important, they need resources to pay for teacher training, materials, and administrative support. This was the unexpected finding from studies of Florida's program, which allows students in lagging schools to transfer out. There was some evidence that these lagging schools were improving (although the one-year gains were vastly overestimated). One researcher claimed that the threat of vouchers alone forced the districts to undertake massive amounts of professional development and to change instruction methods, which improved low-performing schools. However, in an ironic twist, a reanalysis of the one-year achievement gains concluded that competition was not the cause. The improved test scores could be explained by an infusion of new resources and more targeted use of existing resources.[66] Whether that occurred because of competition or because of a general climate throughout the state supporting improvement is hard to say.

Then too, will charters really threaten public schools? How many students have to leave the regular schools before it matters to them? Teachers don't get paid less, nor do principals. The schools don't lose significant resources, forego programs, drop athletic programs, or cease having a school lunch program because a few children left to enroll in a charter school. In fact, if the students who left were not happy or satisfied students, or were achieving below grade level, or were not receiving the level of services their parents demanded, it's entirely possible the district wasn't all that sorry to see them leave. That being the case, the threat of a charter school nearby probably won't do much to foster a competitive spirit in the district.

Flaws in the Research

It may seem plausible that those public schools directly affected by competition will modify some of their practices. And yet, the evidence for that hypothesis is less than persuasive. Certainly it can't be proven with the research models being used. The research is riddled with deficiencies, which include: failure of researchers to take critical circumstances into consideration, lack of information about how policy changes affect student outcomes, conclusions based on puny differences, preoccupation with statistical averages while ignoring the variance, and the absence of explanatory data. We will briefly comment on each.

The Effect of Competition Depends on the Circumstances. Armor and Peiser analyzed choice data collected for Massachusetts school districts between 1995 and 1996 to determine whether districts would take steps to regain market share when they lose students and dollars through interdistrict choice programs.[67] They found that the districts that lost large numbers of students quickly began to gain them back, presumably by changing policies and programs. In a follow-up study, Aud reported that loser districts continued to gain back students in the subsequent two years.[68] Still another observer maintains that when Minnesota began its post-secondary enrollment options program in 1985, which allowed high school seniors to enroll in college courses for dual credit, competition increased among high schools, prompting them to double the number of Advanced Placement courses. However, none of the studies asked about student outcomes, and therefore they provide no evidence, one way or the other, for the idea that competition for students causes test scores to improve.

It may be important to distinguish between competition that comes from outside a district and competition from within. It is plausible that competition from schools within a district will have more impact than competition from outside, because schools within a district communicate with the same district administrators, and are connected through networks of teachers, parents, student friendships, and siblings, sports events, and the like. Still, the impact of competition from any source can be reduced by other conditions. One is the availability of other resources to offset the effects of competition. For example, in Massachusetts, a district that loses tuition gets reimbursed up to a specified "foundation" level. This safety net weakens market pressures. Consequently, in the Armor-Preiser and Aud studies cited above, only those districts that spent above the foundation budget reacted when they lost students. Another condition that can minimize the effect of competition for students is the existing supply of students. Wells learned that districts faced with severe overcrowding are unlikely to be threatened by slight enrollment declines.[69] In public organizations, market forces are modified by political and fiscal policies.

In one novel study, researchers compared Arizona (where charter schools operated) with Nevada (where they did not). They assumed that Arizona schools would report having made more changes than Nevada schools because Arizona schools would be more threatened by competition from charter schools.[70] The authors did find that Arizona schools changed a little more than Nevada schools, although the changes were modest. However, Arizona might simply be more progressive, as witnessed by its readiness to embrace charter schools in the first place. Also, within Arizona, they selected schools that were located in areas where 30 percent of the students were enrolled in charter schools—which was the threshold they used to identify competition for students. These schools were then compared with other schools. Principals of the schools facing competition did report more changes than schools not facing the prospect of enrollment drains. In threatened schools, principals protected teachers from outside pressures, made more effort to inform parents of school programs, and provided more day care. They also stepped up in-service training, encouraged teachers to experiment, consulted with them more and allowed them to exercise more influence over in-service training, curriculum, discipline, and scheduling. However, we question whether these rather marginal actions will be enough to improve student outcomes, especially since the authors themselves rated the amount of change as only slight to moderate.

Variance Is Usually Ignored. As we have mentioned, a pervasive problem in most of the studies is that researchers consider only the average differences and do not report variations among the schools involved. Caroline Hoxby's often cited work is a prime example. She found a relationship in Michigan and in Arizona between competition and improved test scores.[71] She chose to measure competition by the percentage of students within a district who are enrolled in charter schools. She found that public schools located in districts where at least 6 percent of the students enrolled in charter schools improved their test scores after several years. Six percent—that is only 1 percent above normal enrollment fluctuation! The improvement, however, amounted to a modest one or two national percentile points (ranks) over and above other schools, which for some reason she thinks is worth getting excited about. The author reached a similar conclusion about the effect of vouchers on public schools in Milwaukee, where test scores went slightly higher in schools which she thought were more threatened by competition from nearby private schools.

The methods she used focus on average scores, leaving the impression that all schools and districts responded to competition in the same way. But it would be illuminating to know whether districts in the upper quartile of test scores behave differently from those in the bottom quartile. And, the author did not consider the possibility that improved performance in a few neighborhoods and communities might be pulling up the average, thus perhaps masking other areas where competition had a negative impact. For example, the author failed to report differences in the way large and small districts, or high- and low-income districts, respond to competition. Suppose that only high-income districts respond positively to competition and that most charter schools are in these districts. The mean statistic used will obscure a possibly null or negative correlation in low-income districts.

In contrast to Hoxby's findings, Smith and Meier found a negative correlation between (a) competition from the private sector (measured by percentage of students in private schools), and (b) standardized test scores in Florida school districts.[72] The equation included district-level measures of bureaucratic characteristics, income, and academic performance, which they treated as independent control variables. These results were challenged by another study that found a weak but statistically significant relationship between (a) student test-score performance in public schools located in 100 North Carolina counties, and (b) the percentage of students enrolled in private schools.[73] However, using the same North Carolina data, Newmark demonstrated that the relationship between public school student performance and the presence of private school competition was not consistent across different testing areas.[74] A correlation was found in only two of ten separate testing areas. The significance of competition paled in comparison to aggregate levels of parental education and poverty rates as predictors of student achievement.

Newmark's findings were then replicated in Washington State by Simon and Lovrich.[75] They used percentile measures of average district-level student achievement on the Comprehensive Test of Basic Skills (CTBS) for the 104 school districts with private school enrollment. The researchers constructed six regression models, representing three testing areas for the fourth- and eighth-grade levels. Each model included measures to control for parental education level, dollars per pupil expended, and percentage of children living in poverty. Percentage of children enrolled in private schools was used as an indicator of competition. Competition was positively correlated with test scores in only one of the six possibilities, and even then the effect was dwarfed by the effects of socioeconomic context and level of parental education. The authors concluded that there is no clear evidence that competition from private schools for enrollments results in higher test scores in the public schools. Rather, socioeconomic conditions were substantially better indicators of student performance than either district resources expended per pupil or the measure of private school competition. The authors point out that a market-based approach to educational reform cannot alter parental education levels or the socioeconomic conditions prevalent in a particular community.

Studies Provide Few Explanations. What troubles us most about this body of research is that researchers so frequently report a statistical correlation without including data that would help to explain it. A case in point is the Armor and Peiser study cited above. The data do not account for how districts managed to curb the loss of students as a result of losing some money. The escape valve hypothesis and random variation over several years could explain it as easily as administrative actions. That is, perhaps a limited number of families want out of a district and when they have left the exodus stops, except for random fluctuations.

Hoxby's study, described above, is another example of failure to explain. For some reason, the study provides no information to account for how schools managed to improve outcomes in response to a minor amount of competition. The author gives us a lot of speculation, but no empirical explanations. She imagines that maybe administrators were using inducements to make staff work harder, shedding unproductive staff and programs, allocating resources away from nonachievement oriented activities, and renegotiating the teacher contract. In addition, she conjectures, competition may bid up wages, thereby attracting better teachers, or it may force schools to abandon unsuccessful pedagogical techniques.

A better explanation is that choice schools originate in districts that are also undertaking a variety of other initiatives. Many districts are responding to the same community and national forces of discontent that spawned school-choice programs. Some charters have participated in other reforms prior to, or simultaneously with, converting to charter status. Such reforms include state restructuring initiatives, site-based management, Success for All, class-size reduction plans, literacy and curriculum enrichment programs, and beefed up professional development programs. Other initiatives, such as those within a district, have laid the foundation for new practices, such as community councils and site-based management. The No Child Left Behind Act, which requires districts to improve test scores, had been proposed and was being heatedly discussed in congress about the time Hoxby published her findings. It would be prudent then to compare charter schools with schools responding to other pressures. To demonstrate that the introduction of charter schools caused test scores to rise, it would be necessary to show there were no other initiatives being planned or introduced about the same time. Are we supposed to believe that Detroit and Phoenix, which were part of Hoxby's sample, have started no innovative programs other than charter schools? What about Michigan's "schools-of-choice" option that allows parents to transfer to districts of their choice and accounts for a loss of thousands of students from Detroit schools? How did Hoxby factor that into the data? Problem is, her writings reveal no interest in pursuing alternative explanations.

There are still other possible reasons that test scores might improve in districts with charters. For example, perhaps low performers are being excused from the tests, or maybe programs in the arts, music, and theater are being eliminated to make more time to concentrate on tests. Some districts are getting a leg up on others by starting the school year earlier to give students more time to study for the tests. Teaching to the test is another worthy hypothesis. It is widely recognized that school districts that have used a test for a period time tend to show improvement, because teachers (and students) learn to identify the material that is covered on the test and then go over it in class. In addition, some students and teachers may be cheating more. According the Associated Press, more than 200 California teachers in fifty-six schools were investigated during 2004 for helping students cheat on standardized tests.[76] Still another possibility is that competition sometimes prods school districts to find new resources or reallocate existing resources to, for example, pay for longer school days, remedial courses, or more staff. We simply don't know. And, that is the problem. The list of possibilities is endless. Moreover, all these possibilities could be happening independently of charter schools if administrators were responding to the same pressures that are creating charter schools.

Implications

The claim that competition from choice schools is causing school districts to improve cannot be sustained as a general proposition. Reason suggests that some schools, in some districts, will take notice when they start losing enough students and money. However, the research has not identified where that might happen, how much competition it takes, or what actions schools then will take to improve student outcomes. Certainly, test scores will not improve automatically just because a school loses a few students or tinkers with a few policies or programs. To improve outcomes, it takes leadership, skills, and resources—none of which is guaranteed by competition. Nor does competition guarantee that schools will miraculously improve. More likely, it will be corrosive, with the only consequence being a drain on resources from the public sector. Competition might only cause schools to flail blindly without direction. Moreover, a few schools in a district probably are not going provide real competition, although perhaps it's possible.

Several studies have sought to prove that competition from choice schools improves test scores in public schools. They have not yielded convincing support for the proposition nor provided the information needed to explain how it could happen, and they have been plagued with defective analyses, which include: a propensity to inflate the significance of small differences, incorrectly aggregating individual scores to meaningless levels of abstraction, preoccupation with averages that obscure variation, and failure to identify where competition does and does not have an effect. Therefore, even if we grant that competition can have an effect, there is no way to tell whether it is universal or whether it is limited to a few places that are pulling up the correlation under unique conditions (for example, in small districts losing students). In any case, those who espouse the competition ideology have yet to identify the mechanisms that cause student achievement to rise. Supposedly, they would include changes in teaching practices. So, now let's consider those.

THE REFORM LEGEND

Breaking News: "After being released from the stifling clutches of stagnant school districts, charter schools have spearheaded an unprecedented wave of educational reform, which eventually perked up even the sleepiest public schools, miraculously provoking them to produce good education for the first time since Socrates." Well . . . not exactly! That turns out to be another fairy tale. But hold on. It doesn't mean that charter schools have not been innovative. Some have—depending. But like other chapters in the school choice yarn, the actual storyline is more complicated than choice advocates had hoped.

Are Charter Schools Spearheading Reform?

If we shift our focus slightly—away from the general relationship between competition and student outcomes and on to the intervening processes—we come to things charter schools may or may not actually be doing to improve public schools. Are charter schools doing things differently than regular schools? Are they doing things that are causing public schools to change? Are they leading education reform? The answers to those questions depend on how you define the terms. We think of a *reform* as a combination of inventions and widespread innovations. An invention is a practice that is new to the world, whereas an *innovation* is a practice new to a particular setting.

If choice schools were leading reform, they either would be producing breakthrough inventions that regular schools are rushing to adopt, or serving as models to them. They are doing neither. The 2002 AFT's review of charter school research concluded that there is little evidence that competition for students has changed the behavior of host districts. Public school officials in one study said they did not believe charter schools are providing new models or programs, and are not doing anything innovative they wish to emulate.[77] Over half the administrators polled in Arizona said their districts have not been affected by charter schools and do not believe charter schools will improve public education.[78] Dianda and Corwin found that among the first wave of California charter schools, no more than one in four districts was liberalizing its policies governing restructuring as a direct result of the presence of charter schools.[79] And, while charter schools in our follow-up study were implementing more innovations than comparison schools, most districts were not inclined to disseminate practices being used by charter schools; where that occurred, it was usually in smaller districts.[80] A 1998 study of some California charter schools continued to find little evidence that educators in public schools were learning about innovative ideas from charter schools.[81] In fact, there are generally no mechanisms in place for charter schools to share their experiences with conventional schools.[82]

Nearly all superintendents who participated in an early evaluation of Texas charter schools indicated that there had been no changes in educational policies, programs, or services as a result of charter schools in their areas.[83] A later, five-year study revealed that one of every three school officials was not even aware of charter schools within the geographic boundaries.[84] Only 25 percent of the districts reported interacting with charter-school staff. Districts with declining enrollments were more likely than others to report that charter schools had affected their budgets, yet they continued to say that charters had little influence on educational approaches. Most of the officials in the Texas study also expressed concerns about the quality of charter-school instruction, and more than half were especially concerned about whether special needs students were receiving appropriate education.

It seems plausible that competition is causing some schools to reevaluate and tinker with their practices, but so far there is no evidence to support the existence of causal relationships either between the amount of competition and the number of reforms or between competition and improved student achievement. One reason teachers are not looking to charters as models is that many of the innovative things charters are doing are already being widely advocated and used elsewhere. Another is that many teachers do not consider small, experimental charter schools—staffed by uncertified teachers working long hours—to be directly applicable to their situations.

Are Choice Schools More Innovative Than Regular Schools?

If choice schools are not directly affecting the practices of other schools, we still have to wonder whether they are doing things differently than neighboring schools. The evidence is mixed on that.

Private Schools. First, consider private schools. The little research available on the private sector suggests that some private schools are more innovative than others, but there is no basis for saying that they are on the whole highly innovative. From one of the few studies of innovation we could find reporting on private schools, Louis Chandler concluded that a full range of traditional and progressive instructional techniques were operating in the 336 public, Catholic, and independent schools he studied.[85] Principals were asked whether the school commonly used traditional techniques (such as teacher-led instruction, phonics or objective testing), or progressive ideas (like student-initiated discovery learning, whole language, or portfolio assessments). Independent private schools were slightly more likely to use traditional instructional methods, Catholic schools were slightly more likely to try progressive methods, and public schools were in between. But there was more variation within these three categories than between them. This seems to mean that the type of education students receive depends more on the idiosyncratic preferences of their teachers than the kind of school they attend. And, of course, there is plenty of room to quarrel about whether so-called progressive instructional techniques amount to innovation.

Charter Schools. Next, we can consider the more extensive evidence on charter schools. How innovative are they? Again, it largely depends on your definition of innovation. Overall, charter schools do take a wide variety of curriculum approaches, including interdisciplinary, inquiry, and thematic approaches. Manno, Finn, and their associates were impressed with the variety of instructional approaches they have encountered, including a Core Knowledge Program, a Montessori-style school, Waldorf-style schools, schools for former dropouts, work-related programs, virtual computer-based schools, home schools, and the like.[86] Public schools also take a wide variety of approaches of course. The difference could be that a higher proportion of charters than public schools are trying out innovations.

Looking for minor administrative innovations rather than break-through inventions, Finn and Kansotroom describe two studies showing how principals use of the flexibility allowed within the charter to locate good certified and noncertified teachers willing to work long hours, and to pay them more if necessary, as well as to get rid of teachers they do not want.[87] Their point is that the freedom associated with charters opens more possibilities for creative management, though not necessarily creative breakthroughs. Fair enough. We agree and applaud that aspect of charter schools. Corwin, Flaherty, and Dianda also settled for a lower threshold of innovation in 1995 when we asked principals and teachers about curriculum and instruction practices in their schools.[88] The study polled fifty-four administrators and 230 teachers in sixty-six California charter schools and compared their responses to those of forty-six principals representing regular schools the students would otherwise have attended. The analysis showed that some charters were implementing somewhat progressive practices (though not new practices) more frequently than counterpart regular schools. Teachers in charter schools were more likely to: experiment; use alternative assessments; use thematic instruction and include more than one subject in assignments; give individualized assignments; offer a wider variety of subjects; use cooperative learning and cross-age teaching techniques; and involve students in community service. Teachers in charters frequently assessed students through portfolios of their work, often coordinated with other teachers and assigned interdisciplinary work, and frequently reorganized the way they delivered instruction. In addition, charters were far more likely to be using school-based governance techniques, inviting parents to work in classrooms, fostering more parent participation and community partnerships, and employing uncertified teachers.

None of the approaches just mentioned qualifies as an invention as we define it, and the progressive methods themselves probably have more to do with being small schools than being charters. We do think there is a large pool of charters that deserve some credit for using available innovations, especially since we know that many charters are not even ex-pected to be innovative. Back-to-basics and traditional approaches are commonplace in many choice schools, because parents insist on them. However, on the whole, we have to agree with the skeptics who question whether charter schools are being exceptionally innovative. Fiore and Harwell concluded that many charters are not doing anything different from their host districts. Approximately half of the thirty-two schools they visited reported that their curriculum was the same as, or similar to, the curriculum of the state or district.[89] Also, a 1999 study of Michigan school-choice policies found that while many charter schools offer distinct pro-grams, they are not particularly innovative when it comes to teaching and learning.[90] SRI's 1997 study reported that 87 percent of charter schools were using traditional classroom-based approaches to instruction.[91] Horn and Miron found that charter schools were remarkably similar to the reg-ular public schools, but with some notable exceptions.[92] From their analy-sis of Arizona charter schools, Stout and Garn found little going on there that merits of the attention of anyone seeking powerful ways to engage children and youth in learning.[93] Good and Braden could be right. They concluded that innovation in curriculum and instruction is virtually non-existent in charter schools.[94] But again, we caution, there is so much vari-ation among charter schools, it is hazardous to generalize.

Does Autonomy Contribute to Innovation?

Choice proponents think autonomy promotes reform. Some charters op-erate within school districts, while others are totally independent of them. In either case, the amount of autonomy available to teachers varies con-siderably. Corwin and Flaherty found that charter school administrators were far more likely than their counterparts in regular schools to attribute teachers with a high degree of freedom and influence—which meshes with several studies cited in the 2002 AFT review of charter school research.[95] However, among our sample schools, we found some charters were in-dependent in name only, while others controlled key decisions ranging from curriculum, scheduling, and staffing to finance and purchasing.

We wondered if autonomy does make a difference when it comes to in-novation. Therefore, we classified charters in our sample as high or low on a scale of autonomy constructed from the degree of control each school re-ported exercising over sixteen types of decisions. Using this scale to rank schools, we found that high autonomy schools promoted parent involve-ment and made scheduling changes twice as frequently as schools with low autonomy, and by a ratio of five to one, they more frequently reduced class sizes. Other differences we inquired about were negligible. So, it seems that autonomy can make a difference, but only for a limited number of prac-tices. Certainly autonomy is no silver bullet that makes innovation happen.

Do Teachers Make the Difference?

So, where are we? On the one hand, several researchers maintain that charter schools are not doing anything new. On the other hand, in some places at least, charter teachers do seem to be using nonconventional practices more frequently than most other teachers. Differences between these two conclusions can be easily accounted for by whether one focuses on the types of things charters are doing or on how frequently they are being used. Charters may not be doing much that is new to the world, but they could be using unconventional approaches more often than other schools. Is that enough to justify a hyped-up massive national program? Of course not. What it suggests is that regular public schools could use a little more freedom, especially for their most creative teachers. And that could happen without needing to create independent schools.

Apparent inconsistencies in the findings make more sense when the kind of teachers that go into charter schools is taken into account. Since charters bill themselves as reforms, we suppose at least some could be attracting some venturesome, if not always well trained, teachers ready to experiment. But could these same teachers be as creative in other schools? As Marcella Dianda once observed, although most teachers in our study of charters acknowledged that charter status was valuable, few considered it essential for what they were doing—which makes one wonder whether charter status is causing anything.[96] Some administrators also said that charter status was not necessary to implement certain types of innovations. So, charter status may facilitate creative teachers who want to experiment, but that doesn't mean the charter is causing anything to happen. In fact, we found that up to a third of the regular schools in our study reported doing most of the things charters were doing. Moreover, the autonomy that charters sometimes provide seemed important for only a few areas.

Suppose that there is a pool of creative teachers in public education. Then suppose that charter schools attract a disproportionate number of them. It would mean that charters are draining off creative teachers who otherwise would be teaching in public schools. That scenario would easily account for both the possibility that charters are doing progressive things more often than regular schools, and the likelihood that regular schools are doing most of the same things.

Implications

What shall we conclude about the idea that choice schools are leading reform? Judging from the evidence, they are not. They are neither inventing new approaches nor acting as models for public schools. So, if you are looking for big things from choice schools, you are going to be disappointed—unless you are impressed with the few schools using arcane approaches, like the Waldorf program, cyber instruction, home schooling, and the like. But if you are willing to settle for something less than breakthroughs, you can rest content knowing that, although many charter schools are only doing things many other unconventional public schools are already doing, at least many are doing them more frequently, or shall we say, at least in some places. Innovation, after all, only means changing something in a particular setting. And, many charter schools are innovative in that limited sense. But why? Is it the independence and autonomy that comes with charter status? We doubt it. It takes more than releasing a few constraints to make good things happen. Years of research on school-based governance show that granting schools more autonomy will not in itself yield the improved learning results hoped for, unless certain conditions are in place—especially the skills and experience needed to make difficult administrative and policy decisions, the special training often required, and dedicated teachers searching for better approaches.[97]

Is it, after all, the teachers who join charter schools that make the difference? We think the innovations, in some charter schools at least, are a product of freedom in the classroom and exceptional teachers (and probably exceptional self-selected families as well). It appears that, at best, charter status sometimes functions as a facilitating condition in this equation.[98] The freedom a charter offers is probably helpful, but it does not seem to be causing anything to happen by itself. It gives exceptional teachers who join charters opportunities to teach more creatively, or to do what they were doing anyway—only with a little more support and a little less restraint. And, when exceptional levels of autonomy are present, it can give a boost to a limited number of innovations. But, we submit, neither charter status nor exceptional autonomy is sufficient to promote innovation without the selective recruitment of dedicated, creative teachers. There is no evidence that independence from school districts (as opposed to classroom autonomy) plays any part in this. Teachers in public schools use the same techniques as those in charters, if less frequently. In other words, charter status without the right teachers won't pay off in innovation. Conversely, with the right incentives and a generous amount of classroom autonomy, creative teaching can be promoted within the public schools.

THE BUREAUCRACY MYTH

This brings us to the much-maligned, education bureaucracy, which choice proponents portray as the primary problem. But is it? Ironically, as we have just documented, many charter schools are not actually using their autonomy to do much that is different from public schools. And even allowing for a pool of charters experimenting more often than public schools, it doesn't override the fact that a sizeable proportion of public schools are doing the same thing. A report of three states by Fuhrman and Elmore, published in 1995, had already cast doubt at the beginning of the movement about whether state regulations were stifling teachers.[99] The study found that some charter schools never used their flexibility, and that most schools that did create innovative programs stayed within the state's rules. And, as already mentioned, Good and Braden concluded that innovation in curriculum and instruction is virtually nonexistent in charter schools; Stout and Garn found little going on in Arizona charters that merits of the attention of anyone seeking powerful ways to engage children and youth in learning.[100]

Choice apologists use negative stereotypes of bureaucracy as an excuse to justify their ideological quest for independence, which in most cases, is not actually needed. Still, we are told that choice schools should not be regulated because bureaucracy obstructs good teaching. The critics maintain that charter schools and school vouchers are needed because public school bureaucracies have failed and are incapable of changing themselves. Not so. While public education has many failings, as we shall discuss at length in Chapter 5, they can't all be laid off on a fictional bureaucracy. Sure, education has some bureaucratic characteristics, but it is also a complex, loosely coupled system that is inherently receptive to concerted reform efforts. We have already identified a host of innovations going on in school districts, ranging from specialized alternative and magnet schools, to small, site-managed schools, to preschools and middle schools. The point we want to make in the following paragraphs is that many of the problems people think are caused by too much bureaucracy are actually the consequence of too little bureaucracy. In particular, there is no good substitute for bureaucratic rules and specialization.

Big bureaucracies, the critics say, are ossified. When people talk like that, they are thinking only of the organizational pathologies that infect big public and private organizations. Roger's scathing criticism of a fossilized New York City school district in the 1960s survives as a haunting reminder of the organizational pathologies that can be found in public education—from oligarchy to red tape; from inflexibility to abuse of power.[101] Schools are hemmed in on all sides by policies other people control—teacher-training programs, state and federal agencies, school boards, professional bargaining units, parent-teacher associations, and other stakeholders. Ensnared in webs of ambiguous authority, teachers are obligated to obey district regulations governing the curriculum, textbooks, schedules, and the like, which, the story goes, only keeps them from doing what they know should be done for students.

True as that may be, organizational pathologies are not confined to public school districts. The same U.S. Senator, Joseph Lieberman, who calls schools "ossified," leads a set of federal bureaucracies that, to put it mildly, are not known for either innovation or flexibility. Nor is the pri-

vate sector a solution. If you want to experience organizational pathologies firsthand, just try to return a defective automobile to its manu-
facturer. And don't forget Enron. But school choice fans prefer not to be
confused with the facts. They contrast their pathological images of education against a nostalgic, autonomous life of freedom offered by the
mythical free market, unencumbered by the inconvenience of government regulation.[102] If schools could operate in the free market, unshack-
led from political and administrative restrictions, they contend, children
would get a better education. Decisions would be made by the marketplace, eliminating the need for an elaborate managerial apparatus.
Williamson once observed that organizations form when markets fail.
Choice backers have turned Williamson's observation inside out, offering
free markets as the solution to failing organizations.[103]

Those who advocate the free-market doctrine neglect to mention the
Caveat Emptor principle recognized by the courts: buyers beware, because
the merchandise may be misrepresented or defective. They hate to be re-
minded of the army of federal and state bureaucrats who monitor and
enforce laws full time, regulating the so-called free market. Pick up any
newspaper on any particular day and read about businesses failing, executives being prosecuted, and goods being recalled under government
mandate. Charter supporters like to take credit for the fact that the schools
enroll a larger proportion of racial minority and poor students than do
many comparable public schools. But they forget to tell you the schools
do it because they are required to do it. To quote Rothstein:

Not so fast. These data [about serving the underprivileged] are partly driven by
regulations of the sort that conservative charter proponents detest. California's
charter law requires that priority be given to schools serving low-achieving students. Colorado mandates that one-quarter of the state's initial charters must be
for schools primarily serving "at risk" students; Rhode Island requires that half
its charters go to such schools. South Carolina mandates that the racial distribution of a charter school's students must parallel that of its district.[104]

In short, there is no free market for choice schools. It is a luxury no one can
afford. Business and public education alike will be, indeed must be, constrained by laws and rules. We recognize that there are some awful rules
that are unnecessarily cramping public schools and adversely affecting students. However, it isn't necessary to scrap everything to change them.

Education Is a Loosely Coupled System

Bureaucracy is ubiquitous. It permeates society from big business to
baseball, from hospitals to automotive companies. Weber once observed
that one of the most creative organizations modern society has produced,

the symphony orchestra, is the epitome of bureaucracy. The instrumental sections make up the division of labor, and are coordinated through a hierarchy of first chairs, assistant conductors and conductors. Yes, even creative musicians must comply with unforgiving rules embedded in musical scores. So, let's get off the stereotypes. They don't fit any part of modern society, especially not public or private education. Perhaps public education is not the efficient free-market system that choice proponents glorify. But neither is it the inept, calcified organization the critics want us to see. The reality is that a fluid coalition governs education. It consists of state legislatures and departments of education, the courts, labor unions, teacher-training institutions, professional organizations, businesses, and many other stakeholders. One cannot dismiss this complex system as a "bureaucracy." The private sector has no monopoly on diversity. There are over 14,000 school districts, comprising 91,000 schools that vary widely in size, grade-level structure, student composition, course requirements, and funding levels.[105] They cannot possibly fit one mold.

Beneath their bureaucratic skeleton, school districts are complex organizations, operating as natural, loosely coupled systems.[106] Public education is segmented into large and small cities, ghettos and suburbs, and low- and high-income districts. Some decisions are made at centralized levels, but others are decentralized through school-based management, small high schools, specialized alternative schools, and the like. There are big differences among schools within districts that cannot be accounted for by bureaucracy. Consequently, the quality of a student's education depends more on the particular school than whether or not it is a charter, a voucher, or a conventional public school.

What Is Bureaucracy?

This is not to say that school districts have no bureaucratic characteristics. They do, including these:

1. *Specialization,* or in other words, jurisdictions of activity coordinated through a division of labor;
2. *Standardization* through rules, routines, and official documents that guide the activity;
3. *Hierarchy,* which is to say, a system of graded levels of authority;
4. *Compliance* on the part of subordinates to the commands of their official superiors;
5. *Appointment* to office on the basis of *expertise;*
6. *Tenure* and lifetime *careers* that evolve predictably through promotions in rank;
7. Guarded *separation of the bureaucrat's personal life* from his vocation.[107]

Bureaucratic rules in public organizations protect citizens against corrupt employees seeking to promote personal agendas and ready to exploit friendships and family connections for personal gain. Competency standards help protect the public from incompetent employees. Hierarchy is an oversight mechanism to assure that public employees do their jobs, that public funds are used properly, and that citizens have a way to reach higher authorities with their complaints. Documents, that dreaded paperwork, provide memories of an organization's commitments, its activities, and how well it has performed. Bureaucracies are routinized through rules, work habits, and schedules. Routines provide predictable work patterns that facilitate personnel turnover and permit substitute teachers to carry on. Routines are embedded in calendars and daily schedules that tell parents when to send their kids to school, when teachers will be available, and when tests will be given. On a broader, national basis, bureaucratic characteristics—such as standardized curricula at each grade level—facilitate student transfers as they move across the country.

Two principles underlie all of these characteristics, which can be summed up as specialization and coordination. Specialists staff each position and are assigned tasks according to designated spheres of responsibility and authority. A division of labor forms when the work of specialists in different areas is coordinated. Coordination can be achieved through (a) centralized decisions, (b) routines guided by rules, or (c) decisions made by specialists who have been given discretion to apply their expert knowledge as contingencies arise. For the sociologist Max Weber, bureaucracy represented the ultimate form of rational efficiency, because the organization is administered by experts under the rule of law. Employees are appointed, rather than elected to office, and they must qualify on the basis of their training and skills rather than their personality characteristics alone. Advancement opportunities, pensions, seniority, and penalties for noncompliance are all incentives used to secure the bureaucrat's personal, long-term attachment to the organization.

Key Features of Bureaucracy. Some features of bureaucracy that follow from the characteristics just described are worth noting. First, bureaucracies are multifaceted, and the listed characteristics do not always occur together. Bureaucracies are not only about rules and remote decision making. They can be coordinated in a variety of different ways. This multidimensional feature creates different patterns of bureaucracy, and therefore bureaucracies do not all look alike. Thus, one school district is dominated by rules with little need for continual decision making at the top, while another relies on centralized decisions rather than rules, and still another provides discretion to specialists to make their own decisions. Some districts are decentralized, for example, using school-based management techniques. Coordination in such districts occurs through discretion and expertise guided by general rules. Given the variability, public education can be anything someone wants it to be. It is monolithic. It is fragmented. It is both. It depends on the specific localities and policies being considered. It probably also depends on what one would like to believe.

A second important feature is that propensity for change is built into the structure of bureaucracies. Change is a natural response to inconsistencies and power struggles arising from the bureaucratic characteristics themselves. Look no further than many teacher strikes over the years. As trained professionals, teachers have special knowledge that justifies allowing them to make decisions about curriculum. But they are also employees obliged to follow the rules, even rules they consider to be potentially detrimental to students, such as assigning outdated or factually incorrect textbooks. A primary motive (though certainly not the only motive) behind teacher militancy over the past several decades has been to resolve conflicts between these professional and employee roles. Many other role conflicts are inherent to school districts, including conflicting ideas about the roles of parents, students, and administrators.

These role conflicts in turn create pressures for change within school districts. Tensions make districts susceptible to change when resources and expertise are leveraged directly at issues related to the role conflicts. A direct approach to reform—by leveraging existing pressures for change—is a more effective way to produce change than more circuitous routes advocated by choice proponents, such as randomly creating phantom forms of competition that promise no particular outcome. Although competition may make some districts rethink what they are doing, or even change some policies, it does not provide guidance, and it only drains off needed resources. It is no match for targeted reforms designed to make particular changes and backed by necessary resources and skills.

The third point about bureaucracy is that specialization is a key component. In this advanced, knowledge-based, technological society, specialization plays an increasingly important role. Not only is it essential to expand the role of specialists, but more specialization is consistent with the objective of giving teachers more autonomy. Contrary to the myth promulgated by choice proponents, bureaucracy is not opposed to autonomy. Ironically, modern bureaucracies thrive on it. Giving specialists more freedom has become a mandatory requirement for modern service organizations. Since increasing the authority of teachers is doable within the framework of bureaucracy, it is not necessary—as choice advocates want us to believe—to create independent schools in order to expand opportunities for teachers to exercise more freedom within the classroom. In fact, schools require the kind of expertise, support, and resources that school districts provide. When parents opt out, it only compounds their problems, since it is unlikely that the same expertise and resources will be available to teachers working in alternative situations. Many charter school students are learning the hard way that the advantages of being in a small school do not compensate for poor facilities and lack of programs and services.

The last thing to be noted is that bureaucracy has become indispensable. It is so profoundly entrenched in advanced societies that it cannot be abolished. Notwithstanding some pathologies, historically bureaucracy has made possible empires and national and international organizations. And it has served to support public education. Mass public education in this country, in fact, would have been impossible without a bureaucratic system. Formal rules have protected schools against the patronage of corrupt city governments. Thanks to specialization, pupils in the larger school systems have a wider range of curricular alternatives and are more likely to have expert teachers than those in extremely small ones, because of bureaucracy. Moreover, centralized and standardized school systems permitted the country to accommodate the waves of children who inundated the schools at the beginning of the last century in the wake of victories for compulsory free education. Standardization helps guarantee that children will not be shortchanged as they move from school to school, or from one part of the country to another. It also can help to promote equal educational opportunities within a system. Generally speaking, bureaucratic measures are largely responsible for the fact that "school has kept" in the face of fallout from a knowledge explosion, rapid social and technological changes, geographical mobility, and deep-rooted cultural conflicts.

The Bureaucratic Waste Ploy

Critics say public school bureaucracies are wasteful because a huge force of bureaucratic functionaries has swelled the organization charts. Chubb and Moe clocked the growth of administration during the 1980s at 2.5 times faster than the growth of instructional staff.[108] Private schools, by comparison, have much leaner administrative staffs. For example, one-quarter of the Catholic schools, they noted, do not have an administrative apparatus outside of the school board. Presumably, low-level bureaucratization makes private schools more cost-effective than schools in the public sector. Additional savings come from teacher salaries. By some estimates, Catholic teachers earn 40 percent less than public teachers.

However, ability to control waste does not account for the lower overhead in the private sector. If private schools are cheaper, it is largely because they have the luxury of picking and choosing their tasks and their students. Many private schools are subsidized by local parishes, and taxpayers pick up many services, including transportation, textbooks, hot lunches, counseling and speech therapy, and the costs associated with educating disabled and special needs children. Moreover, since private schools can handpick the students they want, they can avoid the costly and perplexing job of dealing with the array of daunting challenges related to concentrations of English learners, special education and vocational education programs, and coping with discipline, violence, chemical dependency, and pregnancies. By some estimates, only 12 percent of schools in the private sector, including nonsectarian specialty schools, are dedicated to special education students.[109] Programs focusing on alternative approaches, or vocational and special education, are available in only 1 percent of the Catholic schools, and in 7 percent of the other religious schools. Nationally, in 1999–2000, only 13 percent of private schools had any students with limited English proficiency, which contrasts with 54 percent of public schools with such students.[110] In California, where nearly a third of the students are learning English, by some accounts only 4 percent of private schools provide language support programs.

Organizational Complexity and Reform

Conventional wisdom holds that big, complex districts are less flexible than simpler ones. However, logic and evidence suggest otherwise. Centralized, complex organizations often are more innovative. Wilson observed that proposals for change increase exponentially with organizational complexity because every unit has its own ideas about how to improve the organization.[111] The likelihood of a large pool of proposals increases the probability that many will survive. Moreover, authoritative centers of power in big places can coordinate system-wide changes and push programs against pockets of resistance. The restructuring and downsizing going on in large school districts across the nation contradicts the myth that change in the public sector is impossible. As will be documented in the next chapter, many districts are adopting innovative structures like small schools and schools within schools, decentralization and school-based management, magnet schools, quality circles, school-business partnerships, and community councils.

Oversight Failures

One of the strengths of bureaucracy is that it provides mechanisms to assure that public funds are being used appropriately. This oversight function is integral to school districts, though granted it does not always work perfectly. However, it has been circumvented and crippled by choice legislation that gives schools with charters and vouchers immunity from most of the laws that govern public school districts. The truth is that the freedom-for-results bargain turns out to be a two-edged sword. Independence opens the door to abuse and impedes oversight without necessarily producing reform. About 10 percent of the almost 3,400 charter schools that have opened in the last decade have closed down, about half of them for financial reasons. RAND found that about 4 percent of charter schools have closed or had their charters revoked, typically for fiscal mismanagement.[112] Abuses involving over 200 charter school campuses and millions of dollars have been reported.[113] Most of these schools have been shut down or penalized financially for a variety of violations, including: failure to serve special education students; grossly inflating enrollment and attendance figures; violating state guidelines; fiscal mismanagement, failure to keep proper records, misusing or stealing millions of dollars; chronic complaints about lax discipline; indebtedness reaching millions of dollars; hiring felons and former convicts; failure to pay teachers or to pay into the teacher retirement system; teaching religion and illegally converting private schools to charters; and hiring un-credentialed teachers (in states where prohibited). One contract allowed the contractor to keep all unspent money without oversight. Some schools have spent huge sums of money without ever opening, while others have folded without notice, displacing hundreds of students and producing an avalanche of litigation.

Operators of the California Charter Academy, which was operating about sixty schools enrolling 10,000 students, are facing criminal charges from the state for misusing $25.6 million (including $2.6 million for personal expenses) and shortchanging students and teachers.[114] Other California charters are also being investigated. Laws protecting the confidential salaries of executives in the private sector blocked the state's investigation of the CEO for conflict of interest. Using school district funds, many of the Academy's campuses enrolled adult students at double the costs of similar programs at community colleges. A decade into the program, the state finally got around to banning that practice and shutting down the Academy, leaving thousands of students in search of new schools. Two years before, the state had reduced funding to forty-six other charter schools after an audit found the schools failed to follow state spending guidelines. And, a state audit in 2002 revealed that four large California school districts were not exercising effective oversight over the academic outcomes and fiscal management of charter schools, and were charging excessive fees for their oversight services.[115] California is only one of several states we could mention. For example, audits of seven Pennsylvania charter schools for the 1997–1998 and 1998–1999 school years found that all twenty-four schools failed to comply with state laws.[116] These are only the cases that have come to light. Who knows how many are going undetected in the unregulated choice school market? No wonder education officials in a number of states have been shaking their heads, exploring how to better monitor charter school funding and spending.[117]

There are also abuses in the private sector, where parents and taxpayers are prohibited by law from monitoring important dimensions of the publicly funded voucher programs. The Associated Press reported in 2004 that one Milwaukee private voucher school (whose employees did not have to undergo criminal background checks) was founded by a convicted rapist, and another pocketed several hundred thousand dollars for no-show students.[118] Moreover, since religious schools often integrate religion throughout their curriculum, vouchers can end up being used to pay for sectarian education, including costs associated with theological training and for religious items such as Bibles, icons and other religious material. Private schools do not have to provide uniform services for special education students or for English learners, or obey state law prohibiting discrimination on the basis of sex, sexual orientation and pregnancy, and marital or parental status.[119] Survey data show that the majority of private schools are unwilling to accept and serve students with learning disabilities, limited English proficiency, low achievement, or permit exemptions from religious instruction/activities. Also, over 40 percent of the surveyed schools are unwilling to either accept voucher students through random assignment or to participate in state tests.[120] Take for example, Wisconsin where about 12 percent of the public students receive special education services. Less than 1 percent of the private school students are enrolled in these programs.[121]

There Are Gaping Holes in State-Level Oversight. Why is the public not being better protected from abuses? Consider first, the hurdles facing state agencies. Private schools in Milwaukee's voucher program do not have to obey the state's open meetings and records laws; release information on employee wages or benefits; provide data such as test scores, attendance figures, or suspension and dropout rates; submit to external performance evaluations, hire certified teachers, or even require a college degree.[122] In the case of charter schools, complex and often ambiguous special laws complicate an already daunting task. Although new federal mandates are changing the picture, only a few states require in their legislation that schools must demonstrate acceptable levels of educational performance or improvement, and states differ in how they interpret the charter school ideal. Not all states have strong accountability requirements, some do not require charter schools to develop programs in compliance with state or local academic standards, and many do not require charters to participate in the state accountability system.[123] Moreover, necessary resources and expertise often are unavailable. In states like Arizona and California, which have a large number of charter schools, diligent monitoring would seem to be nearly impossible for one agency, especially considering the additional overlays of complex laws and regulations in areas like special education. In 2002, an auditor for the state of Ohio concluded that the Ohio Department of Education had not met its responsibility for monitoring the state's ninety-two charter schools.[124]

Education Week observed on March 20, 2002, "Originally designed to inspire innovation and free schools from bureaucracy, in return for showing results, charter schools often remain mired in debate over what they should look like and how they should be regulated and financed."[125] States vary among themselves in the way they are interpreting the idea of charter schools, but it is easier to agree on wrongdoing. A 2003 RAND report on California charter schools laments that "the state continues to face challenges in the areas of charter school finance and accountability." The California Legislative Analyst's Office concedes that: ". . . oversight and accountability have been perennial issues of legislative concern. Much of this concern has arisen as a result of specific instances of wrongdoing. In particular, over the last decade, some charter schools and charter authorizers have engaged in inappropriate fiscal practices and/or have lacked the prerequisite fiscal acumen needed to manage school sites."[126]

Obstacles Faced by Sponsors. So, forget the state. What about oversight from school districts and other sponsors? In theory, charter schools are supposed to be more accountable for educational performance because authorizers have the ability to revoke or not renew charter contracts. But nationally, monitoring of performance has seldom led to charter revocation.[127] Schools seeking renewal have almost always been successful. It isn't always because authorizers have no information. By far the most common tool authorizers use to monitor academic performance is test scores. In California, for example, 85 percent of charters say they report student achievement data to their sponsor. The No Child Left Behind law requires it. Yet, only 4 percent report that the sponsor has ever imposed sanctions or even requested them to make changes.[128]

The sponsors' task is complicated by many factors. For example, often vague goals listed in many charter petitions preclude valid assessments.[129] However, that could be changing. SRI reports that every chartering agency now reports some or all of its schools had measurable goals in the area of student achievement. Even so, confusion exists over how to assess academic progress. Although test scores are commonly used, sponsors often ignore them or haven't decided how to use them.[130] Still other obstacles to good management arise from insufficient resources to monitor, and from proliferating home schools and cyber schools that exist outside traditional school district boundaries. In addition, charter school legislation itself often provides inconsistent guidance.

Although each state has it own unique laws, the dilemmas that can arise are evident in California's continually changing legislation. California is a state that purportedly gives charter schools wide latitude to exercise autonomy. Yet, the actual relationship between sponsors and schools there remains murky.[131] One reason for this is that the law requires each charter school to negotiate its autonomy with the sponsor. As a result, California charter schools relate to sponsors along a broad continuum of independence and dependence. To further complicate matters, the exact boundaries are seldom explicitly spelled out. Some sponsors exert considerable control, while others take a more hands-off approach.

In addition, a contradiction is built into California law itself. On the one hand, the legislation releases charter schools from most state laws governing school districts, and for funding purposes at least, they are considered to be independent school districts. The sponsor's oversight function is therefore effectively limited by the extent to which it buys into the autonomy principle. On the other hand, a sponsor controls the fate of a school, in that it is in charge of approving, renewing, and revoking the school's charter. Any sponsor is free to apply its own requirements as a condition for granting the charter and approving renewals. The way sponsors actually fulfill their oversight responsibilities is an unpredictable outcome of this vacillating tension between the autonomy principle and the fact that sponsors can decide to close any maverick school. The oversight role is also affected by potential liability issues that cannot be easily legislated. Notwithstanding some clarifying legislation, some legal issues will probably be resolved only through litigation. Still another consideration that affects how a sponsor fulfills its oversight responsibility is difficulties associated with evaluating different tasks. Evaluating the effectiveness of instruction, for example, is more difficult than enforcing obvious violations of the rules. Given all the complications, it is no wonder that sponsors often duck their responsibilities for evaluating the charter schools under their jurisdiction.

Parents Too Often Cannot Provide Oversight. If not the state or sponsors, can parents provide oversight? There has not been much discussion about the responsibilities of parents to monitor schools. Instead, charter backers treat parents as passive consumers. If parents like the school and send their children there, it must be good, goes the argument. Some choice allies maintain that market accountability is enough and that performance measures are unnecessary. On their side, it is tremendously difficult to shut down a school that parents and teachers support, no matter what the tests say. However, reducing accountability down to parental choice ignores a state's responsibility to assure that schools are delivering quality education to children in return for public funds.[132] Demand cannot override that. The market model presumes that parents make informed decisions, but that is not always the case. Their access to information varies with factors like publicity and their level of education.

A worst-case example occurred in the San Diego start-up charter school we studied.[133] Half the parents surveyed did not understand the school's highly unorthodox Waldorf program, and moreover, a small but significant number of them were under the mistaken impression that they were required to send their children to the charter school because it was in the neighborhood. Others enrolled their children because the school was close to home, with no knowledge of the highly unconventional program. Parents with less formal education were especially confused about the purpose and philosophy of the school's program and their options. They were also among the least satisfied parents.

Choice schools are not necessarily required to include parents on their governing bodies. In some charter schools, boards are not elected, leaving parents and taxpayers with little opportunity to monitor how money is being spent and whether laws are being followed. Even when parents are included in the governance body, oversight may not be effective. The parents who were on the governance council of the San Diego case had minimal experience with the demanding responsibilities required of them, and they were already busy people serving part-time. Yet, they continually struggled with controversial and complex issues, complicated still further because the governance council's role was not clearly defined. In particular, council members were unsure whether they were responsible for monitoring teaching and instruction, which was the subject of critical newspaper articles and other forms of criticism. Their authority to hire, evaluate and dismiss teaching personnel was continually challenged by the former director; they argued among themselves even about their authority to fire the director.

School Closings. What do choice admirers say about the abuses of freedom just mentioned? Not much, other than dismissing wrongdoing as the missteps of a few "bad apples"—some kind of inevitable overhead. Jeanne Allen, director of the Center for Education Reform, an organization devoted to promoting free-market approaches to education, buries corruption and other forms of malfeasance under the heading of "mismanagement," one of her five types of school closings, and not the one she wants to discuss.[134] Instead, she points the finger at school districts for causing many of the closings. As she puts it, "Sadly, the closures are because most people do not like change." School districts push back against free market schools, she says, under the guise of procedural and bureaucratic obstacles. Possibly, but given numerous documented instances of mismanagement, why shouldn't they be clamping down? She and other critics blame shoddy charter schools on school districts for allowing inexperienced individuals to set up and operate them in the first place. That is a puzzling position for a free-market advocate. Wasn't freedom from district interference the whole idea behind independence? People with good ideas were not supposed to be throttled by sponsors laying on conventional conditions. The intent was to give anyone with a justifiable proposal free rein to start up unconventional schools in competition with traditional districts. Freedom, it seems, is good for thriving charter schools, but school districts are held responsible when they fail. That is a slippery slope. If districts are going to be held responsible, then why should they not also have the authority to set and monitor all parameters of a charter, including its objectives and the clientele it serves? That brings us full cycle back to district planned and operated charter schools.

You might think school closings are a bad thing. Not Allen. She says closings demonstrate that accountability works for charters. What does she say about the frustrated, disappointed parents and students who got on the wrong boat? Not a word. Too bad, she says, that regular schools are not as accountable. Pointing to a federal study that labels 11 percent of the public schools deficient, she says the 7 percent failure rate (actually 10 percent) of charters looks good by comparison. But, wait a minute. The 11 percent figure pertains mainly to academic inadequacies, whereas low academic achievement is a small part of charter school failure, because sponsors aren't holding the schools accountable for it. This apples and oranges comparison glosses over the basic questions about dishonesty and bad education in the two sectors. We do agree, though, that there should be more investigations of possible corruption in the public sector, and that more marginal public schools should be reformed.

According to the Center for Education Reform, 194 charter school closings occurred between 1999 and 2002—about 7 percent of the schools in existence at that time. The Center published the reasons officials gave for each closing. Our tabulation of their reasons is reported in Table 2.1. In many cases, there was more than one reason for closing a school. The numbers in the table appearing in parentheses reflect the number of times each type of reason was mentioned (not the number of schools closed for each reason). Cases of corruption and mismanagement outnumber academic reasons three to one. This tabulation does not include many schools that closed voluntarily without giving reasons. Nor does it include many schools that districts closed to consolidate school sites, often to meet fiscal constraints that many districts were facing.

As the table indicates, academic reasons are overwhelmingly eclipsed by poor planning and corruption/mismanagement events. Clearly, school operators bring most of the problems on themselves through lack of planning, corruption, and mismanagement, which helps explain why charters across the nation are running into trouble paying for facilities and finding suitable classrooms. If most of the closings were because of academic deficiencies, the public might sleep better. But, scholarship doesn't seem to be a primary reason. As we said, most sponsors do not reliably monitor student achievement. While the No Child Left Behind legislation could change that, the fact remains that most closings occur because too many charter schools are engaging in heavy-handed practices. And, given the holes we have noted in the oversight mechanisms, it would be folly to suppose they have all been caught.

Implications. In sum, there is no reliable way to assure effective oversight of self-governing, independent-choice schools. The mechanisms in place are inadequate to monitor and control the complex programs that

Table 2.1
A Tabulation of Reasons Given for Closing Charter Schools

Ineffective Planning

Low Enrollment (28) (usually leading to financial instability)

Indebtedness, Bankruptcy, Lack of Money (27) (including a sponsor who went out of business)

Administrative Conflicts (6)

Corruption, Mismanagement

Fiscal Mismanagement, Fraud, Misappropriation of Funds (25)

Falsifying Enrollment Figures (8) (including one case of falsifying board minutes)

Keeping Inadequate Records (8) (usually including records needed for accountability)

Violating Legal Codes (12) (including health, safety, fire, electrical codes; failure to finger print employees, hiring felons, lack of accreditation, hiring uncertified personnel, violating open meeting laws, IRS violations)

Violating Special Education Codes (6)

Administrative Mismanagement and Leadership Failures (8)

Administrative Problems

Lack of a Facility (14)

Staff Instability (10) (staff and leadership turnover, including two cases where the founder or operator walked away)

School District Closures (5) (includes a school closed for not being innovative)

Academic Deficiencies

Low Student Achievement (13)

Curriculum Deficiencies (6)

are springing up. States are ultimately responsible, but they are strapped for resources and personnel, and the legislation is often muddled. Perhaps just as important, some states are still in a posture of denial. California's Legislative Analyst Office exemplifies this head-in-the-sand approach to oversight. Notice that in the quotation cited, this office refers to "specific instances of wrongdoing." Specific instances? There is a pattern of malfeasance by renegade charter schools that has been allowed to go on because of a confluence of ambiguous and permissive legislation as well as low priority placed on protecting parents and the public from being exploited by private entrepreneurs.

But it isn't just about fiscal wrongdoing. There is virtually no monitoring of educational programs, how they operate, and what outcomes they are producing. And, to the extent they are being monitored, the news is not good. An unknown, but undoubtedly significant, percentage of charters are engaging in illegal, unethical, and otherwise questionable conduct. Add those not meeting academic expectations, and the problem is scary. How many parents are being told about these risks when they enroll their children in these schools? After nearly fifteen years, the risks associated with malfeasance can be no longer passed off as growing pains.

Reemergence of Bureaucracy

Escaping bureaucracy is often mentioned as a reason the public should support independent charters and private schools. Ironically, however, both charter and voucher schools are themselves well on their way to becoming more bureaucratized. It seems inevitable for the following reasons:

- *Demand for more oversight*. As we said, the overlapping layers of oversight built into choice school models are not working as intended; too many independent public and private schools are abusing their freedom. Additional layers of oversight and more effective controls eventually will be required—thus bringing "the autonomous school" fantasy full circle. Some of the abuses connected with charter schools were mentioned above. Private schools also require more rules and oversight. Even the chief proponents of vouchers themselves see a need for more bureaucracy and have recommended a host of rules: rules to ensure that necessary information gets to parents, that admission processes are open and fair, that special funding is available for children with physical and learning disadvantages, and that transportation is provided for those who need it. In addition, legislatures can impose other requirements. For example, the 1992 California voucher initiative would have given the state authority to request participating schools to administer standardized tests.

- *New clientele will require more rules and administrators*. To expand, choice schools must reach a broader market, including students they now avoid. No longer able to cherry-pick the most desirable students, they will have to offer more bilingual, disabled, and vocational programs. The new clientele will in turn subject these schools to more rules, and they will need to hire more staff to administer provisions related to, for example, special education and school lunches. Administrators will be needed to monitor compliance requirements and to supervise and coordinate bigger staffs and more complex programs. At the same time, teachers will eventually balk at spending their time and energy on paperwork and in committee meetings. Charter schools are already more bureaucratized than proponents care to admit. At least two studies found that they are spending more on administration and less on direct classroom instruction than other public schools.[135]

- *Program expansion*. To focus on tests and basic subjects, some choice schools have abandoned the creative side of our culture—art, plays, music, and extracurricular activities such as debate, and sports. Parents will be demanding expanded offerings, and the schools will then face many of the same difficulties encountered by the typical public school.

- *More specialization*. To expand, choice schools will need to find unfilled market niches, which will require them to specialize in areas which public schools are neglecting, or where they are overburdened and not doing well. Parents who at the moment are only looking for a way out will begin to demand more high-capacity public schools with defined missions and specially trained teachers.

- *Certification*. New schools tend to be financially unstable. With no record or reputation to underwrite their competence and reliability, newly founded schools can encounter difficulty attracting backers and customers. Some start-ups will fail; others will languish and remain too weak to spearhead change. Creditors and customers will demand certification of competency.[136]

- *Additional costs*. Additional enrollments will run up the costs connected with building larger school plants, competing for more teachers at standard salaries, and providing costly special education and remedial programs that some parents will demand.

Implications

Charter schools and school vouchers are capable of far more than serving as escape routes for a few families seeking better schools. To appreciate what they can become, we must first understand the system being defiled, the so-called public education bureaucracy. Those who rail against bureaucracy are really complaining about the organizational pathologies inherent to all large organizations. Sometimes the actual problem is the size of the classroom, or the mix of students in the classroom. Sometimes it involves constraining rules, or remote and unresponsive decisions. But these hurdles are not unique to education. This dark side of bureaucracy is easily outweighed by the vital role it plays in modern society. Perhaps bureaucracies are less efficient than so-called free markets. However, market analogies provide no guidance, because there is no free market in education. The public sector is left to do what the private sector sloughs off.

Expertise would be useless without a division of labor, which in turn would be impossible without a hierarchy and the rules necessary for co-ordination. Rules are the only thing standing between legitimate public expenditures and corruption, and indeed the sordid ugliness that has tainted some choice schools occurs in part because they have been released from the usual bureaucratic oversight mechanisms. In fact, bureaucracy has become so indispensable that it automatically emerges as organizations get larger. More bureaucracy, in the form of oversight, specialization, and planning, would alleviate many of the worst handicaps weighing down choice schools that we hear so much about. Indeed, in view of the evidence reviewed in this chapter, it appears that creating schools outside the conventional bureaucracy has created more problems than it has solved.

However, of course, education is more than a bureaucracy. Beneath their bureaucratic skeletons, school districts are complex organizations operating as natural, loosely coupled systems that leave plenty of room for autonomy and reform.[137] We are the first to admit that a sizeable number of public schools are in bad shape, and we shall address that issue at length in Chapter 5. But on the positive side, a host of contradictions and tensions that permeate school districts today pave the way for initiatives designed to give teachers more autonomy without creating independent schools or sending kids to private schools. What it will take is channeling the energy and enthusiasm now being devoted to charters and vouchers back into the task of improving public schools. We are going to propose ways to do that in the following chapters.

CONCLUSIONS

The pitch for school choice—whether in the form of charter schools or vouchers to pay for private schooling—has been disappointing and sometimes dishonest. On July 23, 2004, Herbert Walberg, a former professor at the University of Illinois in Chicago and a visiting fellow at the Hoover Institution, asserted without reservation that no study points to substantially poorer performance of choice schools. He wrote: "Analyses of student achievement indicate that school choice leads to higher levels of learning in various parts of the United States and other countries. Better studies show stronger and more consistent effects, and no study points to substantially poorer performance of choice schools."[138] Professor Walberg didn't bother to mention the studies we have reviewed here reporting mixed and negative results. Not only is his conclusion false, but also his statements grossly distort available evidence. The article exemplifies the kind of misinformation that we fear parents are using to choose schools.

Jeanne Allen cherry-picks the facts that support her views. She labeled as "baseless" data showing that charter school students often do worse on national tests than comparable students in public schools, and accused the analysts of deliberately skewing the data.[139] Her objection? The article didn't mention that charter fourth-graders outperformed their public school counterparts in two of the forty-one states with charter schools. True perhaps, but it is also worth noting that public schools in the two states in question, California and Arizona, enroll lots of English learners, who often do not perform well on tests and who are seldom enrolled in charter schools (because they typically do not offer special language support programs). Writers are quibbling over misleading national-level data, which though incapable of providing conclusive answers, invite anyone to pick and choose the parts of the distribution that confirm their opinions.

Anyone who expected tests to conclusively demonstrate whether or not charters are better than other schools was bound to be disappointed. The promise that it would be possible to demonstrate across-the-board achievement gains in favor of choice schools was impossible from the start, not necessarily because choice schools are inadequate, but because proponents promised too much, and certainly more than can be demonstrated with tests. It is impossible because of the variety of schools and the range of objectives being pursued, because everyone is fixated on misleading averages instead of the enormous variation among schools, and because advocates have seduced the public with an antiquated model of learning that supposes schools are like factories. It is not surprising the evidence has not supported the hopes of charter supporters. Even Chester E. Finn, Jr., an ardent advocate of charter schools from their beginning, now admits: "Not enough charter schools are doing well enough academically to provide evidence that this is a better educational alternative, especially for poor kids."[140] Still, when it comes to poverty schools, one has to be careful. Finn might have backed off too far. It is true that some studies show that minorities who are attending charter schools would probably have better qualified teachers and receive better services in regular public schools.[141] However, that might not be true in the worst parts of the biggest cities where many impoverished minorities sit in classes with unqualified and inexperienced teachers. In Chapter 5 we shall recommend that school districts should start their own charter schools to attack this very problem. More disconcerting to us than their academic track record are the many closures among charter schools reflecting mismanagement, poor planning and chronic shortages of funds, and inadequate classroom space.

But the proponents are not giving up. Quit?—no way! Caroline Hendrie reports in July 2004 that charter school leaders have formed still another national organization devoted to stepping up political pressure on behalf of charters.[142] She writes that the fifth annual national charter school conference was punctuated with pleas for charter activists to "plunge more vigorously into the political fray." And will it work? A former U.S. Secretary of Education, Rod Paige, seems to think so. Not withstanding the fact that the dazzling 70 percent annual charter school growth rate that characterized the late 1990s plummeted to a mere trickle in 2004 (8 percent), he predicts another huge spurt in new charters.[143] He could be right. California's chief legislative analyst, Elizabeth Hill, calls for raising the cap on charters and approving more authorizers, because . . . because of . . . because of what?[144] Certainly not because choice schools are meeting scholastic expectations, at least not as they are currently being measured. Not because there have been no mismanagement scandals. Nor is it because of widespread public demand. Most citizens, including many educators, do not even know what charter schools are.

But if charter schools and school vouchers are not meeting expectations, it can be blamed in large part on the absurdly unrealistic expectations set by choice advocates themselves. In their zeal to push these two reforms, choice fans have inadvertently set standards that are now creating the impression that charters and vouchers are under-performing only because their student outcomes merely match those of regular schools. Choice proponents are drowning in their own bubbly rhetoric. Underperforming is not the real problem. So, let's get off these glib expectations. They were absurdly unrealistic from the start.

Our basic complaints are twofold. First, choice devotees deliberately mislead the public with impossible promises. And second, so-called choice schools are not providing meaningful choices, except for the choice to leave public schools. Why? Even when students in choice schools outperform those in public schools, there is no reason to believe the independent status of charters had anything to do with it. There are good schools within most school districts. So, why should children leave the public schools? And leave them for which alternatives? That is less than clear. Choice schools have the potential to be more than an exit option for unsatisfied parents. They could act as positive forces for attacking definitive challenges within the public school system. There is no hope for public education without improving the school districts that most kids attend. That will not happen while activists and politicians continue to promote reforms that force parents to opt out in order to exercise a choice.

Supporters of school choice want us to believe that charters and vouchers will reform education. Just how will that happen? Evidence for the few instances that purportedly demonstrate success is dubious at best, and the studies provide no information to explain why the presence of a few alternative schools should force the vast pubic school enterprise to turn around. And, all the bureaucracy bashing is only hot air. There is a lot wrong with public schools, but it can't all be laid off on bureaucracy, which performs vital functions—such as supporting specialization and overseeing how public money is actually spent. Public school bureaucracies are plagued by problems, of course, as are all big organizations—including the giant corporations and even the U.S. Congress and the U.S. Department of Education, which are promoting the war on public school districts.

We are not downplaying the serious challenges confronting public education. A class action lawsuit in California, filed in May 2000 by a coalition of civil rights groups, recites a litany of deplorable conditions in many of California's worst schools. The complaint describes more than 100 schools where at least half the teaching staff lacks full credentials.

Many schools have outdated textbooks and not enough seats in class-rooms, while others lack bathrooms and ventilation. These problems are concentrated in schools that primarily serve students of color in urban areas, a problem addressed in Chapter 5. But how will the current school choice approaches help? Few autonomous charters or private schools offer the kind of alternative education programs and services needed, or where they are most needed. Many charters are barely able to stay afloat, lack adequate facilities, and cannot offer music, art, and extracurricular programs, not to mention special services such as speech therapy.

The sad fact is that the charter school system is even more flawed than public education. Oversight systems are not working. Many charter schools are beset with questionable practices, while inadequate planning and feeble leadership dooms hundreds of schools to certain failure. Many have not been resourceful competitors, but instead complain about half-hearted support from the same districts they are supposed to show up. And, there is no good evidence that they boost learning in any predictable way. The concept of charter schools was a good ideal but it is time to re-think the notion of independence.

As we have said, none of this means we want to see charter schools, or school vouchers for that matter, junked. While we object to a policy that gives choice schools unrestrained freedom, at least charter schools have ex-panded opportunities for some exceptional teachers to teach differently, and we can only hope, more effectively. Private schools that accept vouch-ers can provide useful services within a planned system, provided they are willing to accept prescribed missions, cooperate with other schools, and comply with civil rights laws and accountability legislation regulating the use of public funds. But, surely, it is not necessary to create independent schools or to grant vouchers without restrictions in order to increase au-tonomy within classrooms. That can be done by tweaking the flexibility al-ready built into existing models of school-based management, alternative schools, magnets, and other special schools. What we are suggesting is to place conditions on schools of choice to make them responsible for ac-complishing specific tasks and to prevent further abuses. More on that in Chapters 4 and 5. But first, it will be instructive to look closely at other ap-proaches to school choice for clues to improving the charter-school model.

NOTES

1. Chester E. Finn, Jr., Bruno V. Manno, and Gregg Vanourek, *Renewing Pub-lic Education* (Princeton, NJ: Princeton University Press, 2000), 3.

2. E. Paige Robelen, "Bush Upbeat on Making ESEA Work," *Education Week*, 11 September 2002, 23, 25.

3. See, for example, John E. Chubb and Terry M. Moe, *Politics, Markets, and America's Schools* (Washington, DC: Brookings Institution, 1990).

4. California Legislative Analyst's Office, *Assessing California's Charter Schools* (Sacramento, CA: Author, 20 January 2004).

5. Gary K. Hart, "Q & A with Senator Gary Hart," *Operation News* (Fall 1992): 2–3; see also, Gary K. Hart's remarks delivered at the California charter school conference, San Mateo, CA, 30 November 1993.

6. See T. Kolderie, *Beyond Choice to New Public Schools: Withdrawing the Exclusive Franchise in Public Education* (Washington, DC: Progressive Policy Institute, 1990); J. Nathan, *Charter Schools: Creating Hope and Opportunity for American Education* (San Francisco: Josey-Bass, 1996); and R. J. Lake and M. D. Millot, *Autonomy, Accountability, and the Values of Public Education* (Seattle, WA: Institute for Public Policy and Management, University of Washington/RAND, 1996).

7. Kolderie, *Beyond Choice to New Public Schools,* 1990.

8. Ronald G. Corwin and Henry J. Becker, "Parent Involvement," in R. G. Corwin and J. F. Flaherty, eds., *Freedom and Innovation in California's Charter Schools* (Los Alamitos, CA: Southwest Regional Laboratory/WestEd, 1995), 75–104; Henry J. Becker, Kathryn Nakagawa, and Ronald G. Corwin, "Parent Involvement Contracts in California's Charter Schools: Strategy for Educational Improvement or Method of Exclusion?" *Teachers College Record* 98 (Spring 1997), 511–536.

9. Ron Zimmer, Richard Buddin, Derrick Chau, and others, *Charter School Operations and Performance: Evidence from California* (Santa Monica, CA: Rand Corp., 2003), 175; see also Richard Rothstein, "Charter Conundrum," *The American Prospect* 9, 39 (1 August 1998). Available at www.prospect.org/print/V9/39/rothstein-r.html.

10. Ronald G. Corwin, Lisa Carlos, Bart Lagomarsino, and Roger Scott, *From Paper to Practice: Challenges Facing a California Charter School* (San Francisco: WestEd, 1996).

11. See National Center For Education Statistics, *Findings for the Condition of Education 2002: Private Schools* (Washington, DC: U.S. Department of Education, 2002). Available at http://nces.ed.gov/pubs2002/2002013.pdf.

12. James Bogden, "Cyber Schools," *National Association of State Boards of Education Journal* (Autumn 2003), 33–37.

13. See Anne T. Lockwood, *The Charter School Decade* (Lanham, MD: Scarecrow Press, 2004), 62.

14. Joe Schneider, "Five Prevailing Charter Types," *The School Administrator,* August 1999. Web Edition available at www.asa.org/publications/sa/1999_08/schneider.htm.

15. L. Anderson, N. Adelman, K. Finnigan, L. Cotton, M. B. Donnelly, and T. Price, *A Decade of Public Charter Schools: Evaluation of the Public Charter Schools Program, 2000–2001* (Stanford, CA: SRI International, 2002).

16. Lee Sherman, "Homegrown," *Northwest Education Magazine,* Spring 2001.

17. J. S. Coleman, T. Hoffer, and S. Kilgore, *High School Achievement: Public, Catholic, and Private Schools Compared* (New York: Basic Books, 1982).

18. See especially Karl L. Alexander and A. M. Pallas, "School Sector and Cognitive Performance: When Is a Little a Little?" *Sociology of Education* 11 (April 1985), 115–128; for additional information, see the following two references: Henry M. Levin, "The Theory of Choice Applied to Education," in W. Clune and J. Witte, eds., *Choice and Control in American Education, Vol. II: The Practice of Choice,*

Decentralization, and School Restructuring (New York: Falmer Press, 1990), 285–318; Robert H. Meyer, *Applied versus Traditional Mathematics: New Economic Models of the Contributions of High School Courses to Mathematics Proficiency* (Washington, DC: National Assessment of Vocational Education, 1989).

19. Chubb and Moe, *Politics, Markets, and America's Schools*, 1990.

20. B. Rosenberg, "Not a Case for Market Control," *Educational Leadership* 48 (December 1990 and January 1991), 64–65.

21. For more information, see the following sources: J. Witte, *The Market Approach to Education: An Analysis of America's First Voucher Program* (Princeton, NJ: The Princeton University Press, 1999); Jay P. Greene, *The Effect of School Choice: An Evaluation of the Charlotte Children's Scholarship Fund* (New York: The Manhattan Institute for Policy Research, 2000); J. P. Greene, W. G. Howell, and P. E. Peterson, *An Evaluation of the Cleveland Scholarship Program* (Cambridge, MA: Harvard University, Program on Education Policy and Governance, 1999); Jay P. Greene, Marcus A. Winters, and Greg Forster, "Apples to Apples: An Evaluation of Charter Schools Serving General Student Populations," CCI Working Paper (New York: Manhattan Institute, July 2003).

22. Jay P. Greene, "The Surprising Consensus on School Choice," *Public Interest* 144 (Summer 2001). Available at www.thepublicinterest.com.

23. Small and inconsistent differences are evident in the following body of work: J. P. Greene, W. G. Howell, and P. E. Peterson, *An Evaluation of the Cleveland Scholarship Program* (Cambridge, MA: Harvard University, Program on Education Policy and Governance, 1999); K. Metcalf and others, *Evaluation of the Cleveland Scholarship Program* (Bloomington, IN: The Indiana Center for Evaluation, 1998); J. F. Witte, "Who Benefits from the Milwaukee Choice Program?" in Bruce Fuller and Richard F. Elmore, eds., *Who Chooses? Who Loses? Culture, Institutions, and the Unequal Effects of School Choice* (New York: Teachers College Press, 1996), 118–137; J. P. Greene, P. E. Peterson, and J. Du, *The Effectiveness of School Choice in Milwaukee: A Secondary Analysis of Data from the Program's Evaluation* (Cambridge, MA: Program on Education Policy and Governance, Harvard University, 1996); John F Witte, *First Year Report: Milwaukee Parental Choice Program* (Madison, WI: University of Wisconsin-Madison, 1991); J. F. Witte, A. B. Bailey, and C. A. Thorn, *Second Year Report: Milwaukee Parental Choice Program* (Madison, WI: University of Wisconsin-Madison, 1992).

24. See Barbara Minar's review, "Vouchers and the False Promise of Academic Achievement," *Rethinking Schools Online* (February 2002). Available at www.rethinkingschools.org/special_reports/voucher_report/index.shtml.

25. Minar, "Vouchers and the False Promise of Academic Achievement," 2002.

26. Paul E. Peterson and William G. Howell, "Latest Results from the New York City Voucher Experiment," paper presented to the Association of Public Policy and Management, Washington, DC, November 2003.

27. David W. Grissmer and others, *Student Achievement and the Changing American Family* (Santa Monica, CA: RAND Corp., 1994); Coleman, Hoffer, and Kilgore, *High School Achievement*, 1982.

28. National Center for Education Statistics, *Private Schools in the United States: A Statistical Profile* (Washington, DC: U.S. Department of Education, 1993–1994 through 1999–2000).

29. Marcella R. Dianda and Ronald G. Corwin, *What a Voucher Could Buy: A Survey of California's Private Schools* (Los Alamitos, CA: Southwest Regional Laboratory, February 1993).

30. Coleman, Hoffer, and Kilgore, *High School Achievement*, 1982.

31. J. F. Witte, "The Theory of Choice and the Control of Education," in W. Clune and J. Witte, eds., *Choice and Control in American Education, vol. II: The Practice of School Choice, Decentralization, and School Restructuring* (New York: Falmer Press, 1990).

32. Diana Jean Schemo, "Nation's Schools Lagging Behind, U.S. Test Scores Reveal," *New York Times*, 17 August 2004. Available at www.nytimes.com/2004/08/17/education/17charter.html.

33. Edison Schools website, "Edison Schools Post Big Gains on New York State Tests," 27 May 2003. Available at www.edisonproject.com/design/d23.html and www.riverheadcharterschool.com/press_releases/Edison%20schools_05.27.03.htm; see also, Cecil Angel, "Study Questions Edison Schools," *Detroit Free Press*, 22 February 2001. Available at www.freep.com/news/education/edison22_20010222.htm.

34. Caroline M. Hoxby, *Achievement in Charter Schools and Regular Public Schools in the United States: Understanding the Differences* (Cambridge, MA: Harvard University and National Bureau of Economic Research, December 2004).

35. Gary Miron and Christopher Nelson, *Student Academic Achievement in Charter Schools: What We Know and Why We Know So Little*, occasional Paper No. 41 (New York: National Center for the Study of Privatization in Education, Teachers College, Columbia University, 2001): Abstract.

36. Randall W. Eberts and Kevin M. Hollenbeck, *Impact of Charter School Attendance on Student Achievement in Michigan* (Kalamazoo, MI: W. E. Upjohn Institute for Employment Research, 2002).

37. American Federation of Teachers, *Do Charter Schools Measure Up? The Charter School Experiment after Ten Years* (Washington, DC: The American Federation of Teachers, July 2002); L. Mulholland, *Arizona Charter School Progress Evaluation* (Phoenix: Morrison Institute for Public Policy, Arizona State University, 1999).

38. Chester E. Finn, Jr., Bruno V. Manno, and Gregg Vanourek, *Renewing Public Education* (Princeton, NJ: Princeton University Press, 2000), 76.

39. Jo Ann Izu and others, *Los Angeles Unified School District Charter School Evaluation* (San Francisco: WestEd, 1998); Finn, Manno, and Vanourek, *Renewing Public Education*, 2000.

40. American Federation of Teachers, *Do Charter Schools Measure Up?*, 2002.

41. Finn, Manno, and Vanourek, *Renewing Public Education*, 2000.

42. Texas Education Agency (TEA), *Texas Open-Enrollment Charter Schools Fifth-Year Evaluation: Executive Summary* (Arlington, TX: School of Urban and Public Affairs, University of Texas at Arlington, July 2002); see also a report on the same subject in *The Dallas Morning News*, 19 May 2001.

43. American Federation of Teachers, *Do Charter Schools Measure Up?*, 2002.

44. For more detail, see the California Charter Schools Association. Available at www.charterassociation.org.

45. Tom Loveless, *The Brown Center Annual Report on American Education* (Washington, DC: Brookings Institution Press, 2002).

46. Thomas Good and Jennifer S. Braden, "The Charter School Zeitgeist," *Education Week* 19, 27 (15 March 2000), 48.

47. NEA-New York and New York State United Teachers, *Not So Fast: The Unmet Challenges for Charter Schools and Those Who Oversee Them* (PDF, 579k, 26 pages). Available at www.nea.org/charter/notsofast.html.

48. Greene, Winters, and Forster, "Apples to Apples," 2003.

49. T. Good and J. Braden, *The Great School Debate: Choice, Vouchers, and Charters* (Mahwah, NJ: Erlbaum, 2000), 137.

50. Ronald G. Corwin and Krishnan Namboodiri, "Have Test Scores and Individuals Been Overemphasized in the Research on Schools?" in R. G. Corwin, ed., *Research in the Sociology of Education and Socialization* 8 (Greenwich, CT: JAI Press, 1989), 141–176.

51. Karl L. Alexander and Larry J. Griffin, "School District Effects on Academic Achievement: A Reconsideration," *American Sociological Review* 41 (1976), 144–152.

52. Krishnan Namboodiri, Ronald G. Corwin, and Linda Dorsten, "Analyzing Distributions in School Effects Research: An Empirical Illustration," *Sociology of Education* 66 (October 1993), 278–294.

53. Izu et al., *Los Angeles Unified School District Charter School Evaluation*, 1998.

54. Rosenberg, "Not a Case for Market Control," *Educational Leadership*, 1990/1991.

55. See Table 2.1 in this volume.

56. Milton Friedman, "The Role of Government in Education," in *Capitalism and Freedom* (Chicago: University of Chicago Press, 1962); see also Jeffrey R. Henig, *Rethinking School Choice: Limits of the Market Metaphor* (Princeton, NJ: Princeton University Press, 1994).

57. John Merrifield, *The School Choice Wars* (Lanham, MD: Scarecrow Press, 2001), 84.

58. Christopher Jencks, *Education Vouchers: A Report on Financing Education by Parents* (Cambridge, MA: Center for the Study of Public Policy, 1970).

59. Henry M. Levin, "Educational Choice and the Pains of Democracy," in T. James and H. Levin, eds., *Public Dollars for Private Schools: The Case of Tuition Tax Credits* (Philadelphia, PA: Temple University Press, 1983), 38.

60. U.S. Department of Education, *Choosing Better Schools: The Five Regional Meetings on Choice in Education* (Washington, DC: Author, December 1990).

61. Caroline M. Hoxby, "How School Choice Affects the Achievement of *Public* School Students," paper prepared for Koret Task Force meeting, Stanford, CA: Hoover Institution, 20–21 September 2001.

62. Hoxby, "How School Choice Affects the Achievement of *Public* School Students," 2001.

63. John Danner and J. C. Bowman, "The Promise and Peril of Charter Schools," Texas Education Review (Winter 2003–2004) [electronic journal]. Available at www.educationreview.homestead.com/2003charterschools.html.

64. Marcella R. Dianda and Ronald G. Corwin, *Vision and Reality: A First-Year Look at California's Charter Schools* (Los Alamitos, CA: Southwest Regional Laboratory, 1994).

65. Paul Mark Teske, Jack Schneider, and Sara Buckley, *Does Charter School Competition Improve Traditional Public Schools?* (New York: Center for Civic Innovation, June 2000). Available at www.manhattan-institute.org/html/cr_10.htm; see also

The Manhattan Institute, *What Do We Know About Vouchers and Charter Schools? Separating the Rhetoric from the Reality* (Santa Monica, CA: RAND Corp., 2000).

66. Gregory Camilli, "Texas Gains on NAEP: Points of Light?" *Education Policy Analysis Archives* 8 (21 August 2000). Available at http://epaa.asu.edu/epaa/v8n42.html.

67. David L. Armor and Brett M. Peiser, "Interdistrict Choice in Massachusetts," in Paul E. Peterson and Bryan C. Hassel, eds., *Learning from School Choice* (Washington, DC: Brookings Institution, 1998).

68. Susan L. Aud, *Competition in Education: A 1999 Update of School Choice in Massachusetts* (Boston, MA: Pioneer Institute for Public Policy, 1999).

69. Amy Stuart Wells, "Charter School Reform in California: Does It Meet Expectations?" *Phi Delta Kappan* 80 (1998). Available at www.pdkintl.org/kappan/karticle.htm; see also, Wells, *Beyond The Rhetoric of Charter School Reform*, 1998.

70. Robert Maranto, Scott Milliman, Frederick Hess, and April Gresham, eds., *School Choice in the Real World: Lessons from Arizona Charter Schools* (Boulder, CO: Westview Press, 1999).

71. Caroline M. Hoxby, *School Choice and School Productivity (or Could School Choice Be a Tide that Lifts All Boats?)* (Cambridge, MA: National Bureau of Economic Research, Inc., 2001); and Hoxby, "How School Choice Affects the Achievement of *Public* School Students," 2001; see also Thomas S. Dee, "Competition and the Quality of Public Schools," *Economic Education Review* 17 (4) (1998), 419–427.

72. Kevin B. Smith and Kenneth J. Meier, *The Case Against School Choice: Politics, Markets, and Fools* (Armonk, NY: M. E. Sharpe, 1995), Chapter 4.

73. J. F. Couch, W. F. Shughart, and A. L. Williams, "Private School Enrollment and Public School Performance," *Public Choice* 76 (1993), 301–312.

74. M. Newmark, "Another Look at Whether Private Schools Influence Public School Quality: Comment," *Public Choice* 82 (1995), 365–373.

75. Christopher A. Simon and Nicholas P. Lovrich, "Private School Enrollment and Public School Performance: Assessing the Effects of Competition upon Public School Student Achievement in Washington State," *Policy Studies Journal* 24, 4 (1996). Available at www.questia.com/PM.qst?.

76. Associated Press, "Teacher Cheating Is Revealed in Study of Student Testing," *Orange County Register*, 22 May 2004, 16.

77. Good and Braden, *The Great School Debate*, 2000.

78. Good and Braden, *The Great School Debate*, 2000.

79. Dianda and Corwin, *Vision and Reality*, 1994; see also Corwin and Flaherty, *Freedom and Innovation*, 1995.

80. Corwin and Flaherty, *Freedom and Innovation*, 1995.

81. Wells, *Beyond the Rhetoric of Charter School Reform*, 1998.

82. Wells, *Beyond the Rhetoric of Charter School Reform*, 1998.

83. Texas Education Agency (TEA), "Performance of Open-Enrollment Charter Schools," in *Comprehensive Annual Report on Texas Public Schools* (Arlington, TX: School of Urban and Public Affairs, University of Texas at Arlington, 2001).

84. Texas Education Agency, *Texas Open-Enrollment Charter Schools Fifth-Year Evaluation* (Arlington, TX: School of Urban and Public Affairs, University of Texas at Arlington, Arlington, 2002).

85. Louis Chandler, *Traditional Schools, Progressive Schools: Do Parents Have a Choice?* (Washington, DC: The Thomas B. Fordham Institute, 1999).

86. Bruno Manno, Chester E. Finn, Jr., Louann A. Bierlein, and Gregg Vanourek, "How Charter Schools Are Different: Lessons and Implications from a National Study," *Phi Delta Kappan* 79 (1998). Available at www.pdkintl.org/kappan/karticle.htm.

87. Chester E. Finn, Jr., and Marci Kanstoroom, "Do Charter Schools Do It Differently?" *Phi Delta Kappan* 84, 1 (April 3, 2002).

88. Corwin and Flaherty, *Freedom and Innovation*, 1995; see also Dianda and Corwin, *Vision and Reality*, 1994.

89. Lessley Fiore and M. Harwell, *Integration of Other Research Findings with Charter Schools and Students with Disabilities: A National Study* (Washington, DC: Office of Educational Research and Improvement, U.S. Department of Education, 2000).

90. D. Arsen, D. Plank, and G. Sykes, *School Choice Policies in Michigan: The Rules Matter* (East Lansing: Michigan State University, 1999).

91. SRI International, *Evaluation of Charter School Effectiveness: Part 1* (Stanford, CA: Author, 1997), 21.

92. J. Horn and G. Miron, *Evaluation of the Michigan Charter School Initiative* (Kalamazoo: Western Michigan University, July 2000).

93. Robert T. Stout and Gregg A. Garn, "Nothing New: Curricula in Arizona Charter Schools," in Robert Maranto, Scott Milliman, Frederick Hess, and April Gresham, eds., *School Choice in the Real World: Lessons from Arizona Charter Schools* (Boulder, CO: Westview Press, 1999), 159–172.

94. Good and Braden, *The Great School Debate*, 2000.

95. Corwin and Flaherty, *Freedom and Innovation*, 1995.

96. Marcella Dianda, "Teacher Characteristics: Who Teaches in Charter Schools?" in Corwin and Flaherty, *Freedom and Innovation*, 1995, 62.

97. Jane Hannaway and Martin Carnoy, eds., *Decentralization and School Improvement: Can We Fulfill the Promise?* (San Francisco: Jossey-Bass Publishers, 1993).

98. For a typology of variables associated with change, see Ronald G. Corwin, "Strategies for Organizational Innovation: An Empirical Comparison," *American Sociological Review* (August 1972), 441–454.

99. S. H. Fuhrman and R. F. Elmore, *Ruling Out Rules: Evolution and Deregulation in State Educational Policy* (New Brunswick, NJ: The Eagleton Institute of Politics, Rutgers University, 1995).

100. Good and Braden; *The Great Debate*, 2000; Stout and Garn, "Nothing New: Curricula in Arizona Charter Schools," 1999.

101. David Rogers, *110 Livingston Street* (New York: Random House, 1968); Robert Michels, *Political Parties* (Glencoe, IL: The Free Press, 1958 [1915]); Robert K. Merton, ed., *Social Theory and Social Structure* (Glencoe, IL: The Free Press, 1957).

102. Chubb and Moe, *Politics, Markets, and America's Schools*, 1990.

103. Oliver E. Williamson, *Markets and Hierarchies: Analysis and Antitrust Implications* (New York: Free Press, 1975).

104. Rothstein, "Charter Conundrum," 1998, 4. Available at www.prospect.org/print/V9/39/rothstein-r.html.

105. Witte, "The Theory of Choice and the Control of Education," 1990.

106. For detailed discussions of patterns of bureaucracy in public schools, see Ronald G. Corwin, "Patterns of Organizational Control and Teacher Militancy: Theoretical Continuities in the Idea of Loose Coupling," in R. G. Corwin, ed., *Research in the Sociology of Education and Socialization* 2 (Greenwich, CT: JAI Press, 1981), 261–291; Fred Katz, "The School as a Complex Organization," *Harvard Educational Review* 34 (1964), 428–453; Karl E. Weick, "Educational Organizations as Loosely Coupled Systems," *Administrative Science Quarterly* 21 (1976), 1–19; Richard J. Murnane, "Comparisons of Public and Private Schools: Lessons from the Uproar," *Journal of Human Resources* 19, 2 (1984), 269–270.

107. See Max Weber, "Bureaucracy," in H. Gerth and C. W. Mills, eds., *From Max Weber: Essays in Sociology* (New York: Oxford University Press, 1958), 214; Peter Blau, *Bureaucracy in Modern Society* (New York: Random House, 1956); Ronald G. Corwin, *Education in Crisis* (New York: Wiley, 1975), 1–56.

108. Chubb and Moe, *Politics, Markets, and America's Schools*, 1990.

109. National Center for Educational Statistics, *Private School Universe Survey, 1997–98*. Available at http://nces.ed.gov/pubsearch/pubsinfo.asp?pubid= 2001330; *Private Schools in the United States: A Statistical Profile* (Washington, DC: U.S. Department of Education, 1991, 1997, 1999). For more complete information, visit http://nces.ed.gov/pubsearch/pubsinfo.asp?pubid=1999319.

110. Dianda and Corwin, *Vision and Reality*, 1994; Tammy Johnson, "The Voucher Trap," *Color Lines* 3 (Winter 2000–2001) [online journal]. Available at www.arc.org/C_Lines/CLArchive/story3_4_06.html; National Center for Education Statistics, *Findings for the Condition of Education 2002: Private Schools* (Washington, DC: U.S. Department of Education, 2002). Available at http://nces.ed.gov/pubs2002/2002013.pdf.

111. James Q. Wilson, "Innovation in Organizations: Notes toward a Theory," in James Thompson, ed., *Approaches to Organizational Design* (Pittsburgh: University of Pittsburgh Press, 1966).

112. Ron Zimmer, Richard Buddin, Derrick Chau, and others, *Charter School Operations and Performance: Evidence from California* (Santa Monica, CA: RAND Corp., 2003); California Legislative Analyst's Office, *Assessing California's Charter Schools* (Sacramento, CA: Author, 20 January 2004).

113. National Education Association, "Charter Schools: A Look at Accountability" (April 1998). Available at www.nea.org/charter/accnt98.html; California Teachers Association, "Freedom Invites Abuse in Some Schools," *California Educator* 8 (October 2003).

114. There have been several news accounts pertaining to this charter. See, for example, Sarah Tully, "Charter Schools Struggle," *Orange County Register*, 31 July 2004, 1, 4; and Sarah Tully, "Charter Academy Shuts Two O.C. Sites," *Orange County Register*, 2 August 2001, B–1.

115. California Bureau of State Audits, November 2002.

116. Pennsylvania Auditor General, *Charter School Audit* (Harrisburg, PA: Department of the Auditor General, 1 February 2001).

117. Alan Richard, "States' Work on Charters Still Unfolding," *Education Week*, 20 March 2002 [electronic journal]. Available at www.edweek.com/ew/newstory.cfm?slug=27charter.h21.

118. Juliet Williams, "Scandals Rock Milwaukee Voucher Program," *Las Vegas Review Journal*, 6 April 2004.

119. American Federation of Teachers, "Private School Vouchers: The Track Record," Center on Privatization, March 2001. Available at www.aft.org/pubs-reports.

120. Wisconsin Education Association Council, "School Vouchers." Available at www.weac.org/GreatSchools/Issuepapers/vouchers.htm; see also National Center for Education Statistics, "Private School Universe Survey" (Washington, DC: U.S. Department of Education, 1998). Available at www.ed.gov/about/offices/list/oii/nonpublic/statistics.html; Wisconsin Education Association Council, "School Vouchers." Available at www.weac.org/GreatSchools/Issue papers/vouchers.htm.

121. Wisconsin Education Association Council, "School Vouchers."

122. National Education Association, "Charter Schools," 25 August 2004. Available at www.nea.org/charter/.

123. National Education Association, "Charter Schools" [updated 25 August 2004]. www.nea.org/charter/.

124. John Gehring, "Audit Spurs Drive to Revamp Ohio's Charter System," *Education Week* (27 February 2002) [electronic journal]. Available at www.edweek.com; Richard, "States' Work on Charters Still Unfolding," 2002.

125. *Education Week* 20 March 2002 as quoted by the NEA website, "Charter Schools" [updated 25 August 2004]. Available at www.nea.org/charter.

126. California Legislative Analyst's Office, January 2004.

127. SRI International, *Evaluation of the Public Charter Schools Program: Year One Evaluation Report* (Washington, DC: SRI, 2000), 56.

128. SRI International, *Evaluation of the Public Charter Schools Program*, 2000, Part II, 16.

129. SRI International, *Evaluation of the Public Charter Schools Program*, 2000; Wells, *Beyond the Rhetoric of Charter School Reform*, 1998.

130. P. Hill, R. Lake, and others, *A Study of Charter School Accountability* (Seattle, WA: Center on Reinventing Public Education, University of Washington, 2001); SRI, *Evaluation of the Public Charter Schools Program* (2000); K. Bulkley, "Educational Performance and Charter School Authorizers: The Accountability Bind," *Educational Policy Analysis Archives* 9 (1 October 2001), 1–35.

131. Corwin and others, *From Paper to Practice*, 1996, 59–64.

132. See P. Hill, L. Pierce, and J. Guthrie, *Reinventing Public Education: How Contracting Can Transform America's Schools* (Chicago: University of Chicago Press, 1997).

133. Corwin and others, *From Paper to Practice*, 1996, 48–57.

134. Jeanne Allen and Melanie Loony, *Charter School Closures: The Opportunity for Accountability* (Washington, DC: The Center for Educational Reform, October 2002).

135. David Arsen, "Charter School Spending: Autonomous and Accountable?" paper presented at the annual meeting of the American Educational Research Association, Montreal, 1999; Hank Prince, "Follow the Money: An Initial Review of Elementary Charter School Spending in Michigan," *Journal of Education Finance* 25 (1999), 175–199.

136. Arthur Stinchcombe, "Social Structure and Organizations," in J. G. March, ed., *Handbook of Organizations* (Chicago: Rand McNally, 1965), 142–193; Ronald G. Corwin, *Reform and Organizational Survival: The Teacher Corps as an Instrument of Educational Change* (New York: Wiley-Interscience, 1973).

137. Corwin, "Patterns of Organizational Control and Teacher Militancy" (1981); Katz, "The School as a Complex Organization" (1964); Weick, "Educational Organizations as Loosely Coupled Systems" (1976).

138. Herbert Walberg, "School Choice Evidence," *Las Vegas Review Journal* (23 July 2004), 118.

139. Jeanne Allen, "Union Study on Charter Schools Gets 'F' for Inaccuracy," *Orange County Register*, 22 August 2004, E–5; Schemo, "Nation's Schools Lagging Behind," 2004.

140. Chester E. Finn, Jr., "The War on Charter Schools," speech presented at National Charter School Clearinghouse Conference (14 September 2002). Available at www.ncsc.info/newletter/conference/keynote.htm.

141. See *Education Week*, "Charter Schools Found Lacking Resources" (16 April 2003) [electronic journal]. Available at www.edweek.org.

142. See Caroline Hendrie, "New Group to Push for Charter Schools," *Education Week* (28 July 2004) [electronic journal]. Available at www.edweek.org.

143. As reported by Hendrie, *Education Week*, 28 July 2004.

144. Elizabeth Hill is a principal author of the previously cited California Legislative Analyst's Office, *Assessing California's Charter Schools* (2004).

How to Improve Charter Schools: Clues from Open Enrollment Plans, School-Based Management, the Coalition of Essential Schools, and Small Schools Initiatives

Spokespersons for charters and vouchers maintain that it is impossible to create better choices for parents within school districts. That is how they justify using taxpayers' money to send kids to autonomous, deregulated schools beyond the reach of most local taxpayers. It is, of course, another inventive fabrication. We will explain why in this chapter. In the following pages, we return to the idea that choices for parents not only can be made available within public school districts; they already are available. The cacophony of school choice reforms being implemented within school districts demonstrates the pliability of public schools and their receptivity to change. What is missing is a cohesive approach to school choice.

Some forms of school choice have been available for a long time, especially a parent's option to change residence, to pay for private schools, and to teach the children at home. But choices for parents have expanded well beyond these traditional options. Of the many reforms now going on, we have chosen to discuss four in this chapter: Open Enrollment transfers within and between districts, Small Schools Initiatives, School-Based Management, and the Coalition of Essential Schools. We have chosen them not because they are working perfectly, because they are not. We have chosen them because they demonstrate the possibilities for making viable choice programs happen inside school districts, because they can alert us to some of the obstacles that have to be overcome, and because they can teach us something about how to improve charter schools. It is not our purpose to dwell on the details of these complex programs but to paint a large landscape filled with promise and hope.

Open enrollment is a product of political compromises. It reflects the political environment that shapes and guides most educational reform efforts. Because of the political constraints, it has so far helped only limited numbers of students, and yet the potentials of this approach to choice are so compelling that we cannot afford to ignore it. Small Schools programs change the schooling context. We shall review an impressive body of research that overwhelmingly endorses smallness. Not only do small schools produce better academic results, they also seem to facilitate many other types of reforms. School-Based Management (often also referred to as site-based management) is a structural reform. It takes many forms, but in general it can be thought of as a way to decentralize the decision-making process. "SBM," as it is typically called, empowers teachers and parents to create and implement choices, and is a tool for adapting reforms to specific circumstances. The Coalition of Essential Schools is a network of schools devoted to improving pedagogy. The impressive work of this group serves as a reminder that the purpose of school is to help students learn to think clearly. It is too easy to forget that structural reforms cannot work without also changing what goes on in classrooms.

We will identify elements of each approach that we think have genuine potential to become the basis for effective choice programs within school districts. In particular, we advocate integrating them into the charter school model to improve upon it, because we continue to believe the model offers major advantages and is worth the time and effort required to strengthen it. Conversely, we will argue that these reforms could themselves be improved by following some lessons from the charter experience, which we will mention as we go along. But, we will also point to some weaknesses present in some charter schools that should be avoided in any reform program. They include: erratic programs not geared to improving scholastic achievement, blind reliance on untrained teachers, unprepared leaders, and arrogant controls that some charter schools are imposing on parents. Three themes recur in the following discussions: (1) new, start-up schools facilitate reform, (2) schools should be small, and (3) recruiting and rewarding good teachers is critically important.

OPEN ENROLLMENT PLANS

In 1988, Minnesota enacted the first open enrollment program in the nation. This program allows students to attend public schools in any district in the state, provided that space is available. At least twenty-nine states now have laws permitting students to transfer to other schools within their district (intra-district transfers) or into other districts (inter-district transfers). However, the impact of these laws so far has been less than overwhelming. According to National Household Surveys conducted between 1993 and 1999 by the National Center for Education Statistics, the percentage of students enrolled in publicly assigned schools declined by only 4 percent.[1] Currently only 14 percent of children in grades 1–12 attend a public school other than one assigned by their district. It may seem puzzling that more parents are not taking advantage of open enrollment laws, especially since parents who do take advantage of the option are more satisfied with their schools than other parents. In 1999, the NCES found that 62 percent of the parents who selected a specific public school were "very satisfied" with the school compared to only 48 percent whose child was assigned to a specific school.[2]

So, why don't more parents take advantage of open enrollment for their children if they like it so well? A small part of the answer is that the 14 percent figure understates the selection of public school choice for some groups. Black students, in particular, are able to select public schools more often than either white or Hispanic students. In 1999, 23 percent of black students selected their public schools, compared to 18 percent of Hispanics and 11 percent of whites. Those percentages are slightly higher than in 1993. But even so, the fact remains that most students attend their assigned school. There is an easy explanation for this: open enrollment is largely a paper promise. All open enrollment plans are restricted in one way or another by roadblocks designed to limit the number of families that can actually participate in them. For example:

- Almost all plans allow districts to reject incoming transfers; local districts in all but four states can refuse to participate as receiving districts. In Minnesota, all districts must let their students go to another district, but all districts do not have to accept open enrollment students.

- Even where districts are required to, or agree to consider transfer requests, they are not required to honor them; schools are allowed to set transfer quotas based on a variety of considerations, such as maintaining class size, racial balance, and availability of services for special education students.

- Most states also allow districts to control whether a child may transfer out of the district. All plans allow students living within a desired district to attend the district's schools; but no plans require districts to accept students unless space is available. Available space is the primary rationale districts use to limit transfers and it is true that many schools are overcrowded.

- Most states do not provide funds for transportation.

These obstacles exist to protect school district autonomy. As Heise and Ryan point out, any unrestricted transfer plan, especially if it allows transfers between districts, would threaten to undermine the concept of local control, and in particular the ability of suburbanites to restrict who comes into their neighborhoods.[3] Suburbanites have the resources and political clout to erect barriers that guarantee parents the right to send their kids to suburban public schools, to control local revenues, and to protect their children from having to attend schools with more than a handful of "outsiders." At the same time, the authors observe, not many influential groups are pushing for open enrollment. Even civil rights groups seem uninterested in backing efforts to improve open enrollment plans. All of this works against open enrollment as a viable choice approach. Still, any discussion of school choice cannot afford to overlook the vast potential of this approach, or a modified version of it.

How Open Enrollment Actually Works

There is a provision in the federal No Child Left Behind Act of 2001, entitled the Unsafe School Choice Option, that requires each state receiving funds under NCLB to establish and implement a statewide policy permitting a student attending a dangerous school, or a student who has been the victim of a violent criminal offense, the right to attend a safe public school within the district. However, there is a lot of slippage between legislative intent and actual practice. The state, in consultation with school districts, has full authority to determine what is and is not a dangerous environment, and what constitutes a violent criminal offense. Also, the offense must have been committed in or on the grounds of the school the student attends. This provision alone exempts large spheres of student life, including incidents that occur during school-sponsored field trips or after school hours and on weekends; at events taking place at other schools; and while traveling on a school bus, or while walking to and from school. State-level open enrollment plans have been nearly crippled by exceptions like these. To grasp the magnitude of the problem, we need look no further than the multitude of exceptions and complicating hitches in California's legislation that have diluted the promise of open enrollment in that state.

Intradistrict Transfers. California law requires school districts to establish rules and regulations for student transfers within a district. Districts must inform parents of the opportunity to transfer at the beginning of the school year. These transfers must be nondiscriminatory and are on a space-available basis. However, the fine print guarantees each district authority to set its own policy and the criteria for admitting transfers. Each district determines how many openings at each school can be filled by students applying from outside their zoned attendance areas. When requests exceed openings, selection must be random and unbiased. However, the district can establish more than one category for the drawing. For example, there can be a separate drawing for students whose siblings already attend the school and another for students of parents who work for the school district.

Interdistrict Transfers. Each district sets its own policy and regulations regarding interdistrict transfers. Every school district in the state has the option to become an "open enrollment" or "choice" district that allows non-district residents to apply to any school in the district regardless of location. However, no district is under an obligation to accept transfers; moreover, if a transfer request is accepted, the district can assign the child to any school, even though the applicant may have wanted a particular school. Also, accepted students must provide their own transportation. If a transfer request has been denied by an open enrollment school, the parent has no right to appeal, but there is a right to appeal a request to a district that has not agreed to provide open enrollment. In the first case, the district has agreed to establish nondiscriminatory procedures in accepting applications, whereas in the latter case it has not.

Another California law allows districts to draft agreements to consider transfer requests on a case-by-case basis. In some situations, parents have pushed for group transfers on the basis of special needs, such as special education or bilingual programs, arguing that a group of students would be better served in a different district. Still another California law establishes a parent's right to apply to register K–8 children in a district where either parent's job is located. However, such transfers are always on a space-available basis, and districts have the right to determine whether to accept them. Districts that do accept job-related transfers can limit the number and establish other restrictions. Students cannot be discriminated against on the basis of race, sex, income, or achievement. But a student can be denied admission if it would contribute to segregation, or if the district would have to allocate additional funds to educate the student (for example, if the student requires extra, special services).

Official and Subtle Priorities. As noted, communities jealously guard their control over local schools. It is not surprising, therefore, that California school districts have been given wide discretion over the transfer process. The "Schoolwise Press" website, with unusual candor, lays out the criteria California school districts use to act on transfer requests.[4] They include: ethnicity (as it applies to desegregation plans), special education or language needs, location of the child's daycare provider, medical care needs that might require a child to be near a doctor, location of the parent's job, and whether the child's siblings are enrolled in the school. In addition, according to this website, districts take into account how long the student has been at the previous school, how long the parent has worked in the district, and whether the parent's job is full- or part-time.

One of the major considerations relates to expensive special education services. The law allows open enrollment districts to refuse a transfer if the district would have to create a new program or provide a new service to accommodate the student. So, on the one hand, parents want schools that provide better services, but on the other hand, the schools that do provide good services then are at risk of being over-enrolled, and so they restrict transfers. Moreover, the schools that are not providing adequate services can cut back even further as students transfer out, thus accentuating the inequities in special services.

The Schoolwise Press website lists several examples of what constitutes "just cause" that will encourage a district to accept transfers. They include:

- The student desires a particular educational program not offered by his/her district.
- The transfer would get the student away from dangerous circumstances the home district cannot address, or the student needs a change in environment (usually requiring a written professional opinion or court order).
- The transfer will facilitate child care, whereas attending the home school would impose substantial cost or hardship related to providing before-school and/or after-school supervision.
- The student's parent works for the district or within the district.
- A child is having difficulties in the first or second grade at her large K–8 school and would benefit from a small alternative K–5 school with an art program suitable for her interests.
- A fourth-grader has been transferred out of the assigned school where the child had been making solid progress in reading and math, after earlier difficulties.

The website says the following arguments do not work:

- The parent has heard that the assigned school is lax on discipline.
- The parent observes that the school has not done anything about the graffiti.
- The music program at the assigned school is not very good and the child needs to start playing an instrument.

Note that a quest for a high quality education is not the central criterion, and in fact concern about the quality of a school can go against parents who appear to be making invidious distinctions among teachers or between similar programs offered at different schools.

Limitations of Open Enrollment Plans

Open enrollment has been a disappointing approach to school choice for several reasons.

Too Many Restrictions Unrelated to Academic Excellence. While open enrollment plans may seem promising, in practice, they provide only limited options because every state has given school districts control over the transfer process, including whether to become involved. And when they do become involved, districts understandably must erect quotas and other barriers to control the size of their schools and classrooms. Quotas limit transfers even within a district. Most districts already have attendance zones sized according to the number of local households, and schools have been built to accommodate projected numbers of students.

Open enrollment is an unplanned overlay that cannot be easily accommodated within existing school plants.

After a school has decided how many students to admit, it establishes criteria that, while not exactly arbitrary, may be difficult to justify to a concerned mother and father who simply want their child in a better education program. Administrators don't like to acknowledge that some schools are outright better than others, so smart parents will find acceptable excuses, which ironically have nothing to do with the quality of the school. Not that parents are always looking for a better academic environment. Actually, academic priorities often take a backseat to the real priorities, such as getting Johnny into his brother's school, or a school near the babysitter or mom's work place, or maybe a school with a worthy athletic team. Pearson says that nearly half the reasons parents give for wanting transfers have nothing to do with gaining access to excellence.[5] So, how will open enrollment force schools to improve their scholastic programs?

The Downside of Competition. Pearson maintains that from the start, administrators from Minnesota school districts sometimes acknowledged that open enrollment "poisoned the atmosphere" of cooperation between districts and even threatened existing cooperation agreements because of the threatened loss of students. Also, to the extent a school's scholastic quality does count, competition tends to drain off the motivated high achievers. So, what does the competition do to a losing district? The mythology is that it will get up, dust itself off, and start all over again. But can it? Pearson cites a telling example of a small district that lost forty-five students and $200,000 in revenue as a result of open enrollment transfers. She writes:

The administration and school board began proposing reductions in the (next budget). . . . Only 4.5 full-time equivalent (FTE) classroom teachers were proposed for lay-offs. However, this would result in larger class sizes at two elementary grade levels and the loss of one foreign language and five other elective courses in the high school curriculum. Many parents attending the budget meeting . . . were members of the Band Boosters and were particularly upset over proposed reductions in the instrumental music program that would eliminate the summer band program and reduce lesson time at the junior and senior high level. As a result of these reductions, thirty-two students applied to open enrollment transfer for the (next) school year. The district had to prepare for another round of cuts to absorb the additional loss of $140,000 for the next school year. Board members expressed frustration and indicated that they felt trapped in a no-win dilemma. How could they keep or add programs to hold or attract students when they had to cut programs to comply with the budget requirements?[6]

Shuffling Students Does Not Promote School Improvement. But we haven't yet mentioned the major shortcoming with open enrollment: it targets individuals, not the system. Transfers allow some students to change schools, but they leave the schools untouched. They do nothing to improve the schools or to expand the range of options within the public sector. As just noted, transfers may even make things worse for schools that lose students and funds. As it currently operates, open enrollment amounts to little more than a strategy for placating a few parents—a strategy that, by the way, is largely symbolic since districts retain all the control. Open enrollment ultimately leaves all the important choices with the school district, and leaves parents with only the option to switch to another conventional school. It is a way to manage the existing system, when what is needed is an expanded range of options from which parents can chose within the public sector.

Implications for Charter Schools

The forgoing observations about open enrollment suggest several principles that could be used to improve charter schools and schools that accept school vouchers:

- Since, for political reasons, school districts aggressively protect their boundaries from outsiders, districts should not be permitted to control admissions to charter schools, including even charter schools being operated by a district.

- Charter school proponents like to brag about the innovative administrative and scholastic approaches being taken by some schools. It would be ironic, indeed, if all that parents actually want is to be closer to the babysitter. That is a distortion of the facts, of course. But the fact is that many parents seek out choice schools for reasons other than their educational excellence. Any choice school should have the authority to exclude such parents in favor of those searching for a better education for their children.

- Each choice school should emphasize its uniqueness and publicize its distinctive qualities to parents applying for open enrollment; the parent should be given the final say over which school the child is admitted to, provided space is available.

In the final analysis, open enrollment is an exceptionally weak choice option, namely because the option: (1) is a political reform, a product of power and compromise, not thoughtful planning; (2) provides no incentives for districts to release students, since the district would lose money; (3) provides no incentives for high-income districts to open schools to low-income students; (4) is currently limited to a select few individuals, and most fundamental of all; (5) is not designed to expand the range of schools available. Therefore, the remainder of this chapter is devoted to three reforms that hold some promise for improving schools. None requires a child to leave the school district, and each offers features that extend the variety of options available to the fortunate few students who find their way into them.

THE SMALL SCHOOLS MOVEMENT

The small schools movement provides extensive proof that it is possible to create options for parents without insisting they must abandon the public schools to exercise them. In 1974, a New York City high school principal, Deborah Meier, opened Central Park East, the first of about two dozen small elementary and middle schools in the East Harlem district.[7] By 1982, the district's ranking on reading tests climbed from dead last (thirty-second) to fifteenth. In 1985, Meier opened a secondary school, also named Central Park East, with 550 students in grades 7–12. Although most of the students lived in poverty and many had learning disabilities, the school's graduation rate was 90 percent, compared to 55 percent citywide. These schools were precursors of an explosion of small schools in that city and others during the 1990s. Today, with the benefit of help from the Center for Collaborative Education, associated with the Center for Essential Schools, 150 of New York's 1,000 public schools have fewer than 600 students.

As part of the nationwide small schools movement, 150 small schools were created in Chicago between 1990 and 1997.[8] Small schools were not new to Chicago, but historically, they usually served middle-income students, whereas the new wave of schools was targeted to children in impoverished neighborhoods and to children of color. A two-year study of the Chicago experience concluded that creating small schools out of large schools has been a successful means of involving students, parents, and teachers in the process of educational reform. Other cities are following suit.[9] A large batch of small schools is being launched in Oakland, Sacramento, and San Diego. At Cincinnati's Withrow University High School, where 80 percent of the students are African-American and half live in poverty, attendance rates have been over 95 percent since it opened in 2002 and test scores have improved by forty to fifty-five points in state proficiency scores.[10] The San Francisco school district plans to add a few small schools each year, with the goal of ten small schools and ten redesigned schools within five years.[11]

The small schools movement is now getting big boosts from several quarters. In its 1996 report, *Breaking Ranks*, the National Association of Secondary School Principals encouraged high schools to create self-operating units of no more than 600 students to reduce student feelings of anonymity. In 1999, then Secretary of Education Richard W. Riley called for a "national dialogue" on high schools, calling traditional high schools too large and impersonal to nurture teenagers through the often-tough period of adolescence.[12] At least eight large cities, from Sacramento to Boston, have plans for small schools initiatives, and there are several statewide efforts to open more small schools. New York City is pushing to open 200 new small schools in three to five years. In 2001, the U.S. Congress appropriated $125 million for competitive grants to help local education agencies create smaller learning communities.[13] That figure climbed to $174 million in 2004. Still another extremely important source of money and support for small schools is coming from the Gates Foundation. Since 2000 the foundation has pumped over $625 million into districts around the country to establish small schools. It has poured millions into two dozen large cities and is helping underwrite statewide initiatives in a half dozen states. The foundation's goal is to open 1,400 innovative high schools across the nation.[14]

Some Perspective

The movement to downsize high schools is a frustrated reaction to some ill effects of the big high schools that were formed on the heels of a baby boom, which forced schools to grow larger (since bigger schools are cheaper to build than a larger number of small ones). Moreover, big schools were being rationalized by a vigorous school consolidation movement that had gained crushing momentum in the late 1950s, at the outset of the new space age. A spokesperson for the movement, Harvard professor James Conant, was convinced that larger schools would support the kind of advanced science and math programs that he believed were essential to give the country an edge during the cold war competition with Russia.[15] When Russia launched Sputnik in 1957, it marked the beginning of a fierce cold war that would drive school reforms for years to come. Conant was probably right, at the time. In 1950, the school system was an anachronism that needed to be modernized. In 1930, the vast majority of children were still being educated in one-room schoolhouses. The influence of that model lingered on, casting a recalcitrant shadow over an increasingly urban society, desperately struggling to accommodate the baby boom in the midst of rapid urbanization and tight budgets. However, in the name of efficiency and cost reduction, consolidation went madly awry. Between 1940 and 1990, the number of elementary and secondary schools decreased from 200,000 to 62,000, while the population increased 70 percent. Average school-wide enrollments soared from 127 to 653. The number of high schools with more than 1,500 students has doubled in the last decade. Two-fifths of the nation's secondary schools now enroll more than 1,000 students. And schools with 2,000 to 3,000 students are not uncommon.[16]

Experience and a host of studies have confirmed what logic and reason have told us for years. Large high schools breed anonymity and alienation, which paves the way for violence, student dropouts, and low scholastic achievement. Students in large high schools report having little adult contact, as teachers cope with 150 students daily.[17] High schools offer a dizzying array of disconnected courses with little guidance, and schools have created tracks, most of which do not prepare students for college-level course work. Graduation rates hover around 70 percent, and for African-Americans and Hispanic youth, they are closer to 55 percent. Nearly one in five high school seniors cannot identify the main idea in what they have read, and nearly two in five seniors have not mastered fractions, percents, and averages.[18] Only one-third of all students leave high school prepared for a four-year college. Eighty percent of high school graduates go on to college, but half of them require remedial courses. High school reading scores have dropped steadily over the past decade. By twelfth grade, U.S. students score near the bottom of the international scale in math and science—an ironic comment on Conant's consolidation reform, launched primarily to improve student achievement in these two subjects. Conant's mistake was focusing on school size instead of specialization itself. As we shall explain in a moment, the relationship is somewhat complicated, but the bottom line is that specialists function best in middle-size schools, and after a threshold, further increases in size become dysfunctional.

How Big Is Small?

We have to be careful about the term, small schools, because the words "small" and "large" are sliders that have different meanings depending on the context and who is using them. And, more important, they denote a simple dichotomy that obscures the middle category. The middle category is not irrelevant. In fact, we maintain that the middle category is the crucial one. Research and theory both suggest that the so-called small schools model will work best in middle-sized schools—which is to say, schools that are smaller than most but not so small they cannot take advantage of bureaucratic principles.

Look at it this way. If you were to say that very large organizations are more prone to pathologies, and hence function less effectively than smaller ones, you would be right. On a linear scale, the size of a high school tends to be positively correlated with several adverse student outcomes, ranging from low attendance and high dropout rates to substandard grade averages and standardized scores.[19] However, linear correlations can be misleading. For example, while one study reported that violence is over 20 percent higher in schools with more than 2,000 students than in smaller schools, violence and size were not correlated in schools with fewer than 2,000 students.[20] Authorities differ on the optimal school size limit. Some writers set the lower limit at 600 students, and no one seems to recommend high schools below 300 students.[21] According to the National Association of Secondary School Principals, the ideal high school enrollment is about 600 students, about half the typical enrollment. Some researchers suggest a range between 400 and 800 students.[22] Probably an upper limit of 800 does not adversely affect student achievement, but the lower limit (400) is more supportive of communal life styles.[23]

In any case, at some point, small schools sacrifice advantages that larger schools can offer. The main advantage that is lost is specialization. One of the major shortcomings of schools today is that so many teachers are teaching subjects in which they have inadequate academic preparation. Visionaries who believe that generalists can effectively teach a wide array of subjects to secondary students need to explain how they can do it without sacrificing tough, high-level standards. Where is the army of multitalented teachers prepared to teach trigonometry, English literature, and European history? And how many elementary school teachers are prepared to teach students at different ages, grade levels, and performance levels, and then at the same time take on the work of art and music teachers, computer instructors, coordinators of various kinds, and school nurses? Sure, many try it, as they did in the days of the one-room school, but what is wrong with a little help from specialists? That would require schools large enough to justify hiring them.

So, if you were to say that very small organizations are more effective than larger ones, you would probably be wrong. This is an important point, because less is not always better. The apparent contradiction—that neither extremely large nor extremely small organizations are effective—can be accounted for only by introducing a middle category. Focusing on the middle allows us to introduce the *curvilinear principle*. It states that the relationship between size and other bureaucratic characteristics is curvilinear, not linear. This means that the most effective organizations will be somewhere in the middle, between the largest and the smallest. This principle was documented in a study by Lee and Smith, who found that high schools with the highest student achievement growth enroll between 600 and 900 students.[24] Students, they found, learn less in larger schools over 2,100, and (confirming our point) they also learn less in smaller schools below 600 students. Moreover, the mid-size schools produced greater achievement gains regardless of the student's SES or minority status. The curvilinear principle reflects two tendencies:

• Very big schools suffer from poor communication and coordination.
• Very small schools provide neither the division of labor necessary to support specialists nor enough slack resources to cope with spontaneous demands; families looking for small schools must consider whether the required expertise and resources are available there.

The curvilinear principle also explains a well-known correlation between the size of an organization and the degree to which decisions are centralized.[25] Examining this correlation will allow us to go one step deeper into this overview of the curvilinear principle. The correlation can be expressed as follows: as size increases from small to large, decisions become more centralized—but only up to a point. After a threshold, decisions again become decentralized with further increases in size. This pattern is a product of a balance between the three factors: division of labor requirements, difficulty of coordination, and the presence of expert specialists. Putting all three factors together gives us the following explanation:

1. It becomes increasingly difficult to coordinate large organizations from the top as they become progressively larger.
2. As organizations grow larger, they can, and often must, specialize.
3. Coordination can be achieved by giving specialized experts more authority; decentralization occurs as their presence increases.

In sum, the curvilinear pattern favors mid-sized schools—that is, schools no smaller than 400 or 500 students, depending on how closely the school is networked to outside services.

How Small Schools Work

There are three essential requirements for any smaller learning community, according to Raywid.[26] They are complete administrative separation, a clear and distinctive separate identity that is perceptible to students, and identifiable boundaries. Learning communities with these characteristics can take several forms: a new school or a converted (redesigned) existing school; a stand alone school; or one of multiple schools or programs that share space within a single building. Many communities are experimenting with options for sharing space. At minimum there are four types of shared-space structures:

- *Academies* are subgroups within schools, organized around particular themes, for example, career training.
- *House plans* divide students in a large school into groups of several hundred, either across grade levels or by grade levels; students take some or all courses with their house members and from their house teachers; house arrangements may be multiyear or yearlong arrangements; shorter term programs open largely untapped opportunities for promoting rotating racial and SES integration experiences for students; house plans personalize the high school experience but usually have limited effect on curriculum or instruction.
- *Magnet programs* use a specialty core focus (such as creative arts, or a career theme) to attract students from the entire school district; some have competitive admission requirements.
- A *school-within-a-school* is a small, autonomous program housed within a larger school building; it has its own budget, culture, program, and space.

An example of a schools-within-schools model that also employs an academy approach was developed by James McPartland, an extraordinary sociologist who divided a large, nonselective high school in Baltimore into several smaller quasi-autonomous schools of 250–350 students each in grades 10–12. Each of the schools had a special career focus. He writes:

Each Career Academy offered the same common core of demanding academic courses with an appropriate blend of career applications to match the particular Academy theme, so college entrance as well as entry to work was possible from every Career Academy. Each had its own separate section of the building with a unique entrance . . . with marquees announcing the Academy name . . . [which] were important to dramatize the identity of each unit. . . . Each academy had its own faculty for both basic academic courses and career-focused electives. Each had its own management team of Academy Principal and Academy Instructional Leader (drawn from previous school-wide Assistant Principals and Department Chairs) who had major authority for student discipline, instruction, and curriculum. Guidance counselors were also assigned to each Career Academy, as were custodial staff. Patterson had four Career Academies: Arts and Humanities, Business and Finance, Sports Studies and Health/Wellness, and Transportation and Engineering Technology. Each Career Academy developed two or three pathways to provide instruction and internships for more specific sets of occupations within the Academy theme. The daily homeroom period became a mentor-advisor group for students. Each student stayed with the same homeroom teacher for the entire 3 years in the Career Academy.[27]

Drawing on his many years coping with awesome challenges, McPartland also suggests a way to minimize isolation while providing specialized instruction. In his words, "After struggling with a full inclusion model for all special education students during the early reform implementation years, a modified approach was put into place. Most special education students were properly reviewed and placed in regular classrooms with an additional special education teacher in an approved inclusion program. Others who required self-contained classes were drawn together across Career Academies in classes of court-specified size and levels of instructional support."[28] He adds that staff development for regular teachers was provided by special education teachers who worked with them in inclusion classrooms.

Research Findings

The findings from a large batch of studies indicate with unusual consistency that small schools produce superior results in both academic performance and personal conduct. Reviewers have consistently concluded that small schools offer a wide array of advantages, including better graduation rates, higher student and parent satisfaction, and significantly lower levels of absenteeism and crime.[29] In particular, the negative correlation between poverty and school size can become many times greater as schools get extremely large. Also, the impact of size on student misconduct is striking. Only 4 percent of small public schools report serious crimes and 2 percent report physical attacks, including fights with weapons. The comparable rates for large schools are, respectively, 33 percent and 20 percent.

Early documentation came from the National Education Longitudinal Study, which gathered information on the experiences of nearly 12,000 students in 800 high schools nationwide. The data indicated that schools that had restructured to personalize the education experience produced significantly higher and more equitable achievement gains.[30] During the late 1980s and early 1990s, several large-scale studies were reported using students' records to compare performance in large and small schools. One of these studies examined the records of 20,000 students in Philadelphia's public high schools. The investigators concluded that high school students in small schools were more likely than those in large schools to pass major subjects and progress toward graduation.[31] Another study examined the scores of 13,000 youngsters in Alaska and found that disadvantaged students in small schools significantly outperformed those in large schools on standardized tests of basic skills.[32]

Other investigations included schools in entire states.[33] A New Jersey study showed that school size had more influence on student achievement than any other factor controllable by educators. Moreover, findings about the impact of size appeared to hold at all grade levels, but with a tendency for school size and organization to play a larger role as students got older.[34] A four-state regression analysis of the effects of small schools provides still more evidence that student standardized test scores are better in small schools.[35] Elementary schools with fewer than 350 students and high schools having below 900 students were considered small. In three of four states examined, for students in larger schools, the lower the income of the community, the lower the achievement. The well-documented correlation between poverty and low achievement was much stronger—as much as ten times stronger—in the larger schools than in smaller ones in all four states.

In addition to the statistical studies, several studies of particular schools in recent years are noteworthy. One is a seven-year study of the Coalition Campus Schools Project in New York City, which documented the creation of five new small schools that replaced a failing comprehensive high school.[36] Despite serving a more educationally disadvantaged population compared to the previous school, the schools overall produced substantially better attendance, lower rates of misconduct, better performance on reading and writing assignments, higher graduation rates, and more graduates enrolled in college. Still other studies have followed schools in Chicago that serve under 400 students in high schools. Between 1991 and 1996, these schools showed greater improvements in their academic performance, notwithstanding the types of students enrolled.[37] Follow-up research that focused on new small schools serving impoverished neighborhoods supports that conclusion, and also reports lower dropout rates.[38]

Finally, a study of the effects of school size on cost and performance should be mentioned.[39] Most cost studies have confirmed that large schools benefit from economies of scale due to more intensive uses of common spaces (such as gyms and cafeterias), more efficient deployment of teachers, lower administrative costs (which can be spread across more students), and more effective division of labor. Observing that studies of cost seldom take into account school outputs, the authors of this study integrated measures of both economic inputs and school performance measures. They found that smaller schools do have somewhat higher costs per student. However, they maintain that because small schools have substantially higher graduation rates and lower dropout rates, small schools are ultimately more cost-effective than large ones. Bryk also concluded that the envisioned economies of scale are illusive because the marginal inefficiencies of small schools are dwarfed by positive effects on students.[40] But while this is an important point, it also would be useful to weigh the possibility that at some point, smallness can adversely effect specialization and hence the quality of education.

Explanations

Writers have tried to explain these positive effects of smallness in various ways. The favored explanation is that small schools facilitate intensive, personalized relationships and better connections with the students' families. Probably true. To gain more insight on how smallness contributes to personalized relationships, think about how growth in group size affects interaction patterns. Start with the premise that people usually interact in pairs, that is, as members of dyads interacting with one other person at any one time. Each partner can consider an array of unique characteristics of the sole partner. Adding even one additional person complicates the relationship, because now coalitions can form within the new triad. Person A can relate to Persons B and C as a pair, B can relate to A and C as a pair, and so on. This happens, for example, when a father and son have a disagreement with the son's coach. With the addition of each new member, the relationship compounds exponentially, not only because there are more people, but also because higher-order relationships develop among threesomes, foursomes, and larger cliques of people.

It really gets complicated when the same individuals are members of more than one subgroup. For example, some students in the speech club may also be members of the drama group, and find themselves in a role conflict when both groups compete for the same auditorium. As such memberships become more complex and overlapping, it becomes less and less feasible to introduce personal characteristics. Unique personal characteristics of each individual become mute as progressively higher-order groups relate to one another. People begin to use shorthand codes to categorize one another and interact as representatives of groups, cliques, positions, and strata. The larger the group, the more likely that personal qualities will be eclipsed by segmented, formally defined roles and statuses. Eventually, much of the communication occurs through intermediaries rather than through direct face-to-face relationships. At this point, the influence of personal characteristics on relationships drops out almost entirely. Relationships, as they say, become impersonal, and often alienating. Anonymity fosters irresponsibility and misconduct.

George Homans introduced another consideration: status.[41] He observed that the more frequently two people of equal status interact, the more they will tend to either like or dislike one another. But, the higher the status of an individual, the less direct contact the person will have with subordinates in progressively lower strata; feelings about the person's personal qualities are replaced by status-related considerations. They will interact less when occupying different status levels, since status differences create social distance. As groups grow larger, status differences and social distance between individuals increase, and interaction between any given pair declines. Correspondingly, interaction between them becomes guided less by their personal qualities than by their formally defined roles and statuses. Consider a principal, teachers and students in a small school. The principal can directly interact with all teachers and many of the students. But as the school adds more teachers, the principal relates to most teachers through intermediaries (for example, coordinators or chairs), which leaves the principal with less opportunity for direct contact with anyone in the lower echelons.

As a school gets smaller, the opposite patterns occur. With reductions in school enrollments, impersonal status mechanisms can again be supplemented with more personalized and equitable forms of interaction. However, we have to be cautious. Size reduction is no cure-all. One mitigating factor is that teachers and students occupy informal statuses that separate them. The captain of the football team will tend to interact less with marginal nonathletes than with his peers. Another factor is that interaction fosters what Homans called "sentiment," which can be negative as well as positive. In other words, people who associate a lot may find they do not like one another after all. In fact, smallness opens the individual's personal life to closer scrutiny (religion, moral behavior, family life, friendships, etc.), which can invite prejudicial treatment for actions unrelated to the person's formal roles.

Classrooms are still another factor that can mitigate the effects of smallness. Self-contained classrooms can isolate entire groups from one another, even in small schools. Also, larger classrooms probably offer less interaction opportunities. In this context, remember that small schools do not guarantee small classrooms. Class size tends to remain relatively constant across all schools of all sizes. There is some evidence that though charter schools tend to be smaller than other public schools, their student-teacher ratio is only slight lower (16.0 vs. 17.2).[42] To the extent that large classrooms contribute to some of the adverse outcomes of schools, downsizing schools is only a partial solution to impersonality. But, some of these adverse factors can be offset by special mechanisms, such as individualized instruction, personal counseling, and active learning strategies.

Problems and Caveats

While smallness appears to have good effects, it is vulnerable to some of the problems associated with many reforms, as well as a few troubling features of small schools themselves. Accordingly, as the small-school movement expands, some cracks are appearing.

Implementation Woes. Scaling up any kind of reform opens the door to groups who are not fully dedicated to it or who do not understand what it takes to put it into practice. Here are some complications that often arise when something new is put into practice:

- *Scheduling glitches.* An example is construction delays that prevent a new small school from opening on time. Such delays can be disruptive for students who have to start school late or transfer during the year.

- *The way a reform is introduced.* If smaller schools are pushed by lower echelon staff, administrators may be hesitate to give their support. Conversely, if they are introduced from the top down, teachers might be reluctant to buy into them.[43]

- *Role overload.* If an existing school is downsizing, during the transition teachers are often left with the burden of working in several capacities at the same time. They must maintain the old system with one hand, while implementing the new system with the other. Role overload is one of many unspoken "social costs" often associated with implementations. The principle is that social costs associated with a reform are passed progressively down the chain of command to the frontline people who, by default, are left with the responsibility of working out the kinks to carry out their duties. They have to take on the arduous burdens associated with putting elusive plans into practice.[44]

- *Status threats.* Nonparticipating teachers may fear losing some important responsibilities, or worse, are uncertain about how the changes might affect them.[45] Ironically, a person's uncertainty about what might happen is often worse than knowing precisely what will happen. Teachers become at least anxious, if not overtly threatened, when colleagues who are involved in the new program are given preferential treatment in the form of more resources, recognition, released time, and professional support. In some cases, regular schools have been saddled with larger classes and double-session schedules to make room for small schools. Some New York City teachers have called for a moratorium on small schools because of such complaints.[46]

- *Restrictive policies, codes, and employment agreements.* Although public school districts usually can provide the needed flexibility if the reform has sufficient outside and internal support, mobilizing this flexibility is another matter. It requires a concerted effort on the part of the reform advocates.

Limitations of the Small Schools Approach. The forgoing impediments have more to do with the implementation process than with the merits of small schools. But there are two troubling features within the small-schools approach itself that must be resolved. First, smaller schools may have fewer resources to provide students with options that would be available in larger schools, such as school-to-work programs, athletic activities, clubs, driver education, and the like. Second, two or more schools with distinctive missions sharing the same space invites invidious prestige distinctions. The schools, and the students and teachers in them, often tend to become stratified. Competition for resources and recognition is a persistent reality, and the outcomes of conflicts between schools are often decided by differences in their status, power, and connections. But more important, status differences provide groups with differential access to resources. Scheduling the use of common space, for example, can be a constant source of tension. Tensions and conflicts among schools can undermine the shared cultural climate of the larger school. More important, distinctions among schools can lead to tracking, isolating some students while giving others differential access to tough college preparation courses and other high achievement options. Status distinctions can carry over to the teachers as well, creating rivalries and isolating subunits.

While there are no easy solutions to these problems, schools can take some preventative steps. Several writers have mentioned some possibilities and we have added to them below:

- Preceding the implementation, build in time and resources for a planning process that includes meetings with representatives from all administrative echelons, unions, and critical interest groups within the district. Representatives should have authority to make commitments and to commit resources.
- Find ways to compensate teachers for taking on additional responsibilities during the implementation (for example, with released time and public recognitions).

- Communicate clearly and frankly with teachers not included in the new program, explaining how the new program will and will not affect them, giving them special incentives during the transition period, providing hearing and appeal mechanisms, and spelling out their transfer options.
- Create coordinating councils made up of representatives from each school and all competing programs and departments to negotiate differences and to give them a chance to share in the decisions that directly affect them.
- Hold frequent public meetings for students at all schools to inform them about programs and practices at the other schools.
- Provide two or more windows each year during which students can freely transfer between schools without penalty.
- Offer sessions preceding each school year or semester at which all students are required (or at least strongly encouraged) to try a college preparation course; make available intensive tutoring and other forms of assistance for those who need it.
- Establish tough courses in basic subjects offered jointly across all schools that can be taken by any student who applies, regardless of the school of enrollment.
- Establish athletic, speech, art, and music programs and clubs that include students from all schools in the building.[47]

Implications for Charter Schools

In sum, an impressive body of research and theory says with an unusual degree of consensus that smaller schools are far better in many ways than the largest ones. This opinion is shared by government agencies and private benefactors, such as the Gates foundation, whom we commend for supporting this reform. At the same time, the research raises profound questions about the credibility of the choice movement, because choice schools tend to be small. Therefore, we have to wonder whether their outcomes result from their small size rather than their autonomy and programs. It might be entirely possible to produce charter-school-like results only by establishing more small schools within districts without all the autonomy and fanfare. Indeed, all the hoopla over charter schools could be a case of mistaken identity, as charter schools take the bows for another performer's act. Some of the more successful charter schools have done little more than adopt various approaches that are not unique to charter schools and can stand alone without them. School size is one of the most obvious of these.

Therefore, it is crucial to undertake research designed to sort out the effects of autonomy and program, on the one hand, from the size effect on the other. As an example of such a project, consider this. Match highly autonomous, small charter schools with comparable small schools within the same district. Since some charter schools are larger than others, stratify them by size and compare them with comparable public schools of similar sizes. Other characteristics obviously would need to be taken into account, including for example grade level and populations served. The results should illuminate the relative effect of school size and autonomy on outcomes. This type of study also would help identify circumstances that favor large schools so they can stay productively in the overall mix of schools. Finally, classroom size should be included. Small schools do not necessarily have small classrooms, which raises a question about the relative impact of the two measures. While it seems plausible that the combination—small classrooms in small schools—would have the most beneficial effects, for purposes of planning and resource allocation, planners need to know whether to give priority to creating small schools or small classes. We suspect that the positive effects of small schools have been more consistently documented, probably because they impact the school culture.

However, the effectiveness of small schools aside, the main conclusion about small schools that we want to underscore is the one we started with. The large number of successful small schools throughout the nation tells us that options for parents can be created within public school districts. Perhaps, as the critics maintain, undertaking reform within the public sector is not as easy as jumping the fence into the uncontrolled waters of private and deregulated sectors. But we think there is no doubt that it is ultimately more worthwhile to concentrate reform efforts on school districts. Successful implementations of reforms there pave the way for other changes—not only in the participating districts, but in others like them. In stark contrast, reforms that are implemented outside of districts, no matter how successful, cannot have the same impact.

It is worth listening to what school district officials in San Francisco had to say about their experience with starting a small school in that district.[48] They made three salient observations: (1) these district schools were in a better position than charters to impact the district, because as members of the district their experiences rippled across the city; (2) being part of the district, they received their buildings free, enjoyed district salaries and received help from the district; charters, on the other hand, are too isolated to have much influence and cannot count on district support; and (3) rather than waiting for each school to come up with a reform, the district took that responsibility. The San Francisco experience demonstrates that school districts can help identify promising approaches and will support them.

SCHOOL-BASED MANAGEMENT

One can read a lot on the subject of charter schools without ever hearing about one of its leading precursors, a widespread reform that goes back for decades. Since the 1960s, school-based management (SBM) has been operating in some school districts across the nation, and the concept gained new momentum in the 1980s. The reform has many forms and functions, but at the core it aims to decentralize authority, budgets, and decision making to the level of schools. Schools in turn are governed by councils, teams, and committees composed of parents, school-level administrators, teachers, community members, and (sometimes) students. However, though widely used, the reform has never lived up to its promise and potential, perhaps largely because it is not so much a defined model as a philosophical approach that has been interpreted and applied in myriad ways. It addition, the idea often has been thrust upon unprepared, skeptical principals and teachers by mandates from higher levels of authority. Nevertheless, we have chosen to describe this reform here in some detail for two reasons. First, the sheer prevalence of site councils with authority to create flexible programs demonstrates that it is possible to provide choices for parents without going beyond current school districts. Second, understanding how and why school-based management has succeeded, and where it has gone wrong, can supply clues about how to improve charter schools—and equally important, how the charter-school model can enhance the effectiveness of school-based management.

Years ago Michael Katz observed that school systems routinely cycle through periods in which decisions are centralized and then decentralized.[49] In a centralized system, power resides in the office of the superintendent who reports to a board of lay persons. But in recent years, an increasingly vocal segment of the education community has been lobbying for redistributing power from central office administrators to people at the school level. School-based management allows an individual school to make its own decisions related to finances and curriculum. Presumably, a local council can make better decisions because it includes teachers, families and students. Today, in every state, some school districts practice some form of school-based management in some degree, and five states have mandated some form of participatory decision making at every school. In addition, hundreds of districts in other states operate schools using school-based management. Several large urban school systems have taken steps in this direction. By some estimates, over half the public schools in this country have a school-based decision-making body in place.[50]

The philosophy underlying SBM comes from corporate management theories, including the so-called Total Quality Management approach and a stream of participatory management approaches going back more than half a century, which were designed from research showing that employees perform better when they are deeply involved in decisions that affect them.[51] The success of Japanese companies, which allow factory workers to assume significant roles in work teams, gave the idea a big boost in the 1980s, when American businesses took notice and encouraged their employees to use more discretion in doing their jobs. University professors and consultants promoted equivalent reform approaches for schools. Notice that we used the plural, *approaches*, because as already noted, there are many versions of so-called school-based management. This reform resembles charter schools in that respect. Neither reform is based on a uniform, coherent approach to either school management or teaching. This looseness makes it difficult to generalize about either the strategies or consequences of school-based management, just as it has been difficult to form clear conclusions about charter schools.

SBM in Chicago's School Reform

Chicago turned to SBM in a time of crisis, after publicity that fewer than three in five ninth graders would graduate from high school and that only one of those students would read at the national average. In 1988, the Illinois legislature enacted the Chicago School Reform Act, which among other things, required each public school to create a local school council (LSC), chaired by a parent elected by council members, and with power over curriculum and pedagogy, budget and use of resources, and firing the principal. Seven years later, the legislature handed over responsibility for the district to the mayor and reduced the LSCs' independence. Hess credits theories of participatory management, and more important, the "effective schools" literature, for guiding the reforms.[52] Reformers believed that to empower principals to exercise the necessary leadership, it was necessary to remove bureaucratic sanctions. The locus of accountability was transferred to parents and community. Reformers also felt they could raise expectation levels and achievement for students by granting principals the authority to recruit their own faculty and by giving them the flexibility to allocate resources for school-improvement planning.

Multiple Goals and Functions of SBM

Chicago by no means gives us the entire picture. Indeed, school-based management has careened through a twisted history of diverse purposes. As Briggs and Wohlstetter tell the story, up until the 1980s SBM was used for limited purposes.[53] Most often it was part of political reforms designed to give communities more influence over their schools. There was no particular focus other than the hope that redistributing power would somehow produce good things. Beyond placating communities, SBM has also been seen by teacher unions as a way to empower teachers. In addition, some SBM promoters touted it as a tool to improve administrative efficiency, on the grounds that participants closest to students and staff could apply resources more effectively than remote central office staff. Only recently has SBM been given the awesome responsibility of improving stu-

dent achievement. According to Briggs and Wohlstetter, this new academic role has transformed SBM from a stand-alone approach to an aspect of larger reform strategies, embedded within more comprehensive
approaches to reform. Using a theme remarkably similar to that espoused
by charter school proponents, SBM spokespersons are now urging that
the ultimate goal of all school-based management efforts should be to improve student achievement.[54]

These historical shifts in function were accompanied by corresponding
changes in form over the years, as it was implemented in diverse settings under unique circumstances. The variety of terms referring to SBM
reflects some of this diversity. They include: "site-based management,"
"decentralization," "restructuring," "local management of schools,"
"shared decision-making," "self-managing schools," "self-determining
schools," "locally-autonomous schools," "devolution," and "local empowerment." Among the dimensions of SBM that differ from place to
place is the scope of local empowerment. The membership and actual
power of councils varies widely. For simplicity, we can say that, depending on who dominates the council, there are at least four different
forms, which Leithwood and Menzies refer to as: administratively controlled, professionally controlled, community controlled, and balanced.[55]
Administratively controlled, school-based management focuses predominantly on the effective use of resources, while giving local school administrators (guided by site councils) authority over budgets, personnel,
and curriculum. *Professionally controlled* management makes teachers the
primary decision-makers and asks them to use their experience to guide
decisions about budgets and curriculum. Teachers assume leadership
roles in staff development, mentoring, and curriculum development.
Community controlled management allows parents and local community
members the opportunity to introduce local values and preferences to
modify the curriculum. Situations in which parents have obtained disproportionate power have sometimes become adversarial and have gen-
erated conflict with teachers over decisions they traditionally have
controlled. Finally, in *balanced* districts, two or more of the above forms
share power collaboratively.

In practice, the administratively controlled form is typical. According
to Leithwood and Menzies, "Evidence suggests that whatever form of
school-based management that districts or states thought they were leg-
islating, what was implemented was some form of administrative control
school-based management."[56] The principal is exclusively or primarily responsible for making budget decisions in at least five major cities. However, there are some instances of the other forms of control. For example,
the school-level council approves the budget in Chicago and Los Angeles, and in Milwaukee and Denver budget decisions are made collaboratively.

What Is Known About the Effects of SBM?

Given the multiplicity of forms and functions, it is not surprising that assessments of the contributions of SBM to school improvement have been mixed. The research suggests this reform shows promise but has not yet lived up to it. Again, we see a clear parallel with charters and vouchers in this respect. While some early research produced promising findings, later results were often disappointing.[57] Not until recently have some studies begun reporting positive effects. For example, from their 1998 study, Leithwood and Menzies concluded that when teachers participate in school decision making, they express higher levels of commitment and morale. SBM teachers are more likely to collaborate, become engaged in school-wide professional development, and to accept more personal accountability. Other authors have found that SBM is being used as a means for restructuring classroom practice, and that more curriculum and instruction reform takes place when SBM is fully implemented at a school.[58]

In addition, one study, which focused on SBM since it was first conceived in Chicago, provides substantial support for the conclusion that teacher participation in decision making in SBM schools is positively related to improved instructional programs and to increased student learning.[59] A second, smaller study of fourteen Chicago schools corroborated these findings. And, recent studies of the effects of SBM on student achievement have yielded promising results in other places, most notably in Boston.[60] Odden and Wohlstetter have identified two necessary characteristics.[61] First, people on school-site councils must have real authority over budget, personnel, and curriculum. Second, changes must be introduced that directly affect teaching and learning. Some attributes in schools that have successfully implemented school-based management include: dispersal of power throughout the school, ongoing professional development, continual development of the knowledge base, and strong leadership capable of delegating responsibility. Schools that are less successful with school-based management tend to focus on power and housekeeping issues and have less effective communication systems, which often result in information being passed informally.

Boston's Pilot Schools

Boston's Pilot Schools demonstrate that an effective SBM implementation can have a positive impact on student achievement. Pilot Schools are fully autonomous, but unlike independent charter schools, they operate entirely like other schools within the Boston public school district. Created in 1994 to promote increased choice options within the school district, they are unlike most urban public schools, in that they control budgets, staffing, curriculum, governance, and time.[62] As in the case of charters, this flexibility was granted in exchange for stricter accountability. Currently, there are eleven Pilot Schools spanning grades K–12 and serving approximately 2,600 students, or 4 percent of the total Boston Public Schools enrollment. The student assignment process is the same for Pilot elementary and middle schools as for the district as a whole. However, Pilot high schools have special admissions processes that screen for "fit" and commitment to the school's philosophy (but not on prior academic achievement)—which lamentably creates an element of selectivity.

By some accounts, Pilot Schools have used their unusual authority to create a unified learning community in which teaching and learning are personalized and of high quality. An internal report concludes that, "While the Pilot Schools serve a student population generally representative of the Boston Public Schools, Pilot School students perform well on all available measures of student engagement and performance, and are among the top performing of all Boston Public Schools."[63] Pilot Schools rank among the Boston public schools with the highest student attendance rates, and they have the lowest suspension rates of all schools in the public system, which reflects high levels of student engagement. Pilot elementary schools perform at or above the system average in English, Language Arts, Math, and Science, with two schools ranking at or near the top. According to the report, science scores have improved dramatically in all three elementary schools over the last few years. For example:

- A Pilot middle school performed at or above the system average in all three subjects in 1999–2000, ranking fourth of all middle schools in both English, Language Arts, and Mathematics.
- Three of four Pilot high schools outscored other Boston high schools, or placed just behind them in English, Language Arts, and Mathematics.

The authors of the report attribute the schools' apparent successes to their autonomy from the district over budget, staffing, scheduling, governance, and curriculum. In addition, their smallness allows staff and students to know each other well. "The Boston Pilot Schools," says the report, "have begun to demonstrate that when urban public schools are provided increased autonomy and flexibility to adopt innovative practices, and are held accountable for their results, student outcomes across a range of indicators improve."[64] The rationale is that schools struggling to do innovative things are often hampered by the lack of control over budget, staffing, curriculum, governance, and time, all critical conditions to building a unified learning community. Without autonomy, their hands are tied, leaving them unable to use their resources in the best manner possible.

All of this sounds very much like the descriptions—and yes, the hype—used for charter schools. Pilot Schools get self-selected students and actually screen out some high school applicants, and they benefit from smallness. So we have to be wary about some of the claims. The important difference is that unlike charter schools, Pilot Schools operate within the Boston Public Schools (BPS), so when they work, the effects can ripple through the district. All Pilot School teachers are members of the Boston Teachers Union, receive union salaries and benefits, and accrue seniority. It is important to note that this attachment with the district provides the opportunity for Pilot School practices and conditions to influence the larger BPS system—something charters have not been able to do. Their impact is facilitated by the Boston Pilot Schools Network, formed to make the Pilot Schools individually and collectively stronger. An additional advantage of district membership is that Pilot Schools benefit from access to the district's facilities and the services it provides in the areas of payroll and transportation.

Lessons from Pilot Schools for Charters. We have already mentioned one lesson to be learned from Boston's Pilot Schools: choices can be created for parents within school districts. They do not have to skip out of the public schools to exercise their choices. Not only does their existence demonstrate that it is feasible for a large public school district to grant autonomy to some schools, but also (and unlike the charter school situation) the experience shows that school districts can monitor the autonomy-for-results bargain, since as district members, Pilot Schools subscribe to the district's measurement procedures.

Second, whereas the independence of charter schools has isolated them, district membership has enhanced the ability of Pilot Schools to impact other district schools. Third, whereas the independence of charter schools has encouraged them to evolve freewheeling objectives, district membership requires Pilot Schools to focus on improving learning outcomes in agreed upon subject areas. Fourth, when decentralized schools operate as part of a district, instead of independently from it, as most charter schools do, they can call on the district for support in the form of expertise and services, as well as additional resources—something charter schools cannot do.

And finally, the Pilot Schools' project underscores a lesson we cannot afford to overlook, namely that, in hindsight, charter schools would have benefited immensely if promoters had built the charter model on the already viable SBM reforms. Instead, they chose to promote a separate charter school movement driven by a relentless quest for independence. As a consequence of independence, resources and effort were diverted from a promising reform approach (SBM) with a history and a solid potential to do what charters and vouchers are supposed to do, namely give teachers and parents the flexibility they deserve and need to improve student learning. But to be fair, we have to remember that charter schools were invented to serve as a competing alternative to school vouchers. By adopting the language and strategies of vouchers, charter advocates could offer the better of two worlds: the independence and deregulation enjoyed by private schools without sacrificing the big tax bases and a facade of protection offered by the public sector. Still, that doesn't change the prospect that, in the future, parental choice programs would benefit dramatically if a new model were constructed based on a combination of the best of SBM with the charter school model. It isn't too late. Some ideas for how to do it follow.

SBM Principles

Several writers have culled out some principles that separate successful implementations of SBM from unsuccessful ones. We believe that these principles reveal insights about how to improve the charter school model. Conversely, we are convinced that some aspects of the charter-school model would be good contributions to the SBM design. The following paragraphs rely heavily on the work of Briggs and Wholstetter.[65]

Lesson 1: Need for External and Internal Incentives to Overcome Resistance. Perhaps the most important principle is the one least discussed, namely that there will be inherent resistance within school districts to any form of decentralization.[66] It is fair to say that decentralization usually will not happen without incentives from the state level, as well as from within the school district and the schools themselves. In particular, central office administrators, insecure about losing authority, tend to be the most active opponents of decentralization. And, even those principals who gain authority may not entirely welcome it, since it means taking on new responsibilities and bearing the burden of accountability; they can no longer blame the central office for mediocre school performance.[67] Teachers, too, may question SBM if they see it as still another duty assignment in an already busy schedule. Moreover, they might not welcome the closer scrutiny and increased parental involvement. Teachers' unions will be concerned about how their relationships could change, and how the changes could affect their bargaining position. Even some parents may not support the idea, in particular, busy parents who do not have the necessary time or inclination to serve on boards. At least some will be shut out because they are not included on an official council.

Some states have taken steps to combat resistance.[68] Decentralization is mandated by five states. For example, the Indiana 2000 program allows schools to develop a proposal showing their commitment to restructuring along with a workable plan. Several school boards underwrite restructuring efforts with grants to schools or other incentives to help make decentralization work. In New York City, the chancellor allows schools to restructure if the principal and 75 percent of the teachers decide to do so; schools that do choose restructuring receive flexible Chapter 1 federal dollars. Des Moines provides extensive professional development activities. Dolan proposes that a district should form an oversight committee consisting of district-level staff, union representatives, school board members and other stakeholders whose support is essential.[69] In rare cases, teachers might receive extra pay for assuming additional duties. However, recognition can be rewarding, too.[70] These same approaches would definitely help charter schools. In Chapter 5, we will propose giving substantial bonuses to teachers working with low-income children.

Lesson 2: SBM Should Be Part of a Whole School Restructuring Initiative. One principle on which there is general agreement is that SBM involves far more than a change in governance. When done effectively, it requires redesigning the whole school organization, including its relationships with the district. As Dolan puts it, "The entire system is one, and to change a school is to change a district, its union, board, and management. . . . Anything else will be short-lived and false."[71] Wolhstetter and Mohrman emphasize that for SBM to work, the school must control three essential resources: *professional development* and training for teachers and other stakeholders in the areas of management and problem-solving, and curriculum and instruction; *information* about student performance, parent and community satisfaction, and school resources; and *rewards* to acknowledge the increased effort required.[72] The same principles are applicable to charter schools.

Lesson 3: Schools Should Control Staffing. The forgoing two principles, however, would mean nothing without the ability of a school-site council to hire and fire principals and teachers. In particular, research has underscored the importance of the principal's leadership. However, rather than leading in the sense of giving directions, many authorities say, the effective principal is one who distributes authority and then serves as a facilitator to others, creating opportunities and removing barriers so that others can exercise leadership.[73] The principal also concentrates on keeping the school focused on its goals, encourages all teachers to participate in school improvement efforts, collects information, distributes rewards, and finds ways to fulfill standards for student performance.

In addition to recruiting the right principal, it is also necessary to find qualified teachers committed to the reform.[74] That will be difficult in cases where SBM has been suddenly mandated, although over time faculty can be strategically replaced as teachers leave. Not only should staff subscribe to the ideals the school stands for, but they also should be ready to work on the implementation. Willingness to meet the challenge of the unknown is what differentiates teachers in a successful reform program from those accustomed to the routines of ongoing regular school programs. Clearly, they should demonstrate knowledge of their subject matter. For years, studies have shown that student achievement is tied to teachers' knowledge of their subject field, but many regular school teachers are deficient in this regard, as we will document in Chapter 5. For example, more than a third of eighth-grade math teachers in California did not major in either math or math education in college. Autonomy and flexibility mean nothing without competent teachers.

Lesson 4: Autonomy Must Be Shared with Parents and Used to Improve Classrooms. Successful SBM schools have the freedom to create diverse educational programs, just as many charters do. They also have authority to allocate funds, especially funds needed to support the school's initiatives. However, as with charter schools, districts often attempt to reduce the percentage of the budget under the school's discretion, or they restrict how money can be spent, which can undermine the SBM effort.[75] Of course, autonomy alone does not guarantee a successful implementation, particularly if student learning is not the focus, and if empowerment does not extend to parents.

Lesson 5: There Must Be Consensus on the Mission and Standards. None of this makes any difference if the people involved don't understand or agree upon what they are trying to accomplish. Newmann and Wehlage conclude that a "clearly articulated vision" depends on high standards.[76] Briggs and Wohlstetter believe that state curriculum standards, subject matter standards endorsed by national professional associations, and state assessments all provide clear-cut guides for what students ought to learn, and therefore schools should use one or more of these mechanisms to organize the instructional program.[77] While their recommendation seems sensible, too often it has come down to teaching to a test. Schools should be required to use a variety of assessment techniques, including those being used by the Coalition of Successful Schools to be described below.

Standards imply that expectations will be uniformly applied to all students. However, many regular high schools violate that principle by placing students into invidious tracks that limit the range and difficulty of courses they take. Many high schools formally or subtly require only select students to take the courses that qualify them for college. It is critically important for all students to have access to the tougher curriculum. Our suggestion is to make the tough courses the default and then (a) require all students to enroll in at least one upper-tier course, or (b) require them to demonstrate that they cannot do the most challenging work. Under this plan a student would be allowed to enroll in an easier course only after completing option (a) or (b). In addition, schools should be required to tailor remedial courses for students who otherwise would not have a chance to obtain the background necessary to do college-level work. Decentralization is only an empty promise unless schools use their newfound flexibility to support high standards for all students.

Lesson 6: Professional Development Is Essential. Creating a consensus on the mission requires sustained professional development. Even with a dedicated leadership and staff, a school can founder unless the entire faculty and all council members have been trained for their jobs. Unfortunately, in some cases SBM has only taken power from an experienced central office staff and put it in the hands of naïve or incompetent amateurs. In particular, the staff often does not understand how to make the transition from a centralized to a decentralized operation. Once autonomy has been granted, the staff may not fully grasp either their new potentials or the limits of their autonomy.[78] Successful training requires (1) clear division of labor, that is, a guide to "who does what and when," (2) a forum to convey information and techniques related to interpersonal and management skills, especially skills related to shared decision making and implementation tasks, and (3) schedules that include blocks of time for training.

Comparisons between SBM and Charter Schools

It seems clear that charter schools would benefit from incorporating some of the principles of successful SBM schools. It should also be recognized that SBM schools could learn some things from the charter school experience. We shall now go back over each of the SBM principles and comment on how they apply to each reform.

Incentives to Overcome Resistance. Like SBM schools, charters encounter resistance within school districts. Often, boards and superintendents extend only a lukewarm welcome to charter schools, which after all, present themselves as competitors. Overworked or skeptical central office administrators are in a position to erect barriers. Sometimes district-testing requirements, grading practices, or other codes may stand in the way of a charter initiative. Therefore, charter schools also need incentives, support, and resources to help overcome obstacles erected by districts. We shall mention two types of support.

1. *State Legislation.* State legislation can help or hinder charter schools. The amount of deregulation differs greatly from state to state. Pilot Schools and some other SBM schools already have as much flexibility within districts as some charter schools that operate independently, while others could use more help in combating district resistance. Rather than wasting time and energy promoting one form of autonomy, charter school activists should be lobbying for legislation to give all decentralized schools more flexibility within districts, and beyond that they should spearhead a drive to decentralize all schools. The goal should not be to grant autonomous schools independence from public school districts, but to make public school districts more flexible so that all autonomous

schools can function more effectively. This means lobbying simultaneously for revisions in district rules as well as state codes.

2. *Special Resources.* Starting a new school requires a great deal of funding, for things such as training and staff recruitment. Charter and SBM schools each have separate funding sources that should be mutually available. Charters can call on several financial sources, including the money allotted to each child in attendance, federal seed grants during the start-up years, and outside donations. A few states, such as Maine and California, make restructuring grants available to SBM schools, but for reasons only politicians can explain, charter schools are not eligible for these grants, just as SBM schools are ineligible for charter seed grants. They cannot double dip. In most cases, charter schools do not get the overhead associated with the child, which leaves them with little money to pay for facilities, for example. Even though part of the district's budget, SBM schools are also sometimes shortchanged on the percentage of the school-level budget over which they have decision-making authority. In an extreme case, Oakland SBM schools control only 20 percent of the school-level budget.[79] Moreover, the percentage of the total district budget actually allocated for the school level varies widely among SBM schools, and in many cases barely exceeds 50 percent of the amount districts have budgeted to operate them. Reforms require funding, and both SBM and charter schools are being shortchanged. One remedy is for states to provide grants to all autonomous schools, which would give both models a better chance to succeed. Another is legislation mandating that full funding, including the overhead, must be given to all decentralized schools, while preventing districts from placing undue restrictions on legal expenditures.

Whole School Restructuring. The charter school movement has shown no interest in participating in district-restructuring initiatives, or in any way reforming relationships with districts. Indeed, their aggressively competitive stance makes relationship building unlikely. However, it is time to change that. They are not competitive in any meaningful sense of that term. Instead, they should be working with school districts on the big challenges. No one can do it alone, but charters, vouchers, and SBM schools can mutually provide coordinated support for public education's biggest challenges connected with at risk and low-income children, English learners, special education students, college preparation, and vocational education. Coordination requires periods of dedicated planning and training to ease the difficult role transitions that will be required of school staff.

Control over Staffing. Much has been said about the importance of giving parents choices. It is less frequently acknowledged that schools also need choices, especially the authority and resources to recruit hardworking, committed, qualified teachers. Two factors are important. First, the teacher must agree with the school's mission and be ready to work on the implementation details. Second, the teacher must possess the necessary knowledge and skills. Many charter schools hire uncertified teachers. If they have a better grasp of the subject matter than can be obtained from a certified teacher, fine. For example, a drama program might hire an experienced actor without the usual teaching credentials. However, when the primary goal is to obtain run-of-the-mill teachers willing to work for lower salaries, there is something badly awry. As we shall document in Chapter 5, there are simply too many unqualified teachers in many poor minority schools to look the other way when this topic arises. New schools are in the enviable position of being able to selectively recruit faculty suitable to the needs of the reform. They have extensive control over recruiting and training staff fit for the mission. Recruiting options are more problematic for converted schools. When existing schools are in the process of becoming decentralized, professional development becomes the critical strategy that can make or break the reform.

Autonomy and Consensus on Mission. The purpose of decentralization is to give schools enough flexibility to create programs that fit local circumstances. But does this mean that schools need to have total flexibility over not only how instruction is delivered but also over what will be taught? How much control should they have over setting the mission? Analysis of SBM schools shows that the successful ones are focused around concrete goals associated with student learning. Some charter schools seem to be abusing their freedom by pursuing unreliable approaches of dubious merit. An example is the Waldorf charter school mentioned in Chapter 2.[80] The teaching techniques we observed seemed more fitting for producing compliant cult members than students capable of independent thought. Our observations and interviews of this Waldorf School showed that students were being taught by reciting, in unison, fairy tales and fables. The teachers we interviewed expressed the belief that student learning is enhanced when the teaching of facts is associated with musical and body rhythms and other physical activities. Characteristically, teachers would lead students in movements, songs, and choral chants as they counted numbers and recited selections from poetry and other literature. Students participated in drills involving marching and clapping to rhythms. A teacher required children to recite multiplication tables in unison to a musical beat as they stepped forward and backward in time to the music.

The school employed a full-time teacher with over twenty years experience in private Waldorf schools. Her job? To teach knitting and other crafts. In one classroom, for example, during a free-play session, children were hand sewing pieces of felt together into gnome dolls and making finger loom weavings from yarn. In another class, children play-acted a story about twelve dancing princesses, while moving around the room and reciting lines after the teacher. Although Bible stories were used as subject matter in some classes, we did not see direct evidence that the school was teaching religion. But several parents charged the school with teaching a version of religion. While teachers seemed to have a coherent philosophy to justify their approaches, they also acknowledged that they were finding it necessary to adapt the traditional Waldorf approach to circumstances in the district.

In the final analysis, some charter schools are not, on the whole, dedicated to giving students access to intellectually stimulating courses. The quest for total freedom in this regard should not override the principle that a school's mission should be focused around one or more concrete set of standards that clearly identify the knowledge and skills students are expected to acquire.

Professional Development. Most teachers and principals are amateurs concerning decentralization reforms such as charter schools and SBM. Both types of schools have foundered because untrained and inexperienced teachers and administrators have jumped into complex situations without adequate preparation. In this case, successful SBM schools set the standard. Charter schools, it seems, have not pioneered the kind of professional development activities that would be beneficial. Most of them probably would benefit from the experience of successful SBM schools that are providing effective professional development.

THE COALITION OF ESSENTIAL SCHOOLS

In 1984, a leading educational reformer, Theodore R. Sizer, located twelve schools that agreed to redesign themselves on the basis of a dozen simple but penetrating ideas and to form a coalition.[81] Today the coalition has grown to over 1,000 public and private schools and nineteen regional service and support centers. The organization is known as the Coalition of Essential Schools (CES). Each of these schools, most of which are in public school districts, provides a distinct option for parents. The options include private and charter CES schools, but the important point is that parents are not required to leave the public schools to take advantage of CES. Just what are these options? While each school is supposed to be unique, they all share a philosophy guided primarily by the not so astonishing idea that the purpose of school is to help young people learn to use their minds well. The mission of CES represents a stark contrast with many of the reforms being tried and proposed today. Rather than relying exclusively on making structural changes with no particular goal in mind, this approach focuses on teaching practice itself and offers a healthy reminder that ultimately all reforms must somehow transform teaching practice.

But how? One of the main premises is that a student should be expected to master a few important skills and areas of knowledge. The learning strategy aims for depth, not comprehensiveness. The student must direct much of the learning and then be able to demonstrate or "exhibit" the results by showing what he or she can do by performing real tasks, such as exhibiting a project on local history before teachers, other students, and the community. Students are assessed in a variety of ways. They progress individually, at their own rates and independently of their ages. Graduation does not depend upon an accumulation of credits or time spent in class. Instead, the student must be able to demonstrate ability to do important things ("authentic tasks"). Students who have not achieved the appropriate levels of competence are provided with intensive support and resources.

Teachers are the key actors. In principle, they set the tone of the school. Rather than lecturing and doling out scheduled assignments to classes of passive students, they act as coaches and facilitators, guiding the learning process. Instruction is personalized. Ideally, no teacher should have direct responsibility for more than eighty students in high school and middle school, and no more than twenty in elementary school. To capitalize on this personalization, the philosophy directs that decisions about the details of the course of study, the use of students' and teachers' time and the choice of teaching materials and specific pedagogies must be unreservedly placed in the hands of the principal and staff, who in turn are given time to plan. The principal and teachers are expected to perceive themselves as generalists first (teachers and scholars in general education) and specialists second (experts in but one particular discipline). However, be careful about this last one, because encouraging teachers to be generalists only justifies even more unqualified teachers unprepared for the subjects they are teaching.

Structurally, the schools and the classrooms are small. The schools typically serve only half the number of students as the average high school (338 vs. 786), according to a CES survey. Also, they maintain close partnerships with the school's community. The schedule allows ample time for collective planning. The policies and practices strive to be equitable and democratic. Staff are required to assume multiple obligations (teacher-counselor-manager) and to display a sense of commitment to the entire school. Parents are key collaborators and vital members of the school community.

Origins of CES

Sizer says that this vision came to him after participating with colleagues in a five-year study of high schools.[82] The study revealed that American high schools offer an incredible array of courses, ranging from "consumer math" to calculus and from drivers' education to volleyball. Their drive to be comprehensive, he observed, deflects schools from their primary responsibility of helping students learn to use their minds well.

Sizer doesn't like it that high schools are organized around subjects identified by a committee of professors in 1893—subjects such as English, math, and science, with art, theater, and music off to the side. These disciplines, says Sizer, have little relationship to the way the world actually operates today. He saw teachers facing 150 or more students a day and regularly assigning work on the basis of what could be graded quickly rather than on the basis of what would push students to think deeply. Students, traveling from room to room and from teacher to teacher for unrelated fifty-minute classes, rarely had time to delve into any topic and passed their days with little sense of the connections between the various subjects they studied. Consequently, the typical American high school, he concluded, promoted apathy and intellectual lethargy.

Student Achievement

Does the approach work? In 2001, CES conducted a survey of forty-one schools in the national network.[83] The results were entirely positive. For example, by a 21 percent margin CES students entered college more often than the national average. The results were even better for African-American and Latino graduates; the latter entered college at double the national average. CES students were more likely to be enrolled in eighth grade math (a tougher course than most) than most other students (39 percent vs. 25 percent). And, CES students often did well on standardized tests. A study of twenty-two CES schools serving students from diverse backgrounds and with low standardized tests scores, found that the percentage of CES students who passed state achievement tests increased substantially from the initial year of testing. More of them are passing the test than before.

However, we have some concerns about these studies. First, notice that very few of the 1,000 network school have been involved. Second, some of the complaints we have about the selectivity of charter schools apply to CES schools as well. Not only are students and families self-selected, but presumably, so are the teachers. Third, CES schools are small. So, we have to ask the same question that we raised about charters: how much credit should we give to CES, as opposed to smallness? It could turn out that CES is just another opportunity for good teachers to do what they were already doing. We have chosen to spotlight this program because it concerns pedagogy. Definitive proof that it is improving test scores will have to wait.

Comparisons between CES and Charter Schools

What can charter schools learn from CES and what can CES learn from them? The principles operating in successful SBM schools will be used as guides to answering the question.

Incentives to Overcome Resistance. To the envy of both charter schools and SBM schools, CES regional offices make grants available to CES schools. Any choice school should be given the kind of support that CES has been able to give its schools, especially since so many fledgling charter schools have to struggle against high odds with few of the resources they need.

Whole School Restructuring. CES is not a restructuring project in the broadest sense of that term. It does not establish and promote a reform model, and it does not address the distribution of power in schools. In fact, it does not focus on changing much of anything outside the classroom. The focus of CES is on pedagogy, pure and simple, not on school structures. We have to say that it is probably a mistake to ignore the power structure. Even so, we will be the first to recommend that Sizer's focus on pedagogy should be made an essential feature of the charter-school model, if only as an antidote to the preoccupation of charter supporters with structural change.

The premise underlying the charter school model is that autonomy and teacher empowerment will somehow lead to positive (but entirely unpredictable) changes in the classroom. The CES approach, by comparison, focuses on what the classroom should be like, and then assumes that any necessary changes in the structure will follow. It seems to us, though, that either premise by itself is myopic. The CES model would be better if it placed higher priority on redistributing power, just as charters would be more effective if the model addressed intellectual standards that schools are expected to achieve—standards not limited to passing standardized tests. So, combining the two approaches could enhance both models immensely. We don't mean that all charter schools should adopt CES. But is it too much to ask that each school commit to a teaching philosophy and identify the learning outcomes it is trying to achieve?

If CES is not focused on restructuring schools in the usual sense, it is nonetheless a restructuring approach in the more limited sense of curriculum reform. While we applaud many aspects of the CES philosophy, we have some reservations about limiting schooling to a few areas. Depth is important, but many of the aspects of comprehensive academic programs are also important, including art, music, drama, and extracurricular activities. Many charter schools have cut back on these dimensions of the curriculum—to the detriment of students, we think. Although we grant that the CES approach provides a sobering corrective to the "schools can do it all" philosophy that dominates public education, we do not endorse rash attempts to toss out many of the useful programs that schools have developed. If schools have trouble handling the range of responsibilities they have undertaken, it is because of their primitive level of specialization, which forces any given teacher to undertake too much. There is a vast difference between taking on responsibilities and assigning them all to the same people. The solution is restructuring, CES doctrine notwithstanding. This thought will be developed in the following chapters.

One aspect of CES that deserves high praise is the approach to student evaluation. Achievement in CES schools is not supposed to be tied to standardized tests, although students in the limited samples examined seem to measure up well on them. CES students are held accountable for their ability to demonstrate knowledge through "exhibitions" such as projects, speeches, and papers. Some charter schools include aspects of this approach, but because of the buoyant rhetoric promising high levels of achievement, they get little encouragement for using forms of evaluation other than tests. We recommend that they take a careful look at Sizer's approach.

Control over Staffing. In an interview, Sizer identified lack of stable and sustained leadership as a critical issue.[84] This observation supports SBM research, affirming the importance of the principal. The literature on charter schools has not said much about how to select principals to run them, nor the incentives needed to retain good leaders. Yet, the leadership vacuum in many charters has sometimes proven fatal. Also consistent with the SBM literature, Sizer believes that schools falter without a critical mass of teachers committed both to the reform's underlying philosophy, and doing what it takes to implement it. It is they who make the real difference. Again, this is consistent with the SBM research and affirms the importance of recruiting the right faculty (even though we are never told whether or not CES schools are typically in a position to hire new faculty).

However, we think it odd that the CES model does not give the high priority to teacher empowerment that is featured in SBM and charter schools. Indeed, while acknowledging that teachers need a sense of authority, Sizer questions the need for full teacher empowerment, and challenges those teachers looking for more control to justify why they need and deserve it. While we think we know the answer, we also can appreciate Sizer's healthy skepticism. It would behoove all charter schools to justify why teachers deserve more empowerment. The CES experience tells us that charter-school sponsors should require every prospective charter school to guarantee that the principal has made a serious, long-term commitment to the reform; that the school faculty agrees to what they intend to do; and to justify why students will be better off with them in control.

Autonomy and Consensus on Mission. CES schools are far ahead of charter schools, and even successful SBM schools, both in their commitment to establish realistic and practical standards that students are expected to meet, and in establishing reasonable ways to assess whether the goals have been met. The need for higher standards is highlighted by the high percentages of high school graduates who require remedial classes in college. For example, over a third of freshmen admitted to the University of California in 2003 were not proficient in math, and nearly half were not proficient in English.[85] Standards can be based on a number of alternative sources, such as state curriculum standards, and national professional standards (such as math standards endorsed by some national association). Sizer says, "We have to be much clearer as a group of schools about what it is that kids should be able to do to qualify for a diploma."[86] Requiring the faculty to reach consensus on that is a far-reaching stipulation that we think should be part of every reform model, including the charter-school model. As the current front-runner of school reform, charter schools should engage in this dialogue and become backers of alternative standards and other assessment approaches focused on the objective of helping students use their minds more effectively. Instead, state and federal agencies are forcing them to become enslaved by standardized tests that may or may not tap what these schools are trying to accomplish.

Charter schools have gone to one extreme on the amount of autonomy they deem necessary, trying to justify their right to do almost anything, erratically and without accounting to anyone for some strange things that some schools have set out to do. But the CES reform has taken the other, and we think, senseless apathetic extreme by not lobbying for the suspension of selected, obstructing district rules as a condition for joining the coalition. At least, that is the way it looks from the outside. We are not privy to the school-by-school negotiations that determine whether or not a school will be accepted into the program. But in one interview, Sizer admitted that the relentless pressures on schools to perform well on standardized tests are not always compatible with the CES philosophy. At the least, CES schools might want to request being excused from some district and state standardized tests in exchange for demonstrating the desired knowledge and skills in other ways. They could lead the fight for needed correctives to the current preoccupation with the defective standardized testing approach that is forcing many teachers to focus on teaching the answers to test questions.

Professional Development. A remarkable aspect of CES is the unprecedented levels of support being given to the participating schools. The approach being taken to professional development should serve as a standard for both charter schools and SBM schools. There are two important dimensions of CES professional development. First, support is delivered through networks, and in particular collaboration between schools and regional centers. The fundamental importance of networks will be discussed at length in the next chapter. Second, the centers provide substantial and sustained support in the degree that has never been given to charter schools or to SBM schools.

For example, schools that seek to transform their work according to CES philosophy receive support from a regional center in four focus areas: school design, classroom practice, leadership, and community connections.

School design services include a weeklong summer institute on school design; year-round school coaching, consultation, and facilitation of the change process; workshops to help a school measure progress; and courses such as one on how to divide large, comprehensive high schools into small learning communities. Teachers can obtain help on how to undertake teacher collaboration, how to conduct inquiry groups, and how to do peer coaching. They also are given opportunities to visit other CES schools. In addition, regional centers offer institutes for principals and other leaders, and instruction on how to facilitate school-community partnerships. While Sizer may deny CES is a structural reform, the thrust of these workshops and consultations in the areas of school design suggests otherwise. It would be unrealistic to undertake a reform focused solely on classrooms without considering how the organizational context must be altered.

If there is any one area that CES is superior to most, if not all, other reforms, it is in the area of collaboration to deliver professional development. As members of networks, and in conjunction with regional service centers, CES schools benefit as they could in no other way. Networks are at the very foundation not only of this program, but of any good education reform. If charter schools and SBM schools could do no more than adopt this networking, collaborative support dimension of the CES approach, it would be enough to revolutionize both models and put them on the cutting edge of school reform.

CONCLUSIONS

The focus of Chapter 2 was the choice movement, and in particular two major shortcomings with the movement. First, we said that spokespersons for choice have exaggerated the benefits to the point that parents who believe the claims will necessarily be disappointed, if not defrauded. Second, we argued that the idea that it is impossible to create effective choice programs within the public school system is absurd and also misleading. That advocates want schools to be free of restrictions and oversight has more to do with their free-market ideology than with creating viable choices available to most parents. Both criticisms are directed at the movement, not at charter schools themselves, nor even at the idea of sending children to private schools. And they certainly are not intended to cast doubt on the proposition that parents need more choices. We have not said that either form of choice is worthless—only that both have correctable faults.

This chapter has shown that it is possible to create viable reforms within school districts, and that going outside is not necessary—notwithstanding what choice fans want everyone to believe. Apart from free-market ideologies, there is no sound reason that charter schools cannot be part of public school districts. Going well beyond that proposition, we have endeavored to find clues offering ways to improve charter schools, because we believe the reforms we have discussed contain elements that are fundamental to any viable approach to school choice. Some of the most promising ideas embedded in the approaches reviewed here can be summarized as follows:

- At present, open enrollment provides only limited choices for parents, not only because it is a political compromise dominated by school districts, especially suburban districts, but also because it merely shuttles students around without expanding the range of options; however, we are reluctant to give up on the idea entirely because interdistrict programs are operating across district lines in some places, and because intradistrict programs hold out hope for expanding choices within districts.

- Research has consistently confirmed that very large schools produce worse outcomes than smaller ones; however, remember that extremely small schools also produce lower quality education because they do not have the benefits of an effective division of labor; we concluded that middle-size high schools (400–900 students) provide the best outcomes.

- The fact that most charter schools, and many private schools are small, makes it nearly impossible to disentangle the effects of their favorable size from their other features; we raised the possibility that charter schools could be getting credit for outcomes that probably could be obtained by only establishing more small schools within districts; this possibly also applies to CES schools.

- There are two concerns about smaller schools that need to be dealt with. First, their size may limit the scope of programs they can provide students, compared to options usually available in larger schools, such as art, music, school-to-work programs, athletic activities, clubs, driver education, and the like; second, when several schools share the same setting, stratification often develops among the schools, and the students and teachers in them; distinctions among schools can lead to informal tracking and differential access to resources.

- There is emerging evidence which supports the proposition that teacher participation in decision making in SBM schools is positively related to improved instructional programs and to increased student learning.

- Some public school districts have given school-based management schools flexibility in exchange for accountability; Boston's small Pilot Schools rank high in the district on student achievement (although we are skeptical because high schools screen out some high school students on nonacademic criteria).

- Membership in the Boston school district has helped Pilot Schools to impact other district schools, has caused them to remain focused on improving learning outcomes in designated subject areas, subjected them to oversight from the district, and has given them ready access to expertise, services, and additional resources usually provided by a district.

- Due to inconsistencies in state legislation and the way charters do and do not use their autonomy, some SBM schools already have as much flexibility within districts as do some charter schools that operate independently.

- The goal should not be to grant autonomous schools independence from public school districts, but to help all public school districts become more flexible;

choice activists should lobby for legislation promoting more decentralized schools within districts, rather than focusing exclusively on independence applicable only to charter schools.

- While CES schools receive financial support, both SBM and charter schools are being underfunded; charter schools usually do not get much of the overhead associated with the child, while SBM schools are sometimes shortchanged on the percentage of the school-level budget allocated to them.

- There are many directionless charter schools that could take a lesson from CES and successful SBM schools, which have concrete standards that clearly identify the knowledge and skills students are expected to acquire.

- The focus on pedagogy promoted by CES should be a part of every SBM and charter school program; charter schools are especially vulnerable to the criticism that structural reforms typically do not specify how teaching will be changed.

- CES philosophy challenges all SBM and charter schools to justify why teachers deserve more power.

- The CES approach to evaluation, which relies heavily on student demonstrations rather than on standardized tests, should be integrated into the charter-school model along with consensus on the academic standards that will be used to judge student progress.

- Most charter schools would benefit from effective professional development similar to the training experience that CES schools and many successful SBM schools are providing; the CES training model, which relies on forming networks among schools that are then serviced by regional centers, should be adopted by charter schools and SBM schools.

- The extant diverse approaches to school choice should be integrated into a coherent model combining the best of SBM and CES with charter schools.

While each of the approaches discussed in this chapter was treated separately, a truly robust model of choice could be created from combinations of the most promising aspects of each into a cohesive and unified approach. Notice that Small Schools, SBM and CES represent unique dimensions that need to be included in a comprehensive reform model:

- The Small Schools approach tackles the formidable task of creating compatible schooling settings.

- School-Based Management focuses on changing the distribution of power.

- The Coalition of Essential Schools focuses on classroom pedagogy, and in particular goal-oriented teaching and learning strategies.

The introduction of one dimension apart from the others would be unproductive. For example, changing the setting and power structure is meaningless unless it leads to more effective teaching strategies. Conversely, changes in the setting and structure are required to facilitate the implementation of better teaching strategies.

Much of the chapter has been devoted to identifying the strengths and weaknesses of each approach as it bears upon charter schools. Our hope is that proponents and critics alike will unite to improve the already viable charter-school model to make it a more effective option for the parents who want better school choices.

NOTES

1. National Center for Education Statistics, *Trends in the Use of School Choice: 1993 to 1999* (Washington, DC: U.S. Department of Education, 2000).

2. NCES, *Trends in the Use of School Choice.*

3. Michael Heise and James E. Ryan, "The Political Economy of School Choice," *Yale Law Journal* 111, 8 (2002). Available at www.questia.com/PM.qst?a=o&d=5000773591.

4. From the Schoolwise Press website, available at www.schoolwisepress.com.

5. Judith Pearson, *Myths of Educational Choice* (Westport, CT: Praeger Publishers, 1993), 34; see also, Jennifer C. Patterson, "The Truth about School Choice," *Curriculum Administrator* 37 (January 2001). Available at www.questia.com/PM.qst?.

6. Patterson, "The Truth about School Choice," 2001.

7. D. W. Meier, "The Big Benefits of Smallness," *Educational Leadership* 54 (1), 1996, 12–15; see also Michael Winerip, "Going for Depth Instead of Prep," *New York Times*, 11 June 2003.

8. G. Alfred Hess, Jr., *Chicago School Reform: What It Is and How It Came to Be* (Chicago: Panel on Public School Policy and Finance, November 1990).

9. P. A. Wasley, M. Fine, R. M. Gladden, and others, *Small Schools, Great Strides: A Study of New Small Schools in Chicago* (New York: Bank Street College Education, 2000).

10. Melinda French Gates, Remarks before the National School Boards Association, Orlando, FL, 3 March 2004. Available at www.gatesfoundation.org/Education/TransformingHighSchools/ (accessed April 2004).

11. Heather Knight, "The Big Move to Small Schools: S. F. Programs Show New Face of Public Teaching," *San Francisco Chronicle*, 25 August 2003.

12. Joetta Sack, "Riley Says It's Time to Rethink High Schools," *Education Week* (22 September 1999) [electronic journal]. Available at www.edweek.org.

13. Office of Elementary and Secondary Education and Office of Vocational and Adult Education, *An Overview of Smaller Learning Communities in High Schools* (Washington, DC: U.S. Department of Education, November 2001); Joetta Sack, "Riley Says It's Time to Rethink High Schools," *Education Week* (22 September 1999) [electronic journal]. Available at www.edweek.org.

14. Gates, Remarks before the National School Boards Association, 2004.

15. S. Mitchell, "Jack and the Giant School," *The New Rules* 2, 1 (Summer 2000). [Electronic Journal]. Available at www.newrules.org/journal/nrsum00schools.htm (accessed April 2004).

16. Knight, "The Big Move to Small Schools," 2003.

17. J. P. Greene with M. A. Winters, *Public School Graduation Rates in the United*

States, Civic Report No. 31 (New York: The Manhattan Institute for Policy Research, 2002).

18. Gates, "Remarks before the National School Boards Association," 2004.

19. Karen Irmsher, *School Size,* ERIC Digest No. 113 (Eugene, OR: ERIC Clearinghouse on Educational Management, 1997).

20. Ambrose Leung and Stephen J. Farris, "School Size and Youth Violence," paper presented at the Canadian Economic Association Meetings, 15 July 2002.

21. Valerie E. Lee and Julie B. Smith, "High School Size: Which Works Best and for Whom?" *Educational Evaluation and Policy Analysis* 19 (1997), 205–227.

22. K. Cotton, *School Size, School Climate, and Student Performance,* School Improvement Research Series No. 20 (Portland, OR: Northwestern Regional Educational Laboratory, 1996); K. Cotton, *New Small Learning Communities: Findings from Recent Literature* (Portland, OR: Northwest Regional Educational Laboratory, December 2001).

23. M. A. Raywid, *Current Literature on Small Schools* (Charleston, WV: ERIC Clearinghouse on Rural Education and Small Schools, 1999).

24. Lee and Smith, "High School Size: Which Works Best and for Whom?" 1997.

25. Peter M. Blau, "Decentralization in Bureaucracies," in M. N. Zald, ed., *Power in Organizations* (Nashville, TN: Vanderbilt University Press, 1970); Peter M. Blau and Richard Schoenherr, *The Structure of Organizations* (New York: Basic Books, 1971).

26. Mary Anne Raywid, *Taking Stock: The Movement to Create Mini-Schools, Schools-Within-Schools, and Separate Small Schools* (New York: ERIC Clearinghouse on Urban Education, April 1996).

27. James McPartland et al., "Improving Climate and Achievement in a Troubled Urban High School Through the Talent Development Model," *Journal of Education for Students Placed at Risk* 3, 4 (1998), 341.

28. McPartland, "Improving Climate and Achievement in a Troubled Urban High School," 1998, 341.

29. M. A. Raywid, *Current Literature on Small Schools,* 1999; K. Cotton, *New Small Learning Communities: Findings from Recent Literature* (Portland, OR: Northwest Regional Educational Laboratory, 2001); Anthony S. Bryk, *Issues in Restructuring Schools. Commentaries—Different Perspectives on the Lee and Smith Study* (Madison, WI: Center on Organization and Restructuring of Schools, University of Wisconsin-Madison, Fall 1994), 6–7.

30. V. E. Lee and J. B. Smith, "Effects of High School Restructuring and Size on Early Gains in Achievement and Engagement," *Sociology of Education* 68 (1995), 241–270.

31. B. J. McMullan, C. L. Sipe, and W. C. Wolf, *Charters and Student Achievement: Early Evidence from School Restructuring in Philadelphia* (Philadelphia: Center for Assessment and Policy Development, 1994).

32. C. B. Howley and G. Huang, *Extracurricular Participation and Achievement: School Size as Possible Mediator of SES Influence Among Individual Students,* ERIC Document No. ED 336247 (Charleston, WV: Appalachia Educational Laboratory, January 1992).

33. W. J. Fowler, "What Do We Know about School Size? What Should We

Know?" Paper presented at the annual meeting of the American Educational Research Association, San Francisco, April 1992.

34. C. Howley, M. Strange, and R. Bickel, *Research about School Size and School Performance in Impoverished Communities*, ERIC Digest (Charleston, WV: ERIC Clearinghouse on Rural Education and Small Schools, December 2000); Lee and Smith, "Effects of High School Restructuring," 1995.

35. C. Howley and R. Bickel, *School Size, Poverty, and Student Achievement* (Washington, DC: The Rural School and Community Trust, 2002).

36. Linda Darling-Hammond, J. Ancess, and Ort S. Wichterle, "Reinventing High School: Outcomes of the Coalition Campus Schools Project," *American Educational Research Journal* 39, 3 (Fall 2002), 639–673.

37. Bryk, *Issues in Restructuring Schools*, 1994; Valerie E. Lee, ed., *Reforming Chicago's High Schools: Research Perspectives on School and System Level Change* (Chicago: Consortium on Chicago School Research at the University of Chicago, November 2002).

38. L. Stiefel, P. Iatarola, N. Fruchter, and R. Berne, *The Effects of Size of Student Body on School Costs and Performance in New York City High Schools* (New York: Institute for Education and Social Policy, New York University, 1998).

39. L. Stiefel, P. Iatarola, N. Fruchter, and R. Berne, "High School Size: Effects on Budgets and Performance in New York City," *Educational Evaluation and Policy Analysis* 22, 1 (Spring 2000).

40. Bryk, *Issues in Restructuring Schools*, 1994.

41. George C. Homans, *The Human Group* (New York: Harcourt, Brace, 1950).

42. Peter W. Cookson and Kristina Berger, *Expect Miracles: Charter Schools and the Politics of Hope and Despair* (Boulder, CO: Westview Press, 2002), note 74.

43. For further discussion and illustration, see Ronald G. Corwin, "Implementation Problems: The Social Costs of Change," in *Flexible Education for the Health Professions*, R. M. Jacobs, ed. (New York: John Wiley and Sons, 1976), 217–230.

44. Susan Klonsky and Michael Klonsky, "Countering Anonymity through Small Schools," *Educational Leadership* 57, 1 (September 1999), 38–41; K. S. Whitaker, "Implementation Processes, Structures, and Barriers to High School Restructuring: A Case Study," *Journal of School Leadership* 8 (1998), 504–532.

45. W. Ayers, G. Bracey, and G. Smith, *The Ultimate Education Reform? Make Schools Smaller* (Milwaukee, WI: Center for Education Research, Analysis, and Innovation, University of Wisconsin-Milwaukee, 2000); J. T. Fouts, *A School within a School: Evaluation Results of the First Year of a Restructuring Effort* (Seattle, WA: School of Education, Seattle Pacific University, 1994); Raywid, *Taking Stock*, 1996; A. Shorr and J. E. Hon, "They Said It Couldn't Be Done: Implementing a Career Academy Program for a Diverse High School Population," *Journal of Education for Students Placed at Risk* 4 (1999), 379–391; Ronald G. Corwin and Robert E. Herriott, "Occupational Disputes in Mechanical and Organic Systems: An Empirical Study of Elementary and Secondary Schools," *American Sociological Review* 53 (August 1988), 528–543.

46. Caroline Hendrie, "In N.Y.C., Fast-Paced Drive for Small Schools," *Education Week* 23, 41 (23 June 2004), 1, 22–23.

47. McPartland and Raywid, both cited above, have both written about these topics.

48. Knight, "The Big Move to Small Schools," 2003.

49. Michael Katz, "From Voluntarism to Bureaucracy in American Education," *Sociology of Education* 44 (Summer 1971), 297–332.

50. National Center for Education Statistics, *How Widespread Is Site-Based Decision-Making in the Public Schools?* (Washington, DC: U.S. Department of Education, December 1996). Available at http://nces.ed.gov/pubsearch/majorpub.

51. D. W. Drury, *Reinventing School-Based Management: A School Board Guide to School-Based Improvement* (Alexandria, VA: National School Boards Association, 1999).

52. Hess, *Chicago School Reform,* 1990; Wasley, *Small Schools,* 2000; Ronald R. Edmonds, "Some Schools Work and More Can," *Social Policy* (March/April 1979), 28–32; Ronald R. Edmonds, "Making Public Schools Effective," *Social Policy* (September/October 1981), 56–60.

53. Kerri L. Briggs and Priscilla Wohlstetter, *Key Elements of a Successful School-Based Management Strategy* (Austin: University of Texas at Austin and University of Southern California, 21 October 1999).

54. J. L. David, "The Who, What, and Why of Site-Based Management," *Educational Leadership* 53, 4 (1996).

55. K. Leithwood and T. Menzies, "Forms and Effects of School-Based Management: A Review," *Educational Policy* 12, 3 (1998), 325–346.

56. Leithwood and Menzies, "Forms and Effects of School-Based Management," 1998, 341.

57. Education Commission of the States, "School-Based Management," *The Progress of Education Reform 1999–2001* 2, 5 (April/May 2001).

58. Leithwood and Menzies, "Forms and Effects of School-Based Management," 1998.

59. P. J. Robertson, P. Wohlstetter, and S. A. Mohrman, "Generating Curriculum and Instructional Reforms Through School-Based Management," *Educational Administration Quarterly* 31 (1995), 375–404.

60. Hess, *Chicago School Reform,* 1990; Wasley, *Small Schools,* 2000.

61. E. Odden and P. Wohlstetter, "Making School-Based Management Work," *Educational Leadership* 52, 5 (1995), 32–36.

62. Center for Collaborative Education, "How Are the Boston Pilot Schools Faring? An Analysis of Students, Demographics, Engagement, and Performance," Boston Pilot Schools network website, 2002. Available at www.ccebos.org/pilotschools/schools.html.

63. Center for Collaborative Education.

64. Center for Collaborative Education.

65. Briggs and Wohlstetter, "Key Elements of a Successful School-Based Management Strategy," 1999.

66. D. J. Brown, *Decentralization and School-Based Management* (London: Falmer Press, 1990).

67. Drury, *Reinventing School-Based Management,* 1999.

68. NCREL, *Why, How, and toward What Ends?* Decentralization Report 1 (Portland, OR: NCREL, 1993).

69. W. P. Dolan, *Restructuring Our Schools: A Primer on Systemic Change* (Kansas City, MO: Systems and Organization, 1994).

70. Briggs and Wohlstetter, "Key Elements of a Successful School-Based Management Strategy," 1999.

71. Dolan, *Restructuring Our Schools*, 1994, xii.

72. Briggs and Wohlstetter, "Key Elements of a Successful School-Based Management Strategy," 1999.

73. Briggs and Wohlstetter, "Key Elements of a Successful School-Based Management Strategy," 1999.

74. Odden and Wohlstetter, "Making School-Based Management Work," 1995.

75. Odden and Wohlstetter, "Making School-Based Management Work," 1995.

76. John H. Holloway, "The Promise and Pitfalls of Site-Based Management," *Educational Leadership* 57, 7 (April 2000). Available at www.ascd.org/cms/objectlib/ascdframeset/index.cfm.

77. Briggs and Wohlstetter, "Key Elements of a Successful School-Based Management Strategy," 1999.

78. S. Bauer and I. Bogotch, "An Analysis of the Relationship between Site-Council Resources, Council Practices, and Outcomes," *Journal of School Leadership* 11 (1997), 98–119.

79. Cross City Campaign for Urban School Reform, *Annual Decentralization Comparison Across Ten Cities* (Chicago: Author, 2000).

80. Ronald G. Corwin, Lisa Carlos, Bart Lagomarsino, and Roger Scott, *From Paper to Practice: Challenges Facing a California Charter School* (San Francisco: WestEd, 1996), 33–40.

81. See the Coalition of Essential Schools website. Available at www.essentialschools.org.

82. Nexus Interview with Ted Sizer, "How Schools Fail Kids and How They Could Be Better," June 2002; Horace Interview with Ted Sizer, "At the Five Year Mark: The Challenge of Being Essential," November 1989. Both articles are on the CES website. Available at www.essentialschools.org.

83. Coalition for Essential Schools website.

84. Sizer, "How Schools Fail Kids and How They Could Be Better," June 2002, and "At the Five Year Mark," November 1989.

85. G. Hardesty, "Students on List of Shame," *Orange County Register*, 1 June 2004.

86. Nexus Interview with Ted Sizer, "How Schools Fail Kids and How They Could Be Better," June 2002.

4

Why Choice Schools
Should Be Specialized: Charter
Schools and Voucher Schools within
a Planned Division of Labor

In this chapter we propose that to qualify for public funds, a choice school must first agree to function as a specialized school within a division of labor planned and monitored by a school district. All charter and voucher schools would operate under district guidelines that would give them flexibility after they commit to performing specified functions on behalf of districts. We know that requiring charters schools and those accepting vouchers to meet the specifications of a larger plan seems like a major departure from the market-driven, freewheeling, everybody-does-their-own-thing concept of school choice. But the reality is that neither program is now market driven. Both are creatures of politics and restricted by a cacophony of conditions and rules. In particular, many states already require charters to serve specified numbers of at risk or low performing students. Since choice schools don't appear to be doing much better than traditional schools, there is no reason to stay with the fictional market analogy that has promised so much and delivered so little. Adding a requirement that every choice school must be prepared to address a particular type of student need is only an incremental step, not a drastic revision of what has been going on. And, after a qualified school accepts a mission, it would control hiring, curriculum, schedules, and budgets. On a practical level, charters would benefit from more planning, because as noted in Chapter 2, lack of students has caused many of them to fail. Every charter school would have students if it was responsible for a specific underserved group of students, rather than following the whims of its creators.

HOW IT WOULD WORK

Our reasoning on behalf of a planned division of labor is that currently charter schools and school vouchers only promote competition among schools that we believe should be cooperating. School districts need help, not unsettling competition from schools that too frequently are merely duplicating conventional school programs. In the meantime, other students are ignored. Competition is not, as choice advocates want us to believe, the fundamental property of organizations. The fundamental property is interdependency.[1] Schools could not function without the help of other organizations—colleges; neighboring schools; parent and community organizations; district, state, and regional offices; the police; food service providers; suppliers; auditors; and professional organizations. Cooperation and exchange are at the heart of these relationships. A viable model of choice, and of reform, must build on and reinforce this cooperative system.

How Choice Models Would Change

The changes required in current choice models can be summarized as follows:

- Charter schools could be started and operated in one of two ways, First, district officials could start and operate (or perhaps in some cases contract for) charter schools designed to meet specific types of identified needs within the district. Second, any professional employed by a school district (with or without outside collaborators) would be eligible to sponsor or operate a school, provided that (a) the proposal addresses an identified district need, and (b) there is a nucleus of people with the necessary skills who have committed to work on the project.

- Private schools that accept vouchers and have demonstrated expertise in a particular area also could submit applications to a district to work under a special services contract, in compliance with the district's financial and civil rights guidelines and audits; for example, the district might refer students to a voucher school operating a sound program for pregnant teens or potential dropouts.

- To qualify for a charter or a voucher, a school would (a) agree to participate in a network with other specialized and conventional schools, and (b) demonstrate to the district's satisfaction that it has the necessary capacity and competence in an area of specialization.

- All choice schools would be products of deliberate planning, not random market forces, and networks of schools would cooperate, not compete.

- Every school's mission would be tied to a demonstrated need within the district, rather than being the random product of personal predilection, and it would be dedicated to working with students who require special help.

- All choice schools would be required, as part of the mission and contract, to provide services to other choice and conventional schools.
- Parents would apply to, and/or be referred to, a particular choice school that meets their child's special circumstances; no one would be assigned without their consent.
- Students enrolled in a specialized school would also participate in programs, courses, and activities offered by other choice and conventional schools in the network.

The Student Sorting Issue

Specialized schools require separation of students into schools for individualized instruction based on their distinct interests, talents, and needs. Every school district with publicly funded choice schools would assess and group students accordingly. This strategy carries some risks that must be controlled. Sorting students into special settings for even part of the school day or year can be socially and politically hazardous without built-in correctives. There is always a danger that some students will be isolated from contact with other types of students. However, if a good education means no more than compelling everyone to take the same program, with the same teachers, then everyone stands to lose. Moreover, fully integrated heterogeneous schools are already a myth. The truth is that students are sorted into tracks and programs and designated by labels, such as "underachiever," "at risk," "gifted and talented," "slow learner," and "vocational." And, of course, impoverished minorities are firmly segregated from their middle-class peers residing in other parts of the city. When judiciously used, homogeneous grouping can benefit teaching and learning. In response to questions about reforms in their schools, about half the principals participating in a 1998 national study by the National Center for Educational Statistics reported that one of the biggest problems is teaching students who are at different levels.[2] Suppose it turns out that less-able, less-motivated students perform better in settings tailored for them than they do in comprehensive classrooms. And, why wouldn't average students benefit from being in differentiated programs adapted to their varied interests and talents? Certainly, poverty schools deserve to have teachers prepared to cope with their challenges.

While some research suggests that low-income children (and perhaps low achievers) learn more when they are included in classrooms with middle-income, high-achieving children, that information says more about the inability of unprepared teachers working in segregated poverty schools to cope with high concentrations of low-income children than about the integration strategy. Schools for poverty children do not work largely because better, and more experienced, teachers tend to gravitate to classrooms that cater to middle-income students. So, of course any student would benefit from going to these schools. In any case, as we shall document at length in the next chapter, segregated, poverty, minority schools are the reality, like it or not. But it isn't hopeless. Suppose that low-income schools had the resources to attract the best teachers equipped with special techniques designed to help low performers or potential dropouts. Why should we suppose they will not benefit? We are not discounting peer group influences; we assume that a viable strategy must deal with peer pressures. But the point is, teachers working in a school with only one type of student, no matter how challenging, will have a better chance to find and apply solutions than those faced with students who present a wide range of challenges.

RATIONALE

Discussions in this chapter apply to all charter schools and voucher schools that are operating within a school district. They could be working under a variety of different types of arrangements, but for simplicity we shall call them district-*planned* schools. District-*operated* schools are a subtype of these schools, which will be discussed in greater detail in the next chapter. Every choice school in a district would have a special mission and demonstrate the necessary competence to meet it. One school might operate a program for the disabled, another for truants and potential school dropouts, and still another might train students in the performing arts. There could be schools for high achievers, remedial students, the language challenged, and other special cases.

Yes, such schools already exist in many districts, as magnets, specialized or alternative schools, and in some cases, as charter schools. We believe that choice schools should have piggybacked on magnets and alternatives from the beginning, and probably would have if they had not become independent. However, the schools we are proposing would not select students on the basis of skin color as magnets do. Instead, students would be admitted based on the applicability of the school's mission to their needs. Each school would fit into a larger network of schools and would focus on a specific problem area. Teachers could share resources and ideas with their colleagues who may be working with similar students in other network schools. And, all choice schools would make themselves available to serve as resources for conventional schools in the network. Districts would support, not resist, such schools.

Specialization is the hallmark of medicine. For someone who needs heart surgery, a small, general hospital is no match for a major research hospital, staffed with full-time cardiac specialists, supported by trained and experienced staff, and offering facilities designed for heart surgery. But while few hospitals are staffed exclusively by general practitioners, most public schools are staffed almost entirely by teachers with identical job descriptions. In most schools, any given classroom teacher can expect to work with youngsters who may have physical, learning, and language disabilities; youngsters whose parents exhibit varying degrees of support for school policies; and youths from ethnically and socially diverse backgrounds. Moreover, as Merrifield observes, "We stifle specialization by assigning the diverse children of each attendance area to neighborhood 'public' schools. . . . One size fits all for all required classes and lots of elective courses and extracurricular programs."[3]

Although only 12 percent of the U.S. population is foreign born, nationwide, 41 percent of teachers report that they have LEP students (students with limited English proficiency), and only 13 percent of these teachers have received at least eight hours of specialized training in the last three years on how to teach such students.[4] In California, 75 percent of the teachers have LEP students in their classes, but only half of them have received recent training. English learners make up 30 percent of all students in California, and most of those students tested in 2003 did not pass the English proficiency test. We surmise that a given California teacher could be working with students from homes where parents speak only Spanish, or only Japanese, or another language, plus a few physically disabled or behaviorally-challenged students, and perhaps some slow learners and gifted students—all in the same classroom, or at least in the same school. Given the range of challenges that teachers are expected to handle, is it reasonable to suppose that most teachers have either the training or experience to handle them, alone, and within limited time constraints? This situation is not an accident of history; it is a deliberate policy. Could anyone have designed a system that is less likely to succeed?

Although schools have become encumbered by obligations that common sense suggests require special skills and resources, most districts have few specialized schools. In 2002, 98 percent of the public school students in this country attended 91,000 regular schools.[5] More than 9,000 alternative, magnet, vocational or other special schools enroll only 2 percent of them. There are only around 3,000 magnet schools which enroll a million students and around 5,000 alternative schools, which educate fewer than 1 percent of the nation's students. One thousand vocational schools enroll less than a .5 percent of all students. In the private sector, the overwhelming majority of schools emphasize academics. A negligible percentage of private schools focus on either special education or learning alternatives.[6] Nor is the pent-up need for specialized schools being met by choice programs. Most charter schools do not offer a curriculum that differs significantly from regular schools in the same district. Maybe one-in-five serves a special population, such as at risk students, special education students, or disruptive students.[7] Arguably, only one-in-three charter schools enrolls more students of color and low-income students than their parent districts. Even those figures are deceiving, because many of the schools that serve distinct populations are not specialized, as we define it.

The potential role that choice schools could play within a school district is evident in areas of special needs. First, consider some facts. Private schools are not required to provide the same level of special educational services as public schools. Only two of eighty-six voucher schools studied in Wisconsin provided bilingual education and only 38 percent provided transportation. While African-Americans make up over half the enrollment in Milwaukee Public Schools, one study found that they represent only 5 percent of enrollments in the top three academic Catholic high schools.[8]

In a study of Texas charter schools that received on-site evaluations, only one-in-nineteen had a limited English proficiency language committee, even though 40 percent of the charter students were Hispanic.[9] In one Arizona study, Hispanic students participated in charter schools at half the rate of traditional public schools.[10] A number of Texas charter schools have failed to comply with the American with Disability Act.[11] California is among the states that do not require charters to offer school lunch programs, effectively restricting the types of students who can apply. Students who fall between the cracks can be better served by schools designed to deal with their specific types of needs.

Given the seriousness of the special education shortfall in charters, why shouldn't some choice schools be created in most districts to help with that problem, just as many states have laws requiring or urging charter schools to specifically target students at risk. True, some charter schools have evolved specifically for students with disabilities. At the same time, many are finding that this task is presenting bewildering challenges. Mulholland reported that approximately 20 percent of the calls to the Arizona Center for Disability Law were from parents concerned about how charter schools were ignoring special education.[12] One study of California charters found that they enroll about the same percentage of special education students as regular schools, but another twelve-state study reported they generally enroll substantially smaller percentages of special education students than the host district.[13] Still another study says that almost half the charter schools spent no money on special education.[14] In any case, most charters simply mainstream all special education students; relatively few operate special target programs for them. One study found that some charters were counseling special education students back to the traditional public schools.[15] The authors of that study concluded that school operators are generally ill-informed about special education rules and responsibilities. Nearly all of the states sampled in another study reported struggling with a shortage of special education teachers and related services professionals, a problem compounded by substandard pay and the tendency for special education teachers in small charter schools to "wear a lot of hats."[16]

Our point is that special needs students would be better served if each district had one or more choice schools devoted to developing and overseeing programs for them, assistance programs that could be delivered to an alliance of public schools, to make it unnecessary for every school with special-needs students to prepare and administer its own special programs.

Special education is just the tip of the iceberg. The same patterns exist in many special areas, such as remedial work, music, and vocational education. Students with special needs, interests, and talents fall between the cracks when a school is required to take on many tasks it is not prepared for. The solution is—as a condition of funding—to require that every charter school, and every school that accepts vouchers, to demonstrate it has a special competency in a particular area of need within the district, and to work in conjunction with other choice and conventional schools.

THE INDEPENDENCE DOCTRINE

But wouldn't choice schools surrender their distinctive advantages if they were to become part of larger plans for districts? The answer is no. We have talked about the fallacies of independence throughout this book. School choice proponents make a big deal out of school autonomy, and the vast majority of charter schools operating today are located in states that require or allow them to be legally independent. In Chapter 2 we exposed the fallacies being promulgated by choice promoters who tell us that teachers are being held back by repressive public school bureaucracies, and that schools must be free to give students the kind of education they need. These unfounded claims are designed to delude parents into believing that it is impossible to find a suitable education setting within the public school system.

Where Is the Evidence That Membership in a Network Would Undermine Charter Schools?

The independence mystique is misleading on two counts. In the first place, it is fiction that choice schools are (a) not bureaucratized, and (b) function independently. All choice schools are part of a system that makes demands of them. For example, charter schools must file attendance reports to sponsors and states, fill out applications to state and federal agencies for special entitlement funds, negotiate contracts with suppliers, manage financial accounts and submit to audits, administer standardized tests and report results to state agencies, and report to parents. Private schools are dreaming if they think states won't eventually require them to submit to some rules if they are going to take public money. Conditions are, or will be, mandated by outside authorities, and meeting the conditions does require bureaucracy. However, this is not fatal. There are ways around those insensitive rules that impinge on teaching, including school-based management approaches, and magnet and alternative schools, and other approaches discussed in the previous chapter.

Second, apart from whether charter schools can be truly autonomous and free of bureaucracy, research shows that being outside the public school system provides no assurance that teachers will adopt innovative teaching practices. As reported earlier, many private school teachers teach in conventional ways, as do many charter school teachers.[17] As we said in Chapter 2, the contention that teachers would be more creative if only they were released from the clutches of bureaucracy is another fabrication being pushed by zealous choice advocates. Curriculum and teaching styles probably have little to do with whether a school is in the public or private sector, or whether it is part of the public school system or outside of it. The way teachers teach probably has a lot to do with how they have been trained, what parents expect, and especially, the size and culture of the school. If a smaller school encourages adventuresome, creative teachers, and if the parents welcome them, it will attract them. And, if the school then provides a supportive environment, with full parent endorsement, some innovative teaching may actually happen. Independence is not necessary.

The Escape Valve Function

While choice proponents say giving choice schools autonomy will force conventional schools to change, our review in Chapter 2 should have convinced you that this is nonsense. The strategy of choice, as it is now set up, cannot transform public schools, because it is only a mechanism to help a few individuals escape regular public schools. As Cookson and Berger put it, "Ten thousand charter schools educating two million students . . . would only result in more options for individuals but do nothing to [transform] the structure of schooling."[18] Every state, after all, places caps on the number of choice schools that can be authorized. It is clear that these realtively few schools were never intended to produce a revolution. As Cookson and Berger observe, they are escape valves for the few. More important, choice encourages the discontented families to break away. These are families who might otherwise have worked on behalf of public education reforms. By siphoning off the critics, choice schools actually reinforce the educational status quo. To quote Cookson and Berger again, "As the escape valve of public discontent, charter schools—or rather the idea of charter schools—serve a social purpose for those who wish to preserve the social order."[19] In other words, the really angry parents, those who might have tried to change things, get out, leaving the public schools to the people who are less inclined to demand change.

Maybe some charter schools and school vouchers are extending options to some disenfranchised families, but they do nothing to help the students left behind in inadequate public schools. The only way to expand choices for every child is to focus on changing what is happening within the public school districts, and in particular, finding better ways to assist challenged schools. That is precisely what our plan for specialized networks of choice schools is designed to do.

Washington's Hypocrisy

There is no greater advocate for the idea that desperate parents must abandon regular public schools to get help than the U.S. Department of Education. It is ironic that the U.S. Congress and a succession of presidents from both political parties direct a major federal agency to promote a reform movement predicated on the assumption that to be good, a school must bolt the conventional public school system. This is the same agency that funds many conventional education programs, an agency that is supposed to help public schools serve all citizens. Instead, it has squandered money and personnel on a relative handful of schools designed for a select few kids, schools that can damage public education, and are beyond the reach of most local taxpayers who nevertheless must help to pay for them. The escape valve function helps explain the regrettable part that this agency has played in the school choice farce. Rather than working to improve those schools that serve most parents, the Federal government hides behind the enthusiasm associated with the charter-school movement, thus diverting the public's attention from its responsibility for the sorry state of many public schools.

In 1993, President Clinton proposed the Federal Charter School Program, enacted in 1994, as part of the Elementary and Secondary Education Act. Initially, $5 million was appropriated to pay for start-up costs for new charter schools. By 2005 that amount had increased to $255 million and this stately sum continues to grow, and has been expanded to support school vouchers as well with a hefty sum of $64 million. The involvement of the federal government in school choice probably has had a dramatic, positive impact on the enforcement of civil rights legislation, but the U.S. Department of Education became so immersed in the charter-school movement that their successes and failures now reflect upon it. No wonder it has taken bold steps to assure the success of this program, including a grants program, more staff to serve charter schools, conferences on charter schools, and a website promoting the program with a direct

Internet link to the Center for Education Reform, one of the most un-abashed charter-school booster groups in the country.

In 1996, the Department initiated a four-year, comprehensive study of charter schools, which was to be conducted by outside contractors. The study contract was opened to bidders; presumably on the premise it was to be an objective and neutral data-gathering effort. However, we have to wonder, how could bidders escape noticing that this agency, which con-trols a multitude of research contracts and grants on a wide array of top-ics, is not neutral toward charter schools? We were not surprised, then, when the researchers who won the competition to study charters ap-peared very cautious about asking the hard questions that might yield potentially negative information. The data collected were frequently dis-played in complex tables and the interpretation was left to the reader to figure out. Consequently the U.S. Department of Education could take some liberties with the data.

For example, the Department felt free to assert that charter schools were not skimming the best and brightest, but in fact were educating a broad cross section of students, including minorities. Well, not really. If you were to look carefully at the data, you would find that many charter schools segregate by race. Nationally, they do not appear to be segregated only because in several states (for example, Connecticut, Florida, Illinois, Louisiana, Michigan, New Jersey, and South Carolina) lots of black stu-dents are enrolled in charter schools. Examine the data state-by-state, and you can see what is actually going on: a few charters are stuffed with mi-norities while most others enroll only a small handful of minority stu-dents. At the very least, the Department's advocacy role does not promote open and objective criticism of this pet project. What is a researcher's in-centive for criticizing a program being promoted by a powerful and af-fluent funding agency? And, who wouldn't be skeptical of conclusions this agency may draw from the data, which are always open to interpre-tation under the best of circumstances?

Does the Department's advocacy posture make a difference? It might. In 2004, the AFT uncovered test data, some of which was not very flat-tering to charter schools. The information was buried under layers of files in the Department's website. It is not clear that the Department inten-tionally buried the information, but it is clear that it did not actively pub-licize it. But perhaps the most important consequence of its vigorous advocacy role goes back to its initial decision to forcefully back the no-tion that charter schools should operate independently from school dis-tricts, as most of them now do. As already noted, there is no convincing reason why they need to be independent. The resources and effort this agency has expended promoting independent, fully autonomous charter schools has had profound opportunity costs in the form of resources and effort that have been diverted from the central challenge of improving America's public school districts. Rather than using its resources and influence to lead reforms that will directly improve public schools, the Department has chosen to take a manipulative action that will only encourage the critics of regular public schools to get out rather than to stay and work to improve them. The irony is that by backing charters, the Department can appear to be championing reform even though charter schools are having little overall impact on public education.

In any case, the federal role in the charter-school story makes it clear these schools have never been autonomous entities. Nor were they created and shaped by market forces. They are progeny of larger political and bureaucratic systems, taking money and directions from Washington, and cultivated and nurtured by a powerful federal agency. Being independent of school districts was not necessary. The federal government could have just as easily promoted charter schools operating under flexible guidelines within school districts in the tradition of magnet schools, small schools initiatives, and alternative programs. It could have used its clout to persuade districts to give more latitude to charters and other alternative schools wanting to spread their wings, in the manner of Boston's Pilot Schools. Instead, it chose the more politically expedient route of reform on the cheap by backing charter schools under the guise of independence in exchange for accountability and then never stuck around to see to it that one led to the other.

THE COMMON SCHOOL

Specialized schools are polar opposites of the common school, which has dominated the history of education in this country and continues to strangle broadscale reforms. The typical public school system offers a common curriculum for diverse students from all backgrounds. In the ideal common school, students are assigned randomly to schools and to teachers under principles of equitable treatment, rather than on considerations of distinctive needs. Though bent out of shape by segregated housing patterns and tracking practices, the common school prevails in popular mythology as the perfect public school. Even the reality that suburban schools, safely walled off from the inner cities, cater to homogeneous middle classes pursuing a single, college-oriented goal has not tarnished the nation's belief that the common school is *the* most appropriate for a democratic society.

Why the Common School?

The common school is a largely political response to the historic transformations that shattered this society during the early part of the last century. Unprecedented rates of immigration from various countries, drastic shifts in the rural-urban tilt, and disruptive economic, racial, ethnic, and religious distinctions all threatened the solidarity of this nation in the

years between 1850 and 1940, even as it was climbing to world promi-
nence. The comprehensive, common school would, it was believed, serve
as a mechanism for bringing vastly different groups under one roof where
they would come to share a common value system and language.

Once regarded as the first line of defense against elitism, the common
school has now become as obsolete as the general store. It is, after all,
based on an irony, the belief that student diversity itself makes it unnecessary for educators to pay much attention to diverse student needs and
backgrounds. That illusion is grounded in the notion that the common
school would serve as a laboratory for assimilating newcomers who
would be eager to learn the language and customs. Educators bought the
assumption that simply by interacting among themselves in schools, students from different backgrounds would become assimilated. No further
assistance needed. This "school-mix remedy" then allowed educators the
luxury of concentrating on the curriculum without needing to do anything else. This convenient assumption has not been dented by demanding new technologies, unstable job markets, and large concentrations of
physically and emotionally disabled youths, street gangs, a thriving drug
culture, and massive numbers of immigrants who choose to maintain
close contacts with their country of origin and their native languages. Indeed, the school-mix remedy was hauled out again in recent years by reformers pushing desegregation programs with the limited objective of
bringing together students from different racial and socioeconomic backgrounds in the same school.

The flawed hope that assimilation requires no more than putting everyone in the same school continues to thrive. And therefore, educators have
given little attention to structural and procedural changes that might be
necessary to improve admission policies, beyond implementing racial desegregation guidelines. It is no wonder that public schools are not yet
structurally organized to (a) provide an effective socialization experience
for diverse types of students; (b) equip them with distinct types of information and intellectual skills; or (c) help them overcome various hurdles
created by problems at home, language deficiencies, and physical and
emotional disabilities. Schools deal with diversity and a knowledge explosion as afterthoughts tacked onto an organizational form designed for
other purposes. As a result, even in fully desegregated schools, students
can be segregated among classrooms and extracurricular and social activities. At the same time, any teacher can expect to confront a mixture of
students carrying the full spectrum of challenges.

Inadequacies of the Common School

Unfortunately, a school admissions policy devoted only to the goal of
representing students from diverse racial, ethnic, and socioeconomic families is directly contrary to the principle of specialization. Notwithstand-

ing their family backgrounds, students have different interests, talents, abilities, and handicaps. And, notwithstanding their common school tradition, schools are grappling with ways to teach expanding and changing areas of knowledge. In this atomic, electronic age of invisible forces, teaching has become ever more challenging. Students will not comprehend atoms from a field trip through the local milk factory, and theories of economics cannot be easily conveyed with simple household budget models. All of this makes it necessary for teachers to specialize. Teachers need to devise distinctive ways to teach abstract ideas to students with different levels of preparation, and schools need to be reorganized to better prepare students to learn abstract concepts and reasoning, at their own pace.

It is bound to happen. Schools are experiencing a structural lag that will force them to adapt new forms and procedures. Attempting to maintain comprehensive programs in this era is producing several types of strain. One type was already noted. The typical teacher, by design, faces a class of thirty students from different racial heritages and socioeconomic backgrounds, with differing motivations and interests, and with an IQ range of four to six years. Between half- and three-fourths of teachers report having students in class who are not fluent in English, and over three-fourths have students with disabilities.[20] The anomaly is that the teacher—and the school—are condemned to function as a "jack of all trades" in an era of specialization. No wonder so many schools are not doing well.

Another form of strain comes from an astounding array of often conflicting goals, ranging from teaching knowledge to character training. Many of these goals are either logically inconsistent (example, teaching critical thinking along with uncritical patriotism), or they cannot be completely achieved simultaneously because of the limited time and energy of teachers and students. Still another source of strain arises from competition among different programs having competing priorities and seeking limited resources. Schools become bipolar, allowing slower and less motivated learners to slide so teachers can cover material at a pace intended for a hypothetical average student; in the meantime, able students complain of boredom. Far from being democratic, the comprehensive system forces less prepared students to compete with the better prepared ones.

SPECIALIZED SCHOOLS

We suspect that, in the long run, these pressures will force all schools to become more specialized as has already happened in other service sectors. In the meantime, every school district needs a substantial number of specialized schools that not only can serve their own students but also can act as resources for other schools in the district. That is why we are proposing that both charter schools and schools that accept school vouchers should cooperate as part of planned networks of specialized schools operating within districts. Choice schools would collaborate not only among themselves, but also with regular schools that could use their help. The model we have in mind includes and extends salient features of charter schools, existing school-based management, small schools initiatives, and elements of magnet and alternative schools.

Needed Modifications in School Choice Rules

Our proposal requires four fundamental modifications in school choice as currently practiced. First, while retaining most of the freedoms, all charter schools would be part of a larger system. Some new or converted schools would be *planned and monitored* by school districts, operating under contracts in accordance with district guidelines. Others, serving low-income minorities, would be *operated* by districts. Districts could choose to convert any or all schools to charters. The advantages of this will be discussed below and throughout the next chapter. Private voucher schools would also operate under contacts with sponsoring agencies. Otherwise, choice schools would have most of the freedoms that many now enjoy, including: exemptions from many state and local rules governing curriculum; authority to raise funds, hire teachers, and control curriculum and teaching styles (within the constraints of its mission); access to the money attached to the student (including overhead); and opportunities for parents to voluntarily participate in various ways. They would also be accountable for accomplishing realistic missions under the oversight of the district and local controlling boards established to oversee specific aspects of the school's operations.

Second, districts would identify underserved needs and then solicit contracts from anyone interested in starting a school to address an identified mission. A school's mission, in other words, would no longer be defined exclusively by the personal preferences of the individuals who create it, although bidders would be free to propose missions not already identified by the sponsor. Each school's objectives must fit within a systematic plan. Many states already impose similar requirements based on mandates, rather than local conditions, such as restricting charter schools to serve a specified number of low-income or at risk students. However, state mandates do not go far enough either in scope of targeted needs or in certifying the competence of schools to fulfill their commitment.

Third, charter schools and private voucher schools would contribute to joint courses, activities, services, and programs operated by the network of alliance schools. They would be designed to promote racial, ethnic, and socioeconomic integration across schools having different social compositions. For example, all schools could take advantage of computer experts who might be concentrated in a few schools. Every school would not need the same science laboratories, since schools could exchange access to facilities on a scheduled basis. And, a performing arts school with a well-equipped auditorium could share the facility with other students at designated times.

Fourth, schools that enroll charter or voucher students would be required to describe the steps they are taking to prevent erosion from existing levels of racial, ethnic, and socioeconomic integration. Steps taken could include strategic placement of schools throughout a district or region, courses and activities attended by students from more than one school, half-day or one-day programs, and the like. However, it is important to recognize that the main priority in this proposal is academic, not desegregation. Where specialized schools can promote desegregation, by all means, they should do so. But the standard is preventing more, not necessarily promoting less, segregation. The reason is that programs falter when they are expected to accomplish too many objectives. Magnet schools have been serving as instruments of desegregation, and should continue to do so.

Characteristics of a Specialized School

A specialized school is a school with a particular focus and demonstrated competency operating within a planned network of schools. It is part of an interdependent division of labor. Each specialized school in the network is staffed by trained specialists with (a) clearly delineated responsibilities for which they will be held accountable; (b) a supportive knowledge base; (c) specialized training; (d) incentives to work hard at whatever they are expected to achieve; (e) a separate administrative structure; and (f) a supportive environment, which includes specially equipped classrooms, programs, and other critical resources. Note that all of the pieces must be present. For instance, teachers cannot be held accountable for outcomes unless they are backed with the necessary support.

Specialization establishes a mission that, on the one hand, clearly specifies what a school is supposed to achieve, and on the other, describes how it fits in with other schools in the network. The mission makes it possible to tie performance standards and sanctions to each administrator, teacher, and student. The mission also minimizes competition among schools. When providers are undifferentiated, they all compete for the same thing, the same teachers and the good students. A division of labor sorts the population into different domains, thus widening the base and minimizing wasteful competition. In a specialized school, staff members work with a distinct type of student who needs assistance that cannot be as effectively provided within conventional classrooms. Teachers must be trained and have experience and other qualifications appropriate to the school's mission. For example, a school for the emotionally disturbed employs teachers trained in psychology as well as the relevant subject matter. In a school for the performing arts, some teachers have acting experience; the custom facilities might include small auditoriums and sound stages. A school for the physically disabled has health care environments, special toilet facilities, ramps, and desks. All specialized schools need to have a separate administrative structure, with administrators who have been delegated authority to support and coordinate key tasks and to recruit properly trained teachers.

Because "specialization" is a word that has been widely used, and misused, within the education community, it will be helpful to sort out some of the meanings associated with the term.

Special Programs and Homogeneous Types of Students. Specialized schools should not be confused with special programs. The latter operate in a context where most of the effort goes to objectives other than serving the targeted clientele. By design, specialized programs must compete for resources with other programs and activities within a single school. By contrast, within specialized schools, all tasks contribute to a coherent program for a targeted clientele. Other terms that are sometimes confused with specialization are diversity and homogeneous community. Some proponents of choice use the term "diversity" to suggest that schools with specialized programs are abundant in the private sector, while others seem to equate specialization with "homogeneous communities" of students and parents who share the same religious, political, and social backgrounds.[21] Neither term qualifies as specialization as defined above, since neither requires trained staff, special resources, and the like.

Idiosyncratic Specialization. Some schools have evolved almost by accident into a form of specialization that can be called "idiosyncratic." Idiosyncratic specialization is an informal and unplanned form of specialization that schools and teachers work out on the basis of their personal skills and predilections. For example, because of the interests and talents of particular teachers, one school may have become adept at working with at risk students, while another has a reputation for being effective with advanced learners, and still another gives priority to math. Schools also adopt different informal practices for transferring students among teachers with particular strengths, for handling discipline cases in various ways, and for addressing requests from parents for particular teachers.

Sometimes a school becomes highly distinctive as a result of its idiosyncratic features. However, that fact alone does not qualify it as a specialized school if the specialties have evolved in a haphazard manner. Idiosyncratic behavior is uncontrollable, and hence can produce unwanted dysfunctional results. For example, schools sometimes evolve as "dumping grounds" for those students the system chooses not to handle in any other way. Idiosyncratic patterns are unpredictable and unstable because they are so heavily dependent on (a) the personal talents of teachers, who may leave, and (b) the tolerance and encouragement of particular administrators who happen to be in charge at the time. Formal specialization, on the other hand, identifies the special capacities of each school, which then can be held accountable for fulfilling its assigned mission by recruiting certified, experienced teachers. Isolated instances of the kind of specialization we are talking about already exist in embryonic form. They include district specialists, specialized schools, alternative schools, magnet schools, and controlled choice plans. Each is discussed below.

District Specialists. Thousands of nonteaching professional personnel work as school psychologists, reading and language experts, school nurses, bilingual and special education teachers, college job placement counselors, and counselors in the areas of alcohol and other drug abuse, teenage pregnancy, and suicide prevention. During some years, noninstructional staffs have grown at twice the rate of instructional expenditures.[22] The position of district specialist represents the most primitive type of specialization. These specialists usually serve more than one school and are not housed in facilities staffed by others with the same specialty and same special mission. Operating in isolated positions marginal to the basic district structure, specialists cannot count upon resources that effective specialization requires.

Specialized Schools. Specialized schools, by contrast, can count on all of these things. They have been around a long time in one form or another, but are nevertheless relatively rare. Walnut Hills High School in Cincinnati was created in 1918 for academically gifted, college-bound students. Other well-known specialized schools include New York's Bronx High School of Science, Boston's Latin School, and Lowell in San Francisco. Many cities have founded public vocational schools and schools devoted to special education, the arts, and to modern technologies. However, although many states pay most or all of the cost for a public specialized school, there are relatively few specialized schools within any given district. For example, Washington, DC, operates one of the most challenged school districts in the nation. Yet, it has only four early childhood education schools and six specialized high schools (for the arts, careers, student dropouts, multicultural education, and academic achievement). New York City undoubtedly sponsors more specialized schools than any other district in the nation. There are over twenty-four schools for students with learning disabilities, more than 100 for autistic and dyslexic students, and many other schools offering therapy for the hearing or visually impaired, and early childhood education.

Some types of specialized schools are affiliated with one another through professional networks. For example, in 1988 a consortium of eighty specialized secondary schools of mathematics, science, and technology was established to provide opportunities for these types of schools to exchange information. Nevertheless, these schools usually operate as isolated units within their respective districts.

Alternative Schools. Alternative schools, sometimes called "free schools" or "open schools," sprang up in the early 1970s as political expressions of the counterculture movement of that era. They were unique schools that usually offered a special teaching style or curriculum focus. In 1970, with the assistance of $6 million from the federal government, Minneapolis opened four elementary schools and one high school, all with different organizational designs. Of the four elementary schools, the least structured, was referred to as "free" in that students had freedom to direct their own education. The second type was called "open," and had an informal classroom design. The third was "continuous progress," and the fourth had a traditional approach, but Minneapolis chose to call it "contemporary."[23] The city of Berkeley also sponsored a full-scale alternative program featuring basic skills centers, environmentally-oriented programs, independent contracts with businesses to provide curriculum, and other approaches. Alternative schools caught on and spread to major cities across the country during the 1970s. However, within a few years the reform fervor had diminished and most had gone out of existence or drifted back into conventional schools. One study of several alternative schools operating in 1973 found that most already had come to look a lot like conventional schools.[24]

Magnet Schools. Magnet schools evolved along with alternative schools. A magnet school is a school or education center that offers a special curriculum capable of attracting substantial numbers of students of different racial backgrounds. Magnet schools were conceptualized as a political response to remedy racial segregation in school enrollment; and they continue to be part of a broader desegregation plans, often stemming from litigation. According to the Magnet Schools of America website, one of the first schools designed to reduce racial isolation by offering a choice to parents was an elementary school created in 1968 in Tacoma, Washington called McCarver.[25] In 1969, Boston's Trotter Elementary School opened for the same reasons. Both of these early attempts offered a different organizational pattern and guaranteed continuous progress education, by which students would progress at their own rates. As a desegregation strategy, children and faculty could be reassigned to reduce, eliminate, or prevent minority group isolation. Neither of these schools was called a magnet; rather each was referred to as an "alternative." According to the Magnet website, the term magnet caught on after 1971 when a district used it to describe the ability of one school to attract students. The idea behind magnets is that if a school voluntarily attracts students and teachers, it will succeed because, more than for any other reason, those in attendance want to be there.

Now, over one million students attend 3,000 magnet schools, 80 percent of them located in urban areas. At least 60 percent are located in high-minority neighborhoods and are designed to entice white parents to voluntarily transfer their children as a means of improving racial balance. Funds for magnet schools are provided by the U.S. Department of Education's Emergency School Aid Act. By 1980 most major cities had systems of magnets, but it was the federal courts that caused the greatest surge in magnet education. According to the Magnet Schools of America website, today magnet schools are still used to reduce racial isolation, but they are more and more considered superior options within the public sector for all students, even in districts of primarily one race. A key feature of magnet schools is the specialty curriculum designed to embrace a subject matter or teaching methodology not generally offered to students of the same age or grade level in the same local education agency, such as a science-technology center or a center for the performing arts.

The International Network of Performing and Visual Arts Schools and the Magnet Schools of America list at least 500 public schools with a focus on arts education in the United States.[26] The Network defines a school of the performing and visual arts as one in which at least 40 percent of the school day is devoted to arts education. However, not all magnets are school-wide programs. Some operate as programs within a school or as special classes. Some arts schools are "arts-infused," meaning that the arts are used in every aspect of education, without actually teaching the arts as a separate subject. Most magnets focus on one of the following basic skills: individualized learning, math/science concentrations, gifted and talented programs, language immersion, the arts, and at the high school level, vocationally oriented training. Some feature programs in business/finance, justice/law, and technology. Other possibilities for specialization include:

- Health care facilities for alcohol and other drug problems, pregnancy and day care, and sexually transmitted diseases.
- Diagnostic counseling centers for recent immigrants; for students who engage in violence, vandalism, and verbal or sexual harassment, and for students returning to classes after jail sentences or extended truancy.
- Language clinics for limited English proficient students.
- Remedial schools and programs for students with educational and learning deficiencies.
- Centers focused on helping teachers and administrators learn to cope with specific tasks (such as a deaf child or a child who cannot speak English).

Magnet schools resemble charter schools in that they are free to establish their own special focus and missions. Consequently, like charters, they operate as unique isolated entities, not as part of a systemic plan or network of interacting schools. As a result they sometimes develop bizarre programs, such as one devoted to the care and feeding of animals or another focused on athletic skills. Therefore, while instructive precursors of the planned networks, most magnet schools do not provide much insight into how a planned network of specialized schools would operate within a district. However, there are a few models that illustrate what we have in mind. One is Cambridge, Massachusetts, and another is Montclair, New Jersey. Both cities have eliminated attendance zones and assigned each school some distinguishing program features.[27] District 4 in East Harlem also has eliminated attendance zones for junior high students who must apply to any of twenty-four programs throughout the district. In the East Harlem case, several "schools" are housed within a single building. Each school retains a distinct administrative structure and teaching style. These examples can provide insight into the kind of networks we are proposing for charter and voucher schools.

Desegregation and Controlled Choice Plans

Where attendance zones have been eliminated, parents must choose a school. However, their choice is usually restricted, subject to availability of space and the potential impact on racial composition. For this reason the approach is referred to as "controlled choice." Controlled choice differs from other choice plans, such as open enrollment and voucher models, in that it does not rely on market competition between schools to initiate school improvement. The approach attempts to provide choice while maintaining ethnic and racial integration. Instead of neighborhood attendance districts, this approach is based on zones and allows families to choose within their zone, provided that admitting students to their school of choice does not upset the racial and ethnic balance at that school. Most programs are patterned after a plan designed by Michael Alves and Charles Willie, which was first implemented in Cambridge, Massachusetts, in 1981.[28] Under the Cambridge plan, new families visit a central registration area, choose four schools, and rank them in order of preference. The district reviews the lists and tries to assign students to their choices, but it also tries to ensure that no school exceeds its capacity and that all schools reflect the district's racial and ethnic composition.

Controlled choice is used by magnet schools to reduce segregation in schools. It is needed to offset a documented preference on the part of white parents for schools with fewer minorities. However, the practice of denying a student's request for transfer into a school on the basis of skin color has come under fire. From the earliest desegregation plans in the 1960s until today, it has been assumed that basing student and teacher assignments on race was not discrimination when the aim was the advancement of certain racial and ethnic groups. However, that premise is being challenged by critics who maintain that controlled choice is a form of discrimination due to the fact that decisions are based on a student's skin color. They believe that schools should focus on academics, not social engineering. Of course, some language immersion programs rely on social engineering to target a particular ethnic group. However, the critics do have a point. The race issue is complicated by the multiracial backgrounds of many students, and by students who live with families of a different race from their own—making it nearly impossible to categorize some individuals by race or to identify them by skin color. Various Middle Eastern groups may be classified as white, black, or perhaps even Asian. Another complication arises because people with the same racial characteristics have different heritages, as is the case of African-Americans whose ancestors were not born in the United States, who therefore may not easily identity with African-American citizens whose ancestors were slaves. Issues involving race and ethnicity are so complexly intertwined, it is sometimes impossible to develop policies that can be clearly applied to specific individuals.

It is probably a mistake to make racial background a criterion for admission to a particular school. Even when a school has been desegregated, resegregation often occurs in classrooms, activities, and social events. Therefore, desegregation efforts must target program levels. It is often easier to justify using skin color to mix students within classrooms than to deny them admission to a school because of their race. We see at least two ways to accomplish program-level integration. First, even in a school with a high percentage of minority students, it may be possible to integrate the remaining students by using selective course enrollment policies and by designing inclusive activities and events. Second, when there is a coalition among network schools, each with a different student mix, it is possible to promote integration through joint academic and extracurricular programs, especially when they are supported by transportation and incentives to encourage students to participate. It is not necessary to exclude a student from a particular school on the basis of skin color if that student will be participating with students from other backgrounds in classrooms, lectures, team projects, science fairs, contests, assemblies, clubs, dances and other social events, athletics, and meals. For example, students with different backgrounds could be paired in teams to research local history, collaborate on a science project, or participate on a debate team. Therefore, desegregation programs should promote forms of racial interaction that transcend particular schools rather than relying exclusively on manipulating school composition.

Organizational Networks

We believe that specialized schools can be fully effective only as members of organizational networks. A network of organizations consists of all connected relationships among affiliated organizations. Networks are guided and constrained by interdependencies formed through voluntary exchanges, contracts, overlapping memberships, membership in common formal associations, and various forms of communication.[29] Networks operate on their own logic and laws. The members are not governed by an overriding administrative system as organizations are. But they are nonetheless guided and constrained by existing laws and customs, and more important, by relationships they have established with other member organizations. Networks offer the advantages of institutional cooperation and exchange of goods and services while allowing participating organizations to retain wide spheres of autonomy. The ability of an organization to make creative use of networks to its advantage can be the difference between success and failure. For example, a financially weak charter school might be able to survive by establishing a working relationship with a sympathetic donor, or by placing students in a local business in exchange for resources.

A school district is composed of relationships among partially autonomous schools relating to one another not only directly but through district offices. These relationships establish a network, which in turn determines how schools operate. Districts, in turn, are involved in webs of relationships with a wide range of other organizations: colleges and consulting groups, county offices, employers who hire students, unions, courts, the police, suppliers of books and services, building contractors, and so on. District boundaries are further permeated by cross-district student transfers and tuition arrangements, home schooling networks, and Ethernet programs. What is important here is that districts, and schools within them, are assisted—but also constrained—by widely ranging interdependencies among these diverse organizations. These relationships with other organizations are profoundly important and must be thoroughly understood before their performances can be accurately evaluated or improved. Sometimes districts are helped by their partners, as when a police department provides campus security. Sometimes they are hindered by their relationships, as when a building contractor fails to complete remodeling on time, forcing the district to find other temporary housing for students. Sometimes intense controversies (for example, about textbook content) arise because of the actions of network partners (publishers) who cannot be fully controlled.

In sum, a school's effectiveness depends heavily on how it relates with its network partners within a district. Put in the simplest terms, a charter school can either compete with other schools for resources and students, or it can help meet the pragmatic needs of the district. Putting it that way puts choice schools in a different light. If they compete by offering comparable programs to the same students, they are faced with the prospect of demonstrating that their approaches yield better results than their competitors. And, as already noted, that task is proving nearly impossible because of extreme differences among schools, and because of controversies over which outcomes to measure, as well as how to report changes for students in various parts of the distribution. On the other hand, when choice schools perform services other schools are not providing, or are not providing effectively, their help will be welcome. What is expected of them can be adjusted to the known challenges they face and the importance of the role they are playing within the district. Network analysis can reveal the most challenging areas where school districts could use outside help. Programs for the physically disabled, for truant students, and for homeless students are obvious examples of areas in which districts need help, but programs focused on technology, science, or the arts are also needed in many districts. The same school district that resists supporting a competitive school would welcome that school if it offers to take over some of the responsibility for providing special programs like these.

A BLUEPRINT FOR CREATING A NETWORK OF CHOICE SCHOOLS

How would a specialized network be created and how would it work? We will outline the basics here. First, it will help to think through some assumptions.

Presuppositions

Every blueprint for change starts with presuppositions about opportunities and constraints in the existing environment. Some of our assumptions are outlined below.

1. Narrowly focused reform strategies that set out to attack one problem have a better chance of succeeding than broad gauged attacks on several fronts. This is not a desegregation proposal. As we shall document in the next chapter, they have not worked. At the same time, no strategy should in any way exacerbate existing inequities.

2. Schools function most effectively as part of a district-wide plan and can draw on other resources throughout the district. And, school districts function more effectively when schools work together on specific tasks and thus can share information, leadership, and resources. District-wide networks allow each school to focus on a limited number of objectives, thus increasing the overall capacity of the district. Networks also promote the exchange of ideas and experiences among teachers at different schools who face similar situations and work collaboratively to find solutions.

3. It is sometimes impossible to change classroom teaching without changing the school structure. Many problems schools confront reside at the structural level. For example, schools often do not have the capacity to simultaneously meet stu-

dents' academic and nonacademic needs. By increasing the number of schools specifically designed to help particular kinds of students, learning outcomes can improve, even without the benefit of highly innovative classroom techniques.

4. Systematic oversight and powerful incentives are required to prevent goal displacement. So-called "dumping grounds" evolve when schools are not evaluated and sanctioned. One study of charter schools, for example, revealed that those serving low-income children of color were less likely to provide an academic curriculum, and were generally not as rich in educational resources as charter schools serving white middle-class students. This situation is allowed to occur when the proper training, incentives, and oversight are missing.

5. The progress each school makes fulfilling its mission must be periodically evaluated with instruments tailored to each school's commitments. All schools must be accountable, but they cannot be held to identical measures if they are performing dissimilar missions with different types of students. The balance between a school's ability to focus on academic programs and other demands related to special needs students varies among schools, and the magnitude of the challenges must be reflected in assessments.

6. In all modern societies, tensions exist between bureaucratic, professional, and community sources of authority. This balance must be renegotiated as circumstances change. No one group—not bureaucrats, nor teachers, nor parents—should retain total control. While strong public sentiment favors more parental control, we must remember that local control is largely responsible for existing patterns of racial and economic segregation. Therefore, parents should not be the only force behind a school. Notwithstanding widespread suspicion of bureaucracies, the appropriate bureaucratic rules must be maintained and enforced to guard against favoritism and corruption.[30]

7. Communities, especially suburbs, jealously guard their control over local schools. Therefore, regional networks seem less likely to work than intradistrict plans.

Steps to Creating a Network Model

Creating a school network of the type we are proposing is obviously an exceedingly complex undertaking. Our intention here is limited to suggesting some major parameters that need to be taken into account.

Step 1: Identifying the District's/Region's Needs. As a first step, a district or regional agency must identify the most pressing student needs within its jurisdiction. When the system is viewed as a whole, the gaps and the redundancies should become apparent. Students may be motivated or alienated, idealistic or pragmatic, well-prepared or not. Some may have personal problems (for example, drugs, depression), handicaps (for example, language deficiency, dyslexia), or conflicting responsibilities (for example, a job, a baby). Some may have outstanding talents in art, music, literature, or math. The missions of charter and voucher schools should be based on a census of student needs. Schools within the network, in both the public and private sectors, can then work together through mechanisms such as referrals, joint programs, and contracts.

Classifying students is, of course, never easy and sometimes risky, especially so since the same individual may have several types of needs. It is even more complicated when we realize that the students also classify themselves. For example, several researchers have identified different types of student subcultures, including:[31]

- The *fun subculture* stresses sociability and extracurricular activities; it is a world of clothes, cars, movies, and dates.
- The *academic subculture* stresses brains and grades.
- The *delinquent subculture* is characterized by rebellion, defiance and contempt; these students have given up on school but are not yet in the labor market.

Teachers also classify students, using terms such as "underachiever," or "gifted." We think it makes sense to classify students on two dimensions: (1) demonstrated commitment to succeed in school, as reflected in past performance, expressed goals, and self-concept; and (2) scholastic potential, as indicated in behavior, tests, and teacher and parent evaluations.[32] If these categories are treated as hypotheses about the student, rather than fixed boxes, they can be used as starting points for identifying various kinds of student needs. Dividing each dimension into three categories yields nine types of schools (or programs) for students with different needs. They are identified in Table 4.1.

Nine types of schools (or programs) in this hypothetical system are represented by the numbers in the table. The system is predicated on the assumption that working with unmotivated and troubled students requires distinctly different approaches and facilities than teaching scholastically oriented students. School 1, for high-performing, motivated students, is often referred to as a school for "gifted and talented" or for "college-

Table 4.1
Hypothetical Types of Schools Specialized According to Students' Scholastic Performance and Commitment

Prior Commitment to Succeed in School	Prior Scholastic Performance		
	Above Average	**Average**	**Below Average**
Above Average	1	2	3
	(*Gifted/Talented*)		(*Remedial/Vocational*)
Average	4	5	6
Below Average	7	8	9
	(*Underachiever*)		(*At Risk*)

bound" students. Such schools tend to concentrate on a particular area of knowledge such as math, science, or technology; they also might offer courses and experience in the performing arts. A technology school might be heavily stocked with computers, seminar rooms, and science laboratories, and a performing arts school would have an auditorium, sound systems, music rooms, and recording equipment. School 3 is designed to attract hardworking students who have not yet demonstrated high scholastic potential. "Remedial programs," "work-study," and "vocational schools" fall into this category. These types of schools could also be established for students whose primary scholastic handicap is inability to speak fluent English, and for those needing remedial work in particular areas, such as math. School 9 is often referred to as a school for "at risk" students. It provides a second chance for potential dropouts, pregnant teens, and students with a history of drug dependency or discipline problems. The work and programs in this type of school are necessarily highly individualized. Students would have daily access to psychologists, counselors, and social workers. Remedial courses would be available as needed. Students in School 7 are often referred to as "underachievers." Such a school would specialize in preparing students who have high potential, but who need special support and incentives. It might use individualized instruction, or have work programs and extracurricular programs to peak students' interest in school. Unlike comprehensive schools, it is likely that most of the resources of School 7 and School 8 are dedicated to motivating and guiding able students. Students may be bright, but without the experiences and academic backgrounds that schools often require. In such a school, the counselor-student ratio would reasonably be expected to be about twice that of some other types of schools.

Physically disabled and emotionally disturbed students might fall into any of the categories, but if there are enough of these students to justify a separate school, that school might give priority to special education programs operated in conjunction with the other schools, for example, by transporting students, through teacher exchanges, and by using modified computer-based instruction.

Step 2: Creating Porous School Boundaries. We do not want to give the impression that students would be stuck in any one school, as is now true of most existing specialized schools and magnet schools. When schools participate as part of a larger network, students can associate with a broad spectrum of other students outside their base school through joint programs, courses, and extracurricular activities. All students could be required to participate in one or more joint programs, ranging from district-wide athletic programs and social events to lectures, seminars, and workshops. For example, a performing arts school might hold auditions for students at other schools, perhaps giving the drama majors at the school an opportunity to direct plays. A technology-oriented school could offer computer workshops to students throughout the district, and students attending a school for advanced study could, on a regular basis, tutor remedial students from any school in math or science.

Also, students could rotate among schools in half-day or full-day classes at different schools at designated times each week, or in remedial after-school programs, weekend workshops, and summer school. Also, they could rotate among different schools on an annual, a semester, or a trimester basis. As an example, consider Franklin County, Virginia where all 8th-graders enroll for one semester in the Center for Applied Technology and Career Exploration.[33] Each student chooses to participate in three career modules, each six weeks in length, taught by pairs of instructors, one from the world of work and one a certified teacher. Students with varied interests and aspirations have a chance to work together on a specific problem, such as assessing the impact of a toxic spill in a local stream; they then determine how to clean it up. The assumption is that barriers between students from different backgrounds tend to break down as they pool their knowledge to deal with a common problem. Some schools add another twist by offering joint courses for youths and adults.

Finally, cross-school collaboration could be facilitated by supplementing conventional classes with independent study, small seminars and discussion groups, team projects, computer instruction, and even system-wide lectures. Breaking curricula into specific units or course components of varying lengths would smooth transitions for students participating in more than one school program. For example, students who fail a unit on fractions could make it up in a remedial workshop offered at a network school, without requiring them to repeat the entire math course. Flexible scheduling may require teachers to work in teams and divide their work in unconventional ways. While in conventional schools such requirement is likely to meet resistance from unions, charter schools would not be bound by union contracts.

Step 3: Creating and Staffing Schools That Match the Needs. Guided by needs assessments, the school district would identify the schools designated to accomplish each mission identified. The district could convert existing schools or create new ones. In some cases, the district may wish to convert all schools to charters. In addition, as already noted, teachers and other professionals within the district could apply to start a charter school, provided they submit evidence it would meet a district need, and provided that a core of skilled staff is ready to commit to the tasks involved. The district might also encourage or require some community involvement at this and later stages.

A major concern at this proposal stage is to minimize unneeded duplicates and also to weed out schools that could become dumping grounds for less-motivated and below-average students. In the existing common-school framework that dominates school districts, most teachers prefer to work in schools serving higher-income students. Schools serving lower-income students often get ignored or get second best. Many of their students are eventually placed in custodial classes offering ceremonial courses where often inexperienced teachers routinely pass them on, prepared or not. The advantage of specialization is that not only is each school held accountable for helping all students improve, it is also in a position to recruit teachers prepared to help students who are performing at different achievement levels.

Step 4: Establishing Incentives and Rewards for Teachers. Teacher unions generally oppose contracts that permit differentiated assignments and pay scales. They fear that unethical principals will punish strong teachers who question their leadership by giving them undersirable assignments. They also believe that most principals are unqualified to evaluate teacher performance, so they demand a single salary schedule for all teachers. Obviously, the teachers' unions have some justification for their positions. But the consequences are creating a system of "rich schools and poor schools" within most districts. The better, more-experienced teachers eventually use their seniority to settle into the schools serving the higher-income students, leaving the new, less-experienced teachers to serve the schools with the neediest students.

However, the idea of differentiated staffing has been around for over forty years, and at least some districts have a form of it. Since state laws generally exclude charter schools from union contracts, they can offer teachers special incentives in exchange for their commitment to specialize and to work in nontraditional settings. Meaningful incentives—including money, prestige, and opportunity to wield influence—should be offered to teachers and principals willing to work in schools with special missions. In particular, teachers should be rewarded when their students progress to the point where they are prepared to move on to other schools and programs. A large percentage of students enrolled in a program for so-called underachievers should eventually live up to their potential and transfer to other types of programs. Teachers who can make these students successful should be acknowledged and rewarded; if they can't, they shouldn't be retained as faculty in these schools. We are not proposing that teachers who are working with less advantaged children should be held to the same testing outcomes as teachers in more advantaged schools. We are talking only about rewarding improvement, taking the students' circumstances into account.

Step 5: Admitting Students. Admission to any specialized school should be voluntary, based on applications and recommendations. Moreover, no student should be stuck in a school. Mechanisms should be created to allow and encourage student exchanges and transfers among schools, and schools should be held accountable for assuring that a significant number of low-performing students show enough improvement to transfer to more scholastically demanding schools. Three considerations should guide how students are admitted to each school.

The first consideration is the student's personal circumstances. Some students may require language immersion experiences, others may be talented artists, and still others need remedial work. Their parents could submit applications, and teachers would be free to recommend individuals they think would benefit from a school. In some cases—such as applications to schools of visual and performing arts or music—students might be required to audition or otherwise demonstrate minimal qualifications. Choice plans have been justly criticized for leaving some students behind. In the interest of expanding choice opportunities to everyone, when demand for a particular type of school exceeds supply, the sponsor should be required to take steps toward providing another school. In the meantime, admission would have to be based on random assignment. In no case, would residence dictate admission.

Parents would not have to leave the public schools to enroll their children in choice schools, and the range of options available within districts would expand significantly. Some of these options would directly benefit families with special needs, not now being met by charter schools, whose goals often are dictated by the whims of individuals operating them. The real question, though, is a relative one: Is the current involuntary student assignment procedure based on residence really better than a referral plan that matches students to schools capable of addressing their special circumstances?

The second factor that must be considered in any discussion of student admissions concerns the school's boundaries. A choice school's jurisdiction can be either contiguous with district boundaries or it can be regional (or in some cases, perhaps, statewide) in scope. Regional boundaries are problematic whenever suburbs are included, because historically they have resisted more than token numbers of outsiders. As Heise and Ryan have observed:

Politically, school choice seems most likely to succeed when it is confined to districts where there is not a great deal of attachment to neighborhood schools, which is most likely to be true in urban districts where neighborhood schools are not very good. . . . Any effort to extend choice beyond a particular district or to include private schools will be even more difficult politically, in large part because such plans threaten (or will be perceived to threaten) suburban schools. What we should expect to see, in short, are scattered, geographically constrained choice plans in urban areas with a large number of inadequate schools.[34]

The wall of isolation around suburbs opens choice programs to charges of elitism and segregation, but we doubt that much can be done about it. One might hope that a few suburban parents can be enticed to participate if cities open specialized schools offering clearly superior programs.

That is the magnet school strategy. But while those magnets that offered exceptional programs have sometimes attracted a racial mix of students, they do not guarantee that students will actually interact together across color lines. Moreover, the strategy is often symbolic and has never been applied to most schools in a district. Conversely, one might hope that suburbs will agree to accept a limited number of inner city youths. But again, the numbers are likely to be small and amount to little more than a token victory. Still another tack that has been tried to promote regional schools is a coalition among districts that agree to cooperate. There are a few isolated examples of this approach, including the controlled-choice program in Cambridge, Boston's METCO program, and Milwaukee's Chapter 220 program, and a legal settlement between Minneapolis and eight surrounding suburbs. However, by and large, we will probably have to be content with intradistrict approaches to open enrollment.

The third factor that effects student admission options are the transportation arrangements. Some families are able to provide or pay for private transportation, while public transportation may work for others. Most states do not provide funds for transportation in connection with existing choice plans within the public sector. However, without funding, choice will remain an option only for the wealthy, or for the fortunate few with a choice school in their backyard. When transportation funds are not available, choice schools can be located adjacent to or on large public school campuses. As we noted in the previous chapter, "schools-within-schools" models, consisting of several specialized schools that operate within a single building, provide a practical way to minimize transportation hurdles while at the same time facilitating cross-school collaboration.[35] Students at Wyandote High School in Kansas City can enroll in any of eight distinctive schools in the largest building as well as take courses at a nearby community college.

OTHER CONSIDERATIONS

There are two additional features of the model that we are proposing. First, parents must not only participate. They must have real influence. Second, schools must be held accountable to realistic standards and submit to periodic evaluation by teams of educators and parents. Each feature will now be discussed.

Parent Involvement

Researchers and practitioners increasingly recognize that a close-knit community, linking families and schools, can contribute substantially to student commitment and quality of schoolwork. Several empirical studies have found that students whose parents are involved with their learning at home have higher academic achievement, regardless of socioeconomic factors.[36] Homework is a vehicle that promotes such collaboration, and Corwin and his colleagues found evidence that the amount of homework teachers assign correlates positively with a school's standardized test scores.[37] Parent support legitimizes teachers' demands and promotes positive attitudes in children.[38] Epstein describes the ideal family-school relationship as a partnership where both school and family recognize, respect, and support each other. In practice, such partnerships take different forms, as each family chooses how it will participate.[39] Some parents may choose to focus on the primary needs of their child and turn to the school for assistance in doing so. Others concentrate on providing learning activities at home. Still others volunteer their services as aides, clerical workers, and fund raisers. And some want to participate in key decisions.

Types of Parent Involvement. But let's be careful about the term "involvement." It can refer to a wide variety of activities ranging from participation to influence and ultimately, full control. Participating in a school is not the same thing as exercising real influence over it. Schools that use parent contracts like to take credit for encouraging parent "involvement" when what they are really doing is persuading or coercing parents to provide some kind of service to the school, which can range from helping in classrooms to fund raising. As instruments written by schools, not by parents, contracts can be intimidating and manipulative, allowing schools to define involvement in ways that suit them and then coercing parents to participate on the school's terms. The veneer of participation protects the school from actually extending to parents real opportunities to control or influence policies and practices.

To enable us to go deeper into this topic, let's say that the relationship between parents and schools can be described by the two variables, participation and influence.[40] The joint relationship between the two variables forms a profile of a school's partnership with parents. The configuration differs from school to school. For example, in one school there may be high rates of parent participation, but even when they participate, parents may not have much influence on the school's policies or activities. In another school, while a select few parents might have full control over some critical decisions, such as selecting the principal, there might not be much contact beyond that. Three types of participation roles and two types of influence roles can be identified.

1. Participation Roles

- *The client role.* Parents ask the school for assistance or advice pertaining to specified issues. To play this role, citizens must have become aware of a problem and be ready to initiate the relationship. The school then can reserve the right to determine if the request is legitimate and when and how it will respond to the request.

- *The implementer role.* The school initiates this relationship. A person or group of parents is called on to collaborate in implementing an existing policy or procedure. In this case, the school has already made a decision. Parents are asked to assist in carrying it out. Examples include helping with a fund-raising campaign, volunteering to serve as crossing guards or school-lunch aides, or providing party snacks for a special occasion.

- *The consumer role.* Again, the school takes the initiative by establishing programs and communicating information through the mass media, speeches, telephone calls, and personal visits. Parents are treated as passive consumers of the school's programs, who may either choose them or decline as school officials attempt to persuade them or their children to participate in an activity, such as a school festival.

2. *Influence Roles*

- *The consultant role.* This relationship is the reverse of the client role. The school seeks advice from a parent or group of parents. There are at least four ways citizens can influence policies within this type of role: (a) by providing information, (b) by interpreting events, (c) by giving advice, and (d) by recommending and endorsing specific policies. These roles entail fact-finding, analysis, interpretation, and other responsibilities. For example, a group of parents may be convened to gather facts pertaining to the possibility of enlarging a playground. Or, they may be asked to describe neighborhood traditions and ethnic values to a group of teachers, or to find out why a school bond levy was defeated.

- *The decision-maker role.* Of course, all parents exercise indirect influence whenever they choose to enroll or withdraw their child from the school. But they can also directly influence the decision-making process as members of permanent or ad hoc committees and by accepting special assignments. Examples are parents serving on a committee to hire a principal or to evaluate the teachers.

The amount of influence wielded by parents can be measured along several dimensions. One dimension is the number of decisions parents are involved in. For example, a committee might have authority over only one area (hiring) or many areas (discipline, dress codes, and athletic eligibility). A second dimension is the scope of influence. For example, a committee's authority might be limited to a specific neighborhood or school, or it could extend throughout an entire district. A third dimension is the balance of parent representatives on a committee. Parents might dominate a committee in some cases, but in others they might act only as token representatives. Taking all of these factors into account reveals whether parents (a) are in control, (b) are full and equitable partners, or (c) are marginal participants with circumscribed influence.

Parent Involvement in Charter Schools. Most studies indicate that charter schools have higher rates of parent involvement than conventional schools. Ronald Corwin and Henry Becker studied parent involvement in sixty-six charter schools and some comparison conventional schools.[41] Although the study is now a decade old, we want to mention some findings here because we collected details about patterns of participation not available in more recent studies. In general, we found that more charter-school parents than other parents participated in the seven different types of activities measured. In particular, by a two-to-one margin, charter schools more frequently attracted at least 25 percent of the parents to Saturday events. By a wide margin of six-to-one, charter parents were much more likely to have helped or taught in the classroom or volunteered weekly as a class aide. Teachers in charter schools encouraged parent involvement by assigning homework that included parents in some way, and they very often provided suggestions for activities that parents could do at home with their child.

Not only did charter school parents in our study participate more, they also wielded more influence than other parents. In comparison to parents in conventional schools, parents in charter schools held more leadership positions, worked more often on major committees or boards, and were far more likely to have voted for board members. Charter-school parents were more likely to advocate nontraditional approaches and were involved more often in controversial issues. But there was no difference in whether parents had been responsible for changes in policies and practices of the schools.

However, these numbers are tricky. You get different pictures depending on whether you focus on (a) activities that include some parents or (b) percentages of parents who participate in them. For example, we found that a substantial number of charter schools could count on some parents to help in lunchrooms, offices, or playgrounds, and volunteering as classroom aides. However, the absolute percentages of parents involved showed a different picture. Relatively few parents participated in any of these activities. For example, as noted in Chapter 2, only a small minority of charter schools could count on even one-fourth of their parents helping in a classroom, or one-tenth doing committee work or fundraising. Most charter school parents did not even vote in board elections.

By a huge margin, parent contracts were used much more frequently in charter schools than in conventional schools. In lieu of engaging in other types of outreach approaches, charter schools in our sample chose to rely heavily on contracts as the means of gaining additional parent involvement at school. Most of these contracts (seventeen of the twenty-three we analyzed) required parents to participate in the school; only a few allowed some parents to participate by performing chores at home. The median time requirement specified for both home and school participation was thirty hours per year.

Conclusions about Parent Involvement. Charter schools seem to provide ample precedent for providing opportunities for all types of parental involvement. However, we are not sure the high rates of participation and influence can be attributed to their charter status. It could be a combination of their small size and the kind of parents they attract. Perhaps charter schools attract parents ready and willing to become involved, and then their small size makes involvement feasible. If so, we should reconsider whether conventional neighborhood schools are the appropriate comparison group. Rather than using them as the benchmark, perhaps a more appropriate comparison is other small schools in the public sector, especially other schools (like magnets) that attract parents who have taken the initiative to join.

The distinction we have been making between participation and influence is not merely academic. It is an important distinction because, we submit, charter schools have been more excited about getting parents to perform on-site services than about engaging them in meaningful policy decisions or encouraging them to influence what schools actually do. In the model we are advocating, that would all change. Parents would share control with teachers and administrators over all phases of the schools, including policy levels and even evaluation of programs.

Evaluation of School Performance

The final dimension of our model is evaluation. We have to wonder: when advocates promised that charter schools would produce superior students, did they actually think anyone could prove it with standardized test scores? But no matter. As we have previously said, the promise was a big mistake. Analyzing and interpreting test scores is a tricky business, and especially so, given the many schools with different types of students in various states of readiness and attending divergent programs.

Every specialized charter school should only be expected to demonstrate that it is overcoming some of the obstacles it is facing and to show improvement in a variety of ways. Because it is performing a service for the district, it should not be required to produce dazzling test results to justify its existence. Nor should it be expected to serve as a catalyst of reform. Maybe some charters will, but by and large, we are talking about fledgling, small units, many struggling to get up and running and to stay alive. Why should they have to be heroic if they are addressing critical district needs? It is enough to demonstrate capacity and dedication to work on some of the big challenges in public education. It is enough if they have well-trained, professional staff and the resources required to carry out special missions, such as helping low performers in need of remedial help, the disabled, or the behaviorally challenged, or the students who need help with language. It is enough to provide good vocational education, training in technology, or driver training. It is enough to be available for students who need counseling, to provide good college preparation, or to offer experience in the performing or media arts.

But, you may ask, weren't charter schools supposed to be held to a higher standard of student achievement? Yes, they were—in exchange for independence. They haven't lived up to expectations. So, we need to be more realistic about what they can do and how much freedom they really need. We are not proposing that specialized schools should be immune from scrutiny and evaluation. On the contrary, of course they should be evaluated. But the evaluation instruments should be tailored to their individual missions, activities, and challenges. The expectations should be realistic given the circumstances. Certainly, outcome measures should be aggregated across schools only when they are similar. And, any aggregated analysis must report findings for schools in each part to the distribution of outcome measures, so we know what works and does not work for schools in the upper and lower ends.

None of this is unworkable. The first task is to decide what each school realistically can be expected to accomplish in one-, three-, and five-year increments. Then, we recommend that teams of educators and parents should visit each choice school (and some comparable regular schools) on a scheduled basis, talk with administrators, teachers, students, and parents, and make judgments about the effectiveness of policies, programs and teaching styles. They should use an array of assessments in addition to standardized tests, as deemed appropriate to the school's mission, and then offer recommendations. School personnel in turn should have a chance to comment on the observations and recommendations and to challenge procedures and conclusions. The emphasis of the evaluation effort would be on school improvement, not on showing up the competition. Over time, effective schools should be identified and supported. Ineffective ones should be weeded out and their students should be transitioned gradually to other appropriate schools.

CONCLUSIONS

Chapter 2 of this volume was about the past, what choice was intended to be, and its failures. This chapter has been about the future, what charter schools and school vouchers can become. The school choice debate artificially sets schools against one another when competition is not the solution. School districts need help. We have proposed that planned networks of specialized schools should be created to provide targeted services that address unmet special needs and circumstances of different types of students within a district. Under this plan, any school seeking choice status, as a condition for acceptance, would be required to establish a special mission and to demonstrate the necessary competence to meet it. Different choice schools could offer programs for the disabled, truants and potential school dropouts, accelerated learners, science and technology, remedial students, language-challenged students, the performing arts, and other special cases. Then parents would have meaningful options within their district.

When schools for at risk students adopt some of the features we have listed, there is a good chance they can help the students. In Chapter 2, we referred to several studies indicating that charter schools are not, on the whole, producing better test scores than regular schools. However, we also observed that there is a lot of variation, and that some charters seem to be doing very well. We think the success of a charter has a lot to do with its level of specialization. In this connection it is worth mentioning that by some reports, in some California cities between 2002 and 2004, charter-school test score gains for poor students exceed counterpart public schools three to five times.[42] And, a study that examined the scores derived from California's Academic Performance Index showed that low-income, at risk students in charter schools improved more than similar students in other public schools.[43] It is worth entertaining the hypothesis that those charters that have been created specifically to serve this special population eventually develop the kind of expertise we have been talking about. We will say more about that in the next chapter.

The school-choice movement now relies on random, hit-or-miss approaches to solve complex problems. At best, the schools that evolve from these programs provide, in a few instances, idiosyncratic forms of specialization, such as a school here and there prepared to deal seriously with special education or at risk students. But idiosyncratic approaches to specialization are no substitute for planned systems of schools equipped to handle the full range of demanding responsibilities confronting all but the smallest school districts in this country. A specialized school can hire qualified personnel, concentrate on manageable tasks, and be held accountable for results. Wasteful and duplicative competition between identical schools is replaced by mutually beneficial exchanges. Parents should be able to select among schools equipped to meet their children's actual needs. They should be able to choose among specialized schools that have good track records for dealing with specific types of students. They cannot afford to wait for solutions to complex problems to evolve from random market forces, and they should no longer have to bear the risks of damaging competition that guarantees nothing. If choice advocates would devote some of their influence and energy to expanding choices within the public sector, school districts would improve. The benefits now available to the few parents prepared to leave their school district must be weighed against putting choice schools back into school districts where they can function as part of a planned system available to all parents.

When one thinks of public and private schools as part of a larger network, the questions shift from "Which is better and more deserving?" to "What is the best mix to produce a given set of results?" And, "How can all schools, whether in the public or private sectors, work together?" Referrals, joint programs, contracts and cooperative partnerships allow all students to benefit from the unique strengths of diverse types of schools. Although Americans are rightfully suspicious of any program that separates students from their peers, we have suggested a few of a multitude of ways available to overcome segregation and stratification, including: student rotations; schools-within-schools; joint programs, courses, and activities; block scheduling; half-day classes; and short courses.

But the critics will howl that choice was supposed to be a freewheeling opportunity to try out better approaches and allow selected families to opt out of the public schools. True, maybe no one ever intended for charter schools and vouchers to have anything to do with planning, or to be anything other than what their creators wanted them to be. So what? They were granted those freedoms on false pretenses. The boastful promises about the educational superiority of choice schools cannot be demonstrated; their facilities, services, and enrichment programs are below par; they are not reforming education; and the rant against bureaucracy is a distraction. Choice is supposed to be available to all parents, not just those who are willing to abandon the public schools. The choice is hollow when limited to a simple dichotomy between staying and leaving the public schools. The planned networks of schools we have proposed expand on one form of specialization that many states already impose by requiring charter schools to serve at risk populations. Our proposal probably does not go far enough toward extending choice to all families, but it does expand the range of available choices in a rational and equitable way, it makes admission to a school dependent on the student's documented needs, abilities, and talents, and preferences, and it all takes place within school districts.

NOTES

1. For further elaboration on models of organization, see Krishnan Namboodiri and Ronald G. Corwin, *The Logic and Method of Macro Sociology: An Input-Output Approach to Organizational Networks* (Westport, CT: Praeger, 1993), 55–72.

2. National Center for Education Statistics, "Status of Reform: Principal's Perspectives." Common Core of Data. Available at http://nces.ed.gov/surveys; http://nces.ed.gov/pubsearch/majorpubs.

3. John Merrifield, *The School Choice Wars* (Lanham, MD: Scarecrow Press, 2001).

4. Cynthia D. Prince, *Changing Policies to Close the Achievement Gap* (Lanham, MD: Scarecrow Press, 2004).

5. National Center for Educational Statistics, *Overview of Public Elementary and*

Secondary Schools and Districts: Year 2001–2002. Author: Lee Hoffman (Washington, DC: U.S. Department of Education, 2003), Table 9.

6. National Center for Educational Statistics, *Private Schools in the United States: A Statistical Profile* (Washington, DC: U.S. Department of Education, 1993–1994 through 1999–2000). http://nces.ed.gov/pubs/ps/97459008.asp.

7. Thomas L. Good and Jennifer S. Braden (with contributions by Daniel W. Drury), *Charting a New Course: Fact and Fiction about Charter Schools* (Alexandria, VA: National School Boards Association, 2000).

8. American Federation of Teachers, *Private School Vouchers: The Track Record*, Center on Privatization (March 2001). Available at www.aft.org/pubs-reports (accessed June 2004).

9. Texas Education Agency, *Performance of Open-Enrollment Charter Schools: Comprehensive Annual Report on Texas Public Schools* (Austin, TX: Author, 2001), Chapter 13.

10. C. Cobb and G. Glass, "Ethnic Segregation in Arizona Charter Schools," *Education Policy Analysis Archives* 7, 1 (1999).

11. *Jason L. BNF Glen & Crystal L. v. Seashore Learning Center,* Docket No. 075-SE-1098.

12. L. Mulholland, *Arizona Charter School Progress Evaluation* (Phoenix: Morrison Institute for Public Policy, Arizona State University, 1999).

13. F. Nelson, E. Muir, and R. Drown, *Venturesome Capital: State Charter School Finance Systems* (Washington, DC: Office of Educational Research and Improvement, U.S. Department of Education, 2000).

14. G. Garn and R. Stout, "Arizona Charter Schools," manuscript, 1998, as cited by Good and Braden, *Charting a New Course*, 2000.

15. G.L.M. Rhim and M. J. McLaughlin, "Charter Schools and Special Education: Balancing Disparate Visions," paper presented at the 2nd Annual National Charter School Conference, Denver, CO (March 1999).

16. T. A. Fiore, S. H. Warren, and E. R. Cashman, *Review of Existing Data on Charter Schools and Students with Disabilities* (Washington, DC: U.S. Department of Education, Office of Educational Research and Improvement, 1998).

17. Louis Chandler, *Traditional Schools, Progressive Schools: Do Parents Have a Choice?* (Washington, DC: The Thomas B. Fordham Institute, 1999).

18. Peter W. Cookson and Kristina Berger, *Expect Miracles: Charter Schools and the Politics of Hope and Despair* (Boulder, CO: Westview Press, 2002), 135.

19. Cookson and Berger, *Expect Miracles*, 2002.

20. National Center for Education Statistics, *Status of Education Reform in Public Elementary and Secondary Schools: Teachers' Perspectives* (Washington, DC: U.S. Department of Education, 1996).

21. This point was made years ago by J. F. Witte, "The Theory of Choice and the Control of Education," in *Choice and Control in American Education, vol. II: The Practice of School Choice, Decentralization, and School Restructuring,* W. Clune and J. Witte, eds. (New York: Falmer Press, 1990), xviii.

22. G. E. Robinson and N. J. Prothoroe, *Cost of Education: An Investment in America's Future* (Arlington, VA: Educational Research Service, 1987).

23. For a fuller description, see the Magnet Schools of America website. Available at www.magnet.edu.

24. Reported in Margaret Gresser Teuber, "The Dynamics of Free School Sur-

vival: Analysis of Organizational Attributes and Member Perceptions" (Department of Sociology, The Ohio State University, Ph.D. diss., Columbus 1973).

25. See the Magnet Schools of America website. Available at www.magnet.edu/about.htm.

26. For a fuller discussion of the types of schools mentioned here, see Michael Heise and James E. Ryan, "The Political Economy of School Choice," *Yale Law Journal* 111 (8) (2002); see also Cookson and Berger, *Expect Miracles*, 2002.

27. For further discussion of types of networks and how they differ from competitive relations, see Namboodiri and Corwin, *The Logic and Method of Macro Sociology* (1993), 55–72.

28. Michael J. Alves and Charles V. Willie, "Choice, Decentralization, and Desegregation: The Boston 'Controlled Choice Plan'" in *Choice and Control in American Education, Volume 2: The Practice of Choice, Decentralization, and School Restructuring*, William Clune and John White, eds. (New York: The Falmer Press, 1990), 17–75; see also Charles V. Willie and Michael Alves, *Controlled Choice: A New Approach to Desegregated Education and School Improvement* (N.p.: Education Alliance Press, 1996).

29. See Cookson and Berger, *Expect Miracles*, 2002, 72; see also Carol Ascher and Nathalis Wamba, *Charter Schools Serving Low Income Children of Color* (New York: Institute for Education and Social Policy, New York University, 2000).

30. For a fuller discussion of this topic, see Ronald G. Corwin, "Militant Professionalism, Initiative, and Compliance in Public Education," *Sociology of Education* 38 (Summer 1965).

31. Burton R. Clark, *Educating the Expert Society* (San Francisco: Chandler Publishing Co., 1962), Chapter 7; Burton R. Clark and Martin Trow, "The Organizational Context," in *College Peer Groups*, T. N. Newcomb and Everett K. Wilson, eds. (Chicago: Aldine Press, 1966), 17–70.

32. First suggested in Ronald G. Corwin, *A Sociology of Education: Emerging Patterns of Class, Status, and Power in the Public Schools* (New York: Appleton-Century-Crofts, 1965), 140–150.

33. Jessica Portner, "State-of-the-Art School Seeks to Take a Bite Out of Crime," *Education Week* (6 September 1995), 6–7; Daniel L. Duke, *Challenges of Designing the Next Generation of America's Schools* (Charlottesville: University of Virginia, May 1998).

34. Heise and Ryan, "The Political Economy of School Choice," 2002.

35. James McPartland and others, "Improving Climate and Achievement in a Troubled Urban High School through the Talent Development Model," *Journal of Education for Students Placed at Risk* 3, 4 (1998), 337–361.

36. A. S. Bryk, Valerie Lee, and J. B. Smith, "High School Organization and Its Effects on Teachers and Students," in *Choice and Control in American Education* 1, W. H. Clune and J. F. Witte, eds. (London: Falmer Press, 1990).

37. Krishnan Namboodiri, Ronald G. Corwin, and Linda Dorsten, "Analyzing Distributions in School Effects Research: An Empirical Illustration," *Sociology of Education* 66 (October 1993), 278–294.

38. James Coleman, "Families and Schools," *Educational Researcher* 16 (1987), 32–38.

39. See Joyce L. Epstein, "School and Family Partnerships," in *Encyclopedia of Educational Research* 6, M. Alkin, ed. (1992), 1139–1151; see also C. Muller and

D. Kerbow, "Parent Involvement in the Home, School, and Community," in *Parents, Their Children, and Schools*, B. Schneider and J. S. Coleman, eds. (Boulder, CO: Westview Press, 1993), 13–42.

40. For a fuller discussion, see Ronald G. Corwin and Theodore C. Wagenaar, "Boundary Interaction between Service Organizations and Their Publics: A Study of Teacher-Parent Relationships," *Social Forces* (December 1976), 471–492.

41. See also Ronald G. Corwin and Henry J. Becker, "Parent Involvement: How Do Parents Participate?" in *Freedom and Innovation in California's Charter Schools*, Ronald G. Corwin and John F. Flaherty, eds. (Los Alamitos, CA: Southwest Regional Laboratory and WestEd, 1995), 75–88.

42. Daniel Weintraub, "Public Education's Best Hope," *Sacramento Bee*, 9 September 2004. Available at www.sacbee.com/politics/columns.

43. Simeon P. Slovacek, Anthony J. Kunnan, and Hae-Jin Kim, *Student Achievement in Public Schools Serving Low Socio-Economic Status Students* (Los Angeles, CA: The Charter College of Education, California State University, Los Angeles, 2002).

Plight of the Poor and Minority Student in an Uncaring Society: Using District-Operated Charter Schools to Improve Poverty Schools

In this chapter we underscore an obvious truth that most of us take too easily for granted: we live in a society segregated by wealth and race, and despite forty years of well-intentioned social programs, it is more segregated now than ever before. The problem is not going away. Consequently, school districts continue struggling to find innovative ways to educate poor children who come to school without the advantages of their more affluent classmates. So far the challenge has been more than most districts can handle. The educational failures associated with poverty schools all too often are dismissed as the inevitable outcome of crushing challenges associated with high percentages of low-income, single-parent families, where English is not the primary language spoken at home. But there is more to it than that. The schools serving these students also tend to be the oldest and generally the most rundown. In addition, the students have to use out-of-date textbooks, which are often in short supply. To complicate matters, teachers serving minority and poor children in our society are the least experienced, have the highest turnover, and all too often are teaching subjects for which they hold no teaching credentials.

Research and reason say that good teaching is strongly associated with favorable learning outcomes. And yet, as things stand, school districts with concentrations of at risk children are simply unable to place and then hold good teachers in what are commonly described as hard-to-staff schools. The reasons are both obvious and complicated. Nearly every school district has a single salary scale. That means a teacher earns as much working in an upscale, lily-white school with high-achieving, college-bound students (with all the extras) as she earns in a ghetto school where fewer than half the students may show up on any given day. In the latter, she may have to worry about her car being vandalized in the faculty parking lot, and cope with the negative opinions of her peers who think she is working at a "failing" school. Her union has fought for a seniority system that gives her the right to have a say in where she teaches, if she stays in the system long enough to realize that benefit. And like most of her peers, the final payoff for seniority is the opportunity to move into a school with low teacher turnover, strong leadership from the principal, and students who come to school ready to learn. Big districts that argue they ought to have the right to force teachers to work where the central-office administration places them have learned through experience that such a policy only drives out the experienced ones into neighboring suburban schools where the pay is better and the work less challenging.

But clearly, without topflight teachers in every classroom, this society will never ratchet up the quality of education to any significant degree. Any initiative to fix America's schools must have at its core a plan for attracting and retaining quality teachers. In the following pages, we are going to recommend that school districts should create and operate charter schools for students now locked in low-achieving, high-poverty schools. Charters will give districts the flexibility needed to overcome some of their worst problems. In exchange, district-operated charters will be eligible for district resources, technical help, and other forms of support not available to independent charter schools. In addition, we shall cautiously suggest that districts should consider contracting with those private voucher schools that have demonstrated success in working with impoverished children and that agree to comply with civil rights laws and submit to audits of how they spend public money.

But, you may ask, aren't some independent charter schools already serving poor minorities? Some are, in unpredictable places. But not only are they too few in number. More important, districts cannot count on freewheeling independent charters to be available when and where they are most needed. And, as we have noted before, the vast majority of existing charters either are independent or are permitted to become so. We propose expanding the number of district-operated charter schools in poverty neighborhoods, which in some cases could include all poverty schools or even all schools in the district. Before elaborating, let's take a hard look at the kind of society we are living in today.

WE LIVE IN A SOCIETY OF ENCLAVES

Before the torrent of immigrants who flooded the country after the War of 1812, there were no slums in American cities. Sure, poor people huddled in run-down houses, and—by mid-century—thousands of homeless children slept in dirty streets and dingy back alleys. There was plenty of crime, too—but not the intense fear and violence, not the armies of un-employed and homeless, not the street gangs and drug users, not the im-pacted ghettos handily sorted by color, heritage, and occupational status, that define cities today. Now, we take for granted the striking disparities that divide urban areas into *Slums and Suburbs*, as Conant called them in his book by that title.[1] Voters, and suburban voters in particular, tend to believe that the nation is divided into winners and losers. And, they are right of course. One need only look at the deep social chasms that sepa-rate urban neighborhoods into balkanized ghettos and gated communi-ties. The suburbs are full of winners. The slums, or "ghettos" as we think of them today, are packed with losers.

Nobody says it's fair; it's just the way it is. Suburban residents work hard to maintain their lifestyles, which includes ensuring isolation from poor people. For that reason, suburban school districts are always "full" when urban districts look around for slots to place their students seeking choice options. White suburban parents know about ghettos and poor black children. They know they attend terrible schools. But white subur-banites don't believe ghetto schools are their responsibility. Frankly, they live in the suburbs to avoid any contact with them. That's what winners are allowed to do. Keeping minorities out of the neighborhood schools isn't simply a racial issue either. Just as often the battle revolves around poverty. Race and poverty are intertwined, for sure, but it isn't lost on anyone that middle-class minorities don't want to live near low-income families any more than whites do, and so affluent minorities are follow-ing their white counterparts into the suburbs.

It is therefore no mystery why you find vast ranges of wealth and poverty clumped together across and within communities. That spread exists even in generally wealthy areas, such as Orange County, Califor-nia, which is known to have some of the priciest neighborhoods in this country—neighborhoods comfortably nestled behind gated communities in sought-after, headline-grabbing places like San Juan Capistrano, San Clemente, Dana Point, Laguna Beach, and Newport Beach. The city of Irvine—home to a major university and boasting idyllic neighborhoods, scrubbed streets, trimmed lawns, low crime rates, and highly educated parents with solid incomes—is the epitome of Orange County. The city supports a new aquatic center where high school students practice water polo, and in this revered school district, the arts flourish alongside a touted program for gifted and talented students. Yet, only a few miles north stands the city of Santa Ana, which incredibly, in 2004, gained the dubious distinction of being the nation's hardest city to make ends meet (according to a Nelson A. Rockefeller Institute of Government survey of the eighty-six largest cities).[2] No water polo pool here. Actually, that is not so hard to understand, though. The city is a magnet for young, Mexican immigrants; 90 percent of the students are Hispanic, nearly all learning English. While tenement housing is a prominent part of this landscape, the economic situation may not be quite as bad as the survey suggests, because many immigrants are there illegally and working off the books in the underground economy. Still, in stark contrast with Irvine, a sizeable portion of parents are poor, have little education, and speak little English. With an enrollment of 57,700, the school district reported in 2004 that dozens of middle- and high-school classrooms were overflowing with fifty or more students, many having trouble with English. Over 700 additional students showed up even as the district cut out 260 teachers for budgetary reasons. With some students standing or sitting on the floor, teachers, as one put it, were more concerned with crowd control than teaching.[3] After a negotiated salary cut the previous year, what are the chances that those schools are attracting the best teachers? Under one-third of the teachers at Adams Elementary, as only one example, are fully accredited.

While Santa Ana may not fit the image of glistening beaches and shiny white faces that Orange County is known for, it is in fact the harbinger of the county's future, which crossed the so-called "majority-minority" threshold in 2003.[4] From 1990 to 2000, while the county as a whole was growing by 18 percent, Hispanics increased 55 percent and Asians 63 percent. Even affluent Irvine was jarred by a 167 percent increase in Asians. Predominately white in 1970, the county is now one of the most racially and ethnically diverse areas in the country. These transitions will have predictable rippling effects on education, not the least of which will be more struggling schools, finding it difficult to attract qualified teachers.

A Quick Swing through Arlington, Virginia

If you want to see differences in wealth, drive through Prince George's and Montgomery counties outside Washington, DC. Pick any area and you can figure out the relative income of its residents by learning a little bit about its neighborhoods and surrounding suburbs. A distinct hierarchy of neighborhoods and suburbs gives a visitor a sense of what the residents earn and where they stand on the social pecking order. Take the communities where one of the authors lives, for example. In Arlington, Virginia, a visitor need only drive north to south on Glebe Road, which bisects the county. North Arlington County is dominated by single-family housing, with prices that range from $500,000 to $3,000,000. Drive four miles south, and at the intersection of Glebe Road and Lee Highway the driver enters Central Arlington County. There she observes a mixture of old, single-family residences and two- and three-story garden apartment houses that extend for blocks. Then the driver comes to Ballston, the heart of the "new Arlington corridor." Here she is struck by the concentration of high-rise apartment buildings and condominiums commingling with office towers and retail outlets, upscale restaurants, and the remnants of Old Arlington's shops and cafes. Three bedroom condos sell for up to $800,000.

A short drive further south brings the driver to Glebe and Columbia Pike, the heart of South Arlington and home to the concentrated masses of the county's huge number of immigrant residents. Most live in high-rise, low- and moderately-priced apartment houses in the area, many built during World War II, to house workers in the nearby Pentagon. Over 60 percent of the students attending elementary schools in South Arlington, Abingdon, Hoffman-Boston, and Oakridge, qualify for free- and reduced-price lunch, attesting to their poverty levels. As we head back north on Glebe, back up to the Ballston area, we pick up Long Branch, Key, and Ashlawn schools. There, fewer students—between one-third and one-fourth—qualify for free and reduced lunch. Then, crossing Lee Highway, we swoop into North Arlington County to encounter Taylor, Jamestown, Nottingham, and Tuckahoe schools. In Taylor, which draws from a large area, only 7 percent of the students are on free and reduced lunches. And in Tuckahoe, Nottingham, and Jamestown the figure drops to under 4 percent. Arlington County, the smallest county in the country, is an inner-ring suburb, located directly across the Potomac River from Washington, DC. But it typifies what is going on in suburban communities everywhere: segregation of people by class and race.

The best schools are in the white suburbs. They are located there because the white people live there. And white people live there because the poor and minorities do not. If the poor and the minorities were to be relocated to the neighborhoods where the whites live, or the schools where they send their children, the whites would move. Or at a minimum they would place their children in private schools. This is the pattern. Whites by far are the most suburban of the major racial and ethnic groups. Nationwide, nearly 71 percent of whites live in suburbs. Children are more segregated than adults, apparently because the movement of white families with children to predominately white suburban enclaves has left childless whites to live in more integrated settings.[5]

A Tour of Some Long Beach, California Schools

However, of course you need not go into the suburbs to see socioeconomic differences. Some of the most dramatic social class inequities lie within the boundaries of America's large cities. Long Beach, California, close to one of the authors, is a good example. Like schools in other California districts, Long Beach schools are being challenged to raise student achievement. The problem this district faces is evident in the distressing fact that only 30 percent of third graders in California test proficient in the English-language arts, and only 35 percent are proficient in math. Nevertheless, to its credit, in 2003 this school district was declared by the Broad Foundation as America's best urban school system for raising achievement for students from all walks of life.

The Long Beach Unified School District (LBUSD) operates eighty-nine schools, including five charter schools, for over 97,000 students. The district classifies only about 17 percent of them as white.[6] Nearly half of its students are Hispanic (or Latino), and about one in five is an African-American. Two-thirds of all Long Beach students qualify for free or reduced price meals and one-third of them are English learners.

The most challenged schools serve the eastern and northern parts of the city, far from the exclusive properties along Ocean Boulevard. Ocean is a busy, picturesque thoroughfare running east and west through the city, into Naples Island and on into Orange County. Here, on the southwest side of town, in a small quadrant formed by Belmont Shore on the East, Pacific Coast Highway on the south, and 7th Street on the north stands Lowell Elementary in Belmont Heights, within a short walk from the venerable sandy beaches that line the oceanfront. Three-fourths of the 600 students attending Naples are white, and nearly all pay for their own meals. Go west a few miles across the bridge to Naples Island, and we swing past Naples Elementary, a school near the water and blessed with only 300 predominately wealthy white kids. While in the area, take a moment to weave through Naples's quaint narrow streets to observe the ribbons of canals lined with stunning homes offering expansive—and expensive—views. Some of the dads there will pay up to $300 for a round of golf at courses that cost several hundred thousand dollars to join and annual dues upwards to $15,000.

Now, go across the other bridge out of Naples to the west, and detour just a few blocks north to get to Fremont Elementary on Apian Way— that's the wide street that wraps around the bay and leads you to the Long Beach Yacht Club. This school is only slightly larger than Naples Elementary and is still predominately white, but you will see a few more students from Hispanic backgrounds, who account for about one-fifth of the enrollment. Before returning to the other part of the city, we must go a only few miles north to Gant Elementary, host to about 700 predominately white kids who pay for their own meals and, of course, come from English-speaking homes. The school, adjacent to the local branch of California State University, serves one of the most preferred communities in the city, with its tree-lined streets, huge lawns and privacy shrubs. It is home to a university's president and numerous corporate executives.

The district's enrollment may be only 17 percent white, but you would never know it from schools in the part of town we've just visited. Yet, waterfront homes, and of course the money they demand, are limited, as we quickly realize while driving on 7th Street back toward downtown. The downtown area is situated in the eastern part of the city, near the 710 freeway and the bridge leading to the shipping terminals. Traveling toward the east side of the city, we enter the northeast quadrant, located at the opposite end of an imaginary line drawn diagonally from Naples. Approaching the downtown area, we can detour north on any street— Temple, Cherry, Walnut, Atlantic, or Martin Luther King Boulevard— and watch the neighborhoods quickly deteriorate. Even a few blocks north of the refurbished commercial downtown district the run-down housing has gotten shoddier and continues to worsen as we move further from the ocean. Tiny, unpainted houses squeeze between liquor stores, or squat among pawn shops, apartment houses, and small grocery stores, many guarded by iron barricades protecting dingy windows and dilapidated doors opening out onto small cement steps.

A few blocks north of downtown in either direction we find lots of schools to choose from. Butler Elementary has over a thousand students— triple the size of Naples Elementary and more than double Fremont's enrollment. These students all qualify for free or reduced-price lunch, every one of them. Forty-three percent of the students at this school are Hispanic, all English learners. One in five is an African-American. Nearby is Lincoln Elementary, near 11th and Anaheim, with an enrollment exceeding most high schools—a whopping 1,400 students, most from Hispanic homes, and most English learners. There are also some African-American students (8 percent), but only a few white students. And not far from there is Lee Elementary, which looks very much like Butler.

But, to LBUSD's credit, the neighborhood is also home to Polytechnic High, recognized as a California distinguished school. One-third of the 4,600 students are Afro-American, one-third Asian, and the rest pretty much equally divided between Hispanics and whites. Eighty-three percent of its teachers are fully accredited, which probably says a lot about the ability of a good specialized school to attract and hold quality teachers.

Do not get the impression that all poverty schools are situated near the city's downtown. Several are in the far northern part of the city, pushing against the adjacent cities of Paramount and Downey. For example, Grant, with over 1,400 elementary students, and Harte, which enrolls 1,200, are both located in the northernmost end of the city, along with Sutter and its 1,100 students. Nearly 80 percent of the students in each of these schools qualifies for free or reduced meals, and most come from minority families and need help with English.

That pretty much sums it up. A city's schools reflect its residential socioeconomic patterns. Clearly the schools within the city of Long Beach are segregated by neighborhood. Some of the smallest—which tend to offer the best education settings—are in the few predominately white neighborhoods clustered at the western boundary. Many of the largest and most challenged are on the east side, downtown, and to the north. But, does it affect classrooms? We have too little information pertaining to Long Beach to enable us to reach a definitive conclusion. But statistics the district publishes on class size, years of teaching experience, and percentage of fully credentialed teachers in each school shed some light on the question. Some of the figures vary randomly across schools. For example, the largest and smallest class sizes, twenty-seven and twenty-one respectively, are both in the large poverty schools. However, it is telling that nearly all of the extreme cases fall into the predicable patterns. Thus, an upper-end school (Naples) has the highest percentage of fully accredited teachers (all of them), and its teachers are among those with the longest experience (eighteen years). At a low end school (Lee), only 62 percent of the teachers are fully accredited; 25 percent are on an emergency certificate. These teachers have under half the experience as those at Fremont (eight versus twenty years). The classes are relatively small, however, maybe because interns teach at the school.

Butler, a downtown school, doesn't seem to fare well, with twenty-seven students in a class and a relatively inexperienced (though hardly new) faculty with eight years of teaching experience. Thirty percent of them are not fully credentialed. In three other poverty schools we mentioned, 20 percent of the teachers are not fully credentialed; and teachers there have less than ten years of experience. By comparison, at the other end of town, Freeont, Gant, and Lowell can boast that 82–95 percent of the teachers are fully accredited and they have thirteen to twenty years of experience on average.

We have used Long Beach is as an example, not because it's particularly bad, but because both authors lived there and have a high degree of interest in its well-being. Long Beach Unified School District is considered a progressive urban school system and certainly never makes anyone's list of horror stories when urban education is discussed. Notice that teachers have been in most schools on average at least seven years, and even in the worst case, over half are fully accredited. Still the brutal facts remain. Even in this relative good district, impoverished minorities attend elementary schools that are far larger, and have fewer certified teachers, than children in the wealthier part of town. The neighborhood patterns in both Arlington County and Long Beach are typical of urban- and inner-suburban districts where both affluent and poor residents live. They reside within the same cities or suburbs, but segregate by neighborhoods and as such send their children to different schools. In the process, affluent whites end up sending their children to the kind of public schools that poor minorities living in the same school districts can only dream about.

Poverty Schools Are Here to Stay

Many city and suburban school districts in this country operate separate public schools for the affluent and for the poor. We can wring our hands and anguish about it, feel guilty and bemoan our natural tendencies. But the chasm between middle-class schools and ghetto schools is alive and well and isn't likely to change. It didn't change during our generation and it doesn't appear to be changing with our children's generation either. Parents take pride in providing for their own. They believe that if some parents commute the extra miles, make the extra mortgage payments, and work the extra hours, those parents are the ones who should reap the benefits. If other parents want the best for their children, they can do the same, right? That's the conversation around the kitchen table at our daughters' homes when their neighbors gather to talk about who should be giving back to the community. Old liberals may sometimes feel guilty, but most young couples don't seem to be afflicted with guilt. They talk about the sacrifices they are making for their children. They think of life as a big competition and they're doing what they can for their family, giving their kids a leg up on the competition by providing them a comfortable home, a supportive community, and a good school. Bottom line? They know that everybody isn't going to get a quality education, and they don't seem to care very much.

Does anyone really care? Advocates for poor minority students take as a given that most people empathize with them. We too once thought that was the case. But we're not convinced anymore. We have raised children of our own and are currently supervising from a safe distance the way our children are raising the grandchildren. Our experiences tell us that people take care of their own first. Parents want their children to excel at T-ball and soccer and ballet and tap dancing. They want them to be good students and well-liked by their teachers. And they will oppose anything that they perceive to be a threat to the quality of life they want for their children. A rental property down the street turned out to be a threat when it went to a single woman with three teenage girls. While the woman was working at night, the girls often entertained boys "from out of the neighborhood." The extra cars in and out of the neighborhood also were believed to pose a safety risk to local children on their skateboards and bicycles. Police were called and the mother eventually was evicted.

White parents who care about their children often believe this means moving to a neighborhood where people look pretty much like them and where the school children look pretty much the same. Today, that neighborhood is probably a suburb or an exurb (a suburb to other suburbs). Poverty is even creeping over into some suburbs, but on the whole, America's suburbs are the most homogeneous places to live of all in the country; the whitest and wealthiest places on the map. They have excellent schools, less crime, better stores and restaurants, stable and growing property values, and they often have lower tax rates than their urban cousins stuck with the costs of supporting the urban poor. Suburbanites not only work hard to preserve their quality of life, but also they raise a hefty bar across the avenue to ensure that undesirable features are kept at bay, including low-cost or subsidized housing, school busing, industries, and proposals to share taxes with less-wealthy school districts.

Such communities are unlikely to give up their advantages without a fight. And so far, nobody is even asking to do that. State legislators and members of Congress alike understand that nearly three-quarters of the voters today come from suburbia. Since the mid-1990s, the suburban voter increasingly has swung to the Republican Party and its "values-driven" agenda. One thing we don't hear the Republican Party saying is that the suburban voter ought to be fretting about the plight of the less-fortunate residents of inner-city ghetto. Even the Democratic Party isn't suggesting the suburban voter make room in their community or school for the poorly served child stuck in an inner-city school. To make that argument, a politician would have to convince a white voter to suffer a loss of all the rights, privileges, and entitlements he has built up for himself over time. The politician willing to make that argument might get himself elected mayor of San Francisco, but he'd be run out of nearly every other town in the country.

As a consequence of all this, public schools became more segregated in the 1990s, even more so than their surrounding neighborhoods. Black and Latino children attend high-poverty, overwhelmingly minority public schools characterized by poor test scores, less-experienced teachers, and fewer resources than most white public schools. This is no secret. Nobody disputes this fact. Collectively, we shrug and say there are winners and losers and then we do the best we can to ensure that our loved ones are provided for. It begins by ensuring they are enrolled in the best schools possible. Because everyone understands: America's public schools are not of equal quality. And the simplest test of that quality is the skin color and family income of the students who occupy the seats.

OUR SOCIETY IS BECOMING INCREASINGLY SEGREGATED

As stated, suburbs are predominately white. But, increasingly, they have been attracting minorities. The rate at which minorities are moving to the suburbs is up from 18 percent minority in 1990 to 25 percent in

2000. Over time, that trend might suggest that neighborhoods and schools are becoming more integrated. However, that is not what is happening, and it probably won't happen any time soon. Segregation by neighborhood hasn't changed much at all, because minorities moving to the suburbs go into neighborhoods already populated by folks who look a lot like them. This is particularly the case for blacks. Latinos and Asians are more likely to be in co-ethnic neighborhoods. But regardless, the whites are still pretty much left alone in their own neighborhoods. Regional variations exist, of course. Blacks are more likely to live in suburbs in Atlanta, Washington, DC, Richmond, New Orleans, and Florida cities, while Latinos are the biggest minority suburban dwellers in Miami, Los Angeles, Riverside, and San Diego. Asians constitute about 10 percent of the suburban populations around cites such as San Francisco and Oakland, Los Angeles, and Orange County, and northern New Jersey. When minorities in small numbers move into suburbs, they can generally integrate the white neighborhoods. When the growth of minority populations in suburban communities becomes substantial, segregation follows, and the likelihood of an ethnic enclave results.[7]

Basically, there are two main types of integrated neighborhoods. The first type tends to be an older suburb bordering a central city. Central Arlington County, Virginia, which we described earlier, is a good example. This type can be biracial or even multiracial. Central Arlington is multiracial, owing to the influx of Latinos and Asian immigrants, along with resident blacks and whites who have lived there for generations. Such communities also tend to be decidedly middle class, both in perspective and demographics, with higher-median incomes than the regional average. The second type of integrated community tends to be multiracial and multiclass, such as South Arlington County. This type of community is poorer, but it represents what may be a more common possibility in our majority-minority future. It is most commonly found in cities or areas with an abundance of affordable rental housing, especially areas that have become magnets for recent immigrants. We shall return to them later.

Resegregation and Demographic Compartmentalization

As America moves toward majority-minority nationhood, the demographics tell a story of even less melding and still more compartmentalization in our future. This division is occurring even as, or perhaps because, the numbers of racial minorities are exploding. The Latino population grew by 58 percent in the 1990s, emerging as our nation's largest minority group. The Asian population grew by 48 percent, blacks by 16 percent, and whites by only 6 percent. Yet there has been essentially no progress in integrating Latinos or Asians with whites in the past two decades. Instead, for the most part, existing Latino and Asian neighborhoods are simply extending. Granted, these groups are not nearly as seg-regated as blacks. But it is surprising that Latinos, the largest minority and the fastest growing demographic group, are largely being contained by, or channeled into, their own enclaves rather than becoming inte-grated.[8] This means that even though racial minorities have moved to the suburbs in vast numbers, their movement, interestingly, has had little im-pact on integration. It appears that minorities tend to move into neigh-borhoods that attract other minorities. When that happens, their white neighbors depart and soon the minorities predominate.

Growth of Segregated, White, Wealthy Communities

At the same time, as of 2000, the average white person in America lived in a neighborhood that was 71 percent white. Millions of whites, partic-ularly those with children, live in neighborhoods that are much more racially homogenous. As a consequence, says Sheryll Cashin:

Both poverty and affluence have become more concentrated over time, meaning that they occupy more tightly compact physical space than in the past. But the overall concentration of affluence in America now exceeds the concentration of poverty. Not only are the affluent coming to inhabit their own neighborhoods, but over the last five decades of the 20th century, they increasingly came to inhabit certain states and metropolitan areas. Affluent people are following the money. The growing concentration of the affluent into their own social and residential environments reinforces the advantages enjoyed by high-income families.[9]

Growth of Segregated Minority Communities

Minorities display a similar pattern. The data show that if blacks exist in large numbers, say more than 20 percent of the metropolitan popula-tion, they are likely to live in predominately black neighborhoods. No other minority is so segregated. Half of all black people live in a metro-politan region with extremely high segregation levels.[10] As we have stated previously, the typical white child attends a school that is close to 80 per-cent white. Even when white children do not attend a neighborhood school, the racial composition of the school they do attend closely matches that of their own white neighborhood.

At the other end of the scale, the average black child attends a school that is more than half black (57 percent). Latino students find on average about the same number of Latino students in their schools (over half). Asian students, while constituting only 4 percent of the elementary pop-ulation, are in schools that average 19 percent Asian. Considering that in many parts of the country there are few or no minority students, leaving other regions with large numbers of minorities, one can appreciate how some schools are heavily impacted with minority enrollments. Meanwhile, each minority group's exposure to white students is declining. In 1989–1990, a third of the average black child's schoolmates were white; that dropped to 28 percent in 1999–2000. Similar drops were experienced by Latinos (from 30 percent to 25 percent) and Asians (52 percent to 46 percent). Black and Latino students are now more separated into racially identifiable schools than at any time in the past thirty years. Nowhere are the effects of this retreat more evident than in the Southern states.

The Growth of Segregated Schools. The segregation in city schools that took place in the last decade of the twentieth century was not always deliberate. Some segregation appears related to what was going on in neighborhoods surrounding schools. But in other cities and other schools, the increase in segregation over the last part of the century was clearly the consequence of policy decisions. The policies that once worked to reduce school segregation were simply reversed in the 1990s to allow segregation to return.

As a result of this resegregation trend, seven out of ten black and Latino students attended predominately minority schools in 2000. The most extreme case is Detroit. A black child in that city is likely going to a school where 87 percent of his classmates are also black. Other cities where 80 percent or more of all the students in the schools are black are Memphis, Jackson, New Orleans, and Birmingham. Similar percentages of Latino students crowd schools in Salinas, California, Las Cruces, New Mexico, and the Texas cities of El Paso, Brownsville, McAllen, and Laredo. The latter three cities enroll nearly all Latino students. San Francisco says about half of its students are Asian. In San Jose, down the peninsula, about 40 percent of the enrollment is Asian. With declining racial integration, we are also witnessing economic segregation, which in turn is creating separate educational tracks that vary greatly in quality. White elementary school students, on average, are in schools that are 30 percent poor. Asian children are in schools that are 43 percent poor. By contrast, black and Latino elementary children are in schools where two-thirds of their classmates are poor.

The urban-suburban divide explains much of this class dichotomy. Urban schools are attended primarily by black and Latino students. The middle classes of all races have been moving to suburbs, leaving behind large numbers of minority poor students, especially in the school districts of America's largest cities. As of 2000, 85–90 percent of the students in New York, Los Angeles, Chicago, Miami-Dade, and Houston—the five largest central-city school districts—were composed predominately of minorities. In Detroit, New Orleans, and Santa Ana, 96 percent of the students were minorities, as were 95 percent in Washington, DC, 92 percent in Dallas, and 88 percent in Baltimore. Overall, the twenty-seven largest school districts, which serve almost 25 percent of all black and Latino public school students, have lost the vast majority of their white enrollment. Not surprisingly, a large percentage of the students remaining in urban school systems are poor. For example, in the five largest urban school systems, typically more than 70 percent of the students are eligible to receive free or reduced price lunches.[11]

"Separate but Equal" Starting to Sound Okay to Middle-Class Blacks

In America today, a growing frustration exists among middle-class and professional blacks. It is becoming increasingly obvious to them that integration is a one-way street. If they want it, they have to move into a white community; their children have to assimilate with white children. White adults and their children are not about to integrate into black communities. Even in the few multiracial communities where blacks, Latinos, Asians, and others live, the schools generally are pretty much devoid of white students, because they tend to be shipped off to private schools. "Consequently, for many blacks at least, integration that happens only when blacks are willing to give up their identity and accept terms that meet white comfort levels, is beginning to be too much to ask," says Cashin.[12] "Integration is simply not a priority in the way that getting ahead is. What black people now seem most ardent about is equality of opportunity." As one of her black acquaintances once put it, "Rather than wanting to integrate with whites, black people now seem more interested in having what whites have. In 2004, 'separate but equal' may not sound so bad to many a black ear because, after the civil rights revolution, it can no longer mean state-imposed segregation, and the hope is that maybe this time around, 'equal' really could mean 'equal.' "

Ironically, however, "black flight" doesn't appear to be working the way some blacks had hoped. Cashin has come to the conclusion that prejudice against black neighborhoods makes it virtually impossible for the black middle class to form havens of their own that approximate the economic opportunity benefits of a white enclave. Black communities, even affluent ones, bear burdens and costs that predominately white ones do not have to pay. Most of these costs are tied to race-laden decisions on the part of whites and predominately white institutions to avoid black communities, and the propensity (in part fueled by discriminatory attitudes) of black communities to attract low-income people. Waves of black suburbanization have been fueled by the desire to escape the social distress of "the hood," including its crime and weak schools. But, as Cashin observes, within the space of a decade, most black suburban movers will find that the social distress they sought to escape has migrated with them.[13]

"As a consequence," she writes, "predominately middle-class African American schools tend to impoverish rapidly because majority-black communities tend to attract lower-income populations over time, which in turn discourages middle-class parents from choosing such schools."[14]

THE NEED FOR QUALITY TEACHERS

What the evidence to date suggests is that we will always have low-income populations and they will congregate together in low-income neighborhoods served by schools attended by low-income students. That has become a fact of life. Perhaps social engineers with a lot more wisdom and foresight than we have, can figure out a way to bring the races together and have us all live in harmony. But educational planners are confronted with the challenge of finding ways to ensure that children who attend schools in low-income neighborhoods receive an education on a par with children who attend schools in more affluent neighborhoods.

First and foremost, of course, it is necessary to ensure that these schools are staffed with qualified teachers. An amazing number of them today are not. The task of recruiting and retaining quality teachers challenges most district superintendents. But it is particularly difficult for districts in which some or all schools serve concentrated numbers of poor and minority students.

Hard-to-Staff Schools

Administrators call them "hard-to-staff" schools. That is an understatement. Many are nearly impossible to staff with qualified teachers, largely because they pose so many challenges to the teaching staff, only some of which have to do with teaching. For example, as we have mentioned earlier, schools serving poor and minority students tend to be less well-maintained, have a higher incidence of student absenteeism, and more frequent leadership turnover. We define a hard-to-staff school as one with higher than average teacher turnover, a high percentage of teachers working with provisional or emergency certification, and significant numbers of poor children below grade level. If pushed to identify explicit criteria, we would say that a hard-to-staff school has the following characteristics:

- 50 percent or more of the students achieving below grade level
- 50 percent or more of the students eligible for free- and reduced-price lunches in elementary schools (40 percent for high schools)
- 15–18 percent annual teacher-turnover rate
- 30 percent or more of the teachers are less than fully credentialed
- 25 percent or more of the teachers holding provisional licenses are lateral entry (up to five years to earn full licensure), emergency or temporary, or are probationary.[15]

Hard-to-staff schools do not exist in every district. They predominate in the 226 large districts having at least 25,000 students. These districts, though accounting for only 1 percent of all districts in the country, enroll nearly one-third of all the nation's students. They are also the districts with the greatest concentration of poor and minority students. As Chubb observes, their sheer size and rules create obstacles to focused efforts to produce good results.[16] The medium-sized districts, between 2,500 and 25,000 students, are generally located in suburbs or small towns and educate about 50 percent of the nation's students. About 25 percent of the districts in the country (3,662) fall into this category. In most, but not all, of these districts there are fewer hard-to-staff schools than in the large districts. All other districts are small. What they lack in size they make up for in numbers—roughly 10,000. They account for about 75 percent of the nation's school districts, but they educate only about 20 percent of the total student enrollment. Because many are poor and geographically isolated, these districts often have hard-to-staff schools. But because rural districts have so few schools, the number of rural hard-to-staff schools pales in comparison to the number found in large districts.

Recruiting and retaining quality educators in hard-to-staff schools isn't a new challenge. Some districts—particularly in urban areas—have always had schools with large percentages of poor and minority students that do not attract the most qualified teachers. As we indicated above, 70 percent of the nation's black students and three-fourths of its Latino students attend schools where minority enrollment exceeds 50 percent. The notion of "concentrated" numbers has meaning when you realize that nearly 40 percent of black and Latino students attend schools in which they make up over 90 percent of the enrollment. Ninety percent of these intensely segregated minority schools are also characterized by concentrated poverty. As Harvard University's Gary Orfield puts it, "Segregated minority schools are on islands of poverty and offer vastly unequal opportunities."[17]

Approaches to Staffing Impoverished Minority Schools

To some extent school districts have tried to meet the demand for better teachers in impoverished minority schools by staffing them with teachers and administrators who come from minority backgrounds. These efforts have been assisted by the career patterns of minority teachers. African-American teachers, regardless of their initial placement, tend to move to schools with higher black enrollment shares than the schools they left.[18] But those talent pools are rapidly disappearing. Overall, African-American teachers currently comprise 13 percent of the nation's teaching force, and that figure is expected to drop to only 5 percent by

2005. Even in central cities today, minority teachers comprise only a third of the teaching faculty.[19]

Another approach that districts have used to improve the quality of poor schools is to encourage top-of-the-line teachers to work there. Interestingly, some good, veteran teachers have volunteered for the toughest assignments, which helps account for an occasional beacon of brilliance among the worst-performing schools. However, a few showcase schools do not override the stark fact that overall, teachers in impoverished minority schools tend to be among the least qualified educators on a large district's payroll. Arthur Wise, president of the National Council for the Accreditation of Teacher Education, Washington, DC, confides that one of education's dirty little secrets is the large numbers of unqualified individuals teaching, and the fact that they are disproportionately assigned to teach children of color and children from impoverished backgrounds.[20] But of course it is no secret at all, except perhaps in the sense that so few people want to acknowledge it.

Mixed and Fluctuating Priorities

So, why aren't districts doing more to place more teachers in poverty schools? The truth is that providing a first-class education to all students is not the only priority in most school districts, and often not the most pressing one. Take for example, Cleveland. It has a long history of troubled schools, many of which are old and in bad physical condition. But even as the city council was considering a bond levy for school construction, it was asking taxpayers to pay for a new convention center. The episode illustrates a disconnect that often occurs between the economic elite and the people who depend on the schools to educate their children.[21]

If urban political leaders are struggling with priorities, so are public school superintendents. They have their hands full trying to satisfy a host of community and state mandates, not to mention coping with the often petty politics that haunt school system leaders. District officials have so many legitimate priorities from which to choose, and so many reasonable approaches available to satisfy them, that poverty schools sometimes get lost in the shuffle. The awesome responsibility of putting quality staff in front of the neediest students often succumbs to easier-to-solve problems that push to the top of the priority list. Besides, remember that poverty schools are not being totally ignored. Many well-intentioned state and federal programs target them. The controversial No Child Left Behind Act signed into law in 2001, which punishes schools that get federal money for failing to meet testing goals is but one example.[22] In the meantime, policymakers are pushing a smorgasbord of fixes, including whole-school reform, smaller classes, smaller schools, standards-based reform, scientifically based reading programs, lengthening the school day, lengthening the school year, greater parental involvement, and of course, charter schools. But, underlying this potpourri, there are two constants: all parents want only the best teachers for their children, and the best teachers want to teach with qualified colleagues in settings where they can succeed with children who come to school every day from supportive families and are ready to learn.

However, a new law has suddenly sparked their attention. Almost overnight, legislators, governors, and the president of the United States decided that educators would no longer be allowed "to leave any child behind." Before superintendents could shout, "Wait a minute, that challenge is a whole lot tougher than you think," they were told, "Fix it, or lose your federal funds." But the harsh fact is that state and federal legislation alike has imposed standards on districts, mandated student testing to ensure compliance, and threatens to withdraw federal funding or to even close schools that do not meet standards after a period of time. Under the cloud of a potent buzzword, "accountability," districts are jumping at ways to meet the challenge of placing qualified teachers in every classroom. Doing less could provoke authorities to impose penalties, including more charter schools and vouchers, both of which take revenue from already financially strapped districts.

We submit that the most effective way for school systems to make sure that no child is left behind is to staff poverty schools with highly qualified teachers and strong, supportive principals. This society must find ways to do that. The No Child Left Behind law is forcing it to do so. We propose that district-operated charter schools can be a key to the answer. We shall return to that suggestion at the end of this chapter. But first, consider the magnitude of the problem and some reasons behind it.

A Shortage of Qualified Teachers for Impoverished Minority Schools

Neither the public in general, nor policy makers in particular, seem to appreciate the severity of the shortage of qualified teachers. A glance at any major daily newspaper in the country could easily convince you that public school systems are satisfied with less-than-the-best teachers. Philadelphia, for example, dominated the education news in early 2002, following the state's takeover of its school system. At least 30,000 students were being taught by teachers working under emergency certifications. Overall, the district had more than 900 apprentice teachers and an additional 367 who failed at least a portion of their state certification exam.[23] The same year in California, more than 40,000 classroom teachers were teaching on emergency permits or waivers.[24] And then you have Chicago. In a hard-hitting series, the *Chicago Sun-Times* in 2001 documented the sorry condition of teacher quality in that city's public schools. The newspaper told its readers that nearly one-fifth of Chicago's teachers tested between July 1988 and April 2001 failed at least one teacher test—3.5 times the suburban teacher failure rate. In a dozen Chicago schools, at least 40 percent of the teachers tested failed the exam at least once. The newspaper lamented that, while Chicago only employs 18 percent of the state's educators, they accounted for 85 percent of those who failed the teacher exam ten or more times.[25]

Of course, when politicians read those stories, they feel obligated to act. Consequently, after the series was published, the Illinois Board of Higher Education said that all aspiring teachers would have to pass a basic skills test before declaring their college majors, and that current education students would have to pass a test in their specialty areas before student teaching. The Board also called on state lawmakers and the Chicago School Board to reexamine a state law permitting the city school system to employ substitute teachers who have not passed any state certification exams.[26] Getting tough like that always makes policy makers feel good. And while it's probably necessary, it doesn't always produce the intended results. In 2000, the New York State Board of Education ordered the New York City Schools Chancellor Harold O. Levy to ensure that only certified teachers would be hired to fill the vacancies in ninety-four schools defined as "failing." Levy snapped back that this was unfeasible in a seller's market. Teachers, he said, will go where they want to go. In fact, more than 1,200 newly certified teachers turned down jobs in New York City because they would have been assigned to the city's lowest-performing schools.[27]

A Philadelphia principal was even more candid. "I'm lucky if I have a breathing body for every classroom, and the ones I end up with are the very bottom of the barrel. I'm not only in a bad part of the city; I'm in a school with a bad reputation in a bad part of the city."[28] Teachers with the best credentials have choices and tend to be selective about where they work. That leaves the others for the toughest jobs in the oldest facilities in the worst part of town. Take, for example, the case of two large districts in Maryland: Baltimore, the state's largest city, and Montgomery County, a large suburb outside of Washington, DC. Baltimore is a poor, overwhelmingly minority district. Montgomery is a wealthy, primarily Anglo district. In the 1996–1997 school years, both districts hung out "for hire" signs. Baltimore needed to fill 826 teaching vacancies. It received roughly 1,800 applicants. To fill its vacancies, in other words, Baltimore had to hire 46 percent of the applicants. Meanwhile, Montgomery County had 6,109 applicants for its 665 vacancies. It was able to cream the top 10 percent of the applicant pool. These stark realities can easily escape a local parent and her elected representative, who might just wonder if superintendents aren't intentionally stacking deadwood into certain classrooms.

Inequities of Teacher Placements

In a perfect universe, the best teachers in a district would be distributed evenly. That way every child, regardless of family circumstance, neighborhood, or the condition of the facility, would have an equal chance to receive topflight instruction. It's not a perfect world. The fact is, teaching talent follows wealth, and if districts want to keep their best teachers, they had better respect that fact. It's simple. The greater the concentration of wealthy and nonminority students, the more attractive the teaching post.

Experienced Teachers Avoid Poverty Schools. Experienced teachers choose the most desirable schools. A poor, minority child is much more likely than his or her more affluent Anglo neighbor to be educated in schools with the least-experienced, uncredentialed teachers. It makes a difference, too. Teachers in schools with high proportions of minority students and low-income students report lower quality teaching in their schools than do teachers in schools with fewer minorities and poor students.[29] This phenomenon occurs even in districts where nearly all the schools are filled with poor and minority students. For example, there is little variation in student backgrounds across Baltimore City Schools. For the most part, the overwhelming majority of its students are poor and minority. Yet even in this environment, experienced teachers tend to cluster in schools with the lowest minority enrollment and the highest income levels. You are more likely to find novice teachers, on the other hand, concentrated in schools with the highest percentages of minority students, the highest percentages of poor students, and the highest percentages of students achieving at an unsatisfactory level.[30] The same can be said of Philadelphia's public schools.[31]

Teachers without Full Certification Wind Up in the Worst Schools. Of course, experience isn't everything. But when inexperience is coupled with little or no preparation in the subject fields being taught, it can make a big difference. Yet, in district after district in this country the children with the greatest need to obtain the highest level of instruction are saddled with teachers with the weakest preparation and training. Again, Philadelphia resurfaces to make the point. In that city in the 1999–2000 school year, 22 percent of teachers in middle schools with the lowest poverty rates were teaching without the proper credentials.[32]

In California that same year, more than 40,000 teachers were working under emergency permits. Low-achieving schools were nearly five times as likely as high-achieving schools to employ these teachers; high-minority schools were nearly seven times as likely as low-minority schools to employ them.[33] And, remember Chicago? As we said, the vast majority of teachers there repeatedly failed the teacher competence test.[34] Moreover, among high school teachers in Chicago's Region 4, which includes schools with some of the district's highest poverty levels, 29 percent were improperly certified. But over in Region 1, which enrolls the fewest low-income students, only 15 percent had not met all their certification requirements.[35]

Rigid Salary Schedules Prevent Districts from Rewarding Teachers for Volunteering to Work in Poverty Schools. In nonunionized companies, employers can use higher wages to entice workers to take undesirable jobs. However, negotiated salary schedules prevent school districts from tying salary to supply and demand associated with different teaching positions. Consequently, they have relatively few options for rewarding teachers who take the tough jobs.

Several states have recently passed legislation that pegs teachers' pay to their students' test scores, a move that will only diminish the desirability of low-performing poverty schools. If their salaries depend on good scores, guess where teachers will go. Basing pay on improved performance may sound like a logical alternative, but the fact remains that the job will be infinitely tougher in the bottom schools. Proposals have been made to adjust improvement expectations for "levels of risk" associated with each student. This approach seems impractical because of the enormous cost and time-consuming effort that would be required to collect and analyze the necessary personal information on each student. Additional incentives are needed to steer good teachers into these schools.

REMOVING BARRIERS AND APPLYING INCENTIVES

What can be done to get better teachers into the worst schools? To answer that question, we must first identify the barriers and then we must find incentives to overcome them. First, consider some of the critical barriers to placing good teachers in troubled schools.

Barriers Related to Teacher Seniority Rights

In almost any other endeavor the solution would be to put your best people where the greatest need exists. You would replace a disappointing sales manager on the West Coast with a proven winner from the Midwest. A national retail store starts to lose money and a team of problem-solvers flies in from corporate headquarters and works with the local staff until the situation turns around. Why is it so difficult for school district officials to do the same for failing schools?

For one thing, through seniority clauses in their contracts with districts, teacher unions have done a good job ensuring that their members can choose their places of employment. Entry-level teachers may have little to no say over placement, but by the time they have three years of experience, they will be in a position to exercise some choice over their assignments. They use this discretion to position themselves in the schools with the most experienced teachers having the best credentials, the schools with the best facilities and most up-to-date curriculum and instructional programs, and probably the district's best principals. These schools just so happen to also have the highest achieving white children and the fewest minorities and poor students. Once ensconced, they can resist any attempt to move them where they don't want to work. There can be no mistake about it. They will resist going into the worst schools. Consider the reaction of the California Teachers Association president when he heard about a state commission's recommendation to shift quality teachers into low-performing schools. "If you think you have a teacher shortage now," he said, "wait until you do that and people know they have no right to teach where they . . . want to teach. . . ."[36]

Cynthia D. Prince found that principals in New York City complain that teacher-seniority rules are preventing them from assigning experienced teachers to schools and classrooms where they're most in need.[37] Yes, technically principals can veto a teacher's request, but they rarely do because of the threat of lengthy grievances filed by the offended employees.[38] In Philadelphia, before the state took over the schools in early 2002, the union contract granted teachers—not principals—the right to control teacher transfers between schools.[39]

In 1997, Chicago's top administrators reconstituted seven failing high schools. In theory, their principals were dismissed and the teachers had to reapply for their jobs. In reality, two-thirds of those same teachers were simply rehired at their old schools. An additional 174 were shuffled to other schools within the district, moves that were "widely seen as an olive branch to the powerful Chicago Teachers Union, which vociferously opposed the high school shakeups."[40] When the superintendent in Hartford, Connecticut, tried to turn around his failing schools by reconstituting some of them, union officials became angry because they hadn't been invited to contribute to his plan. Consequently, the president of the local teachers' union publicly called for the reconstitution of the school district's central office.[41]

More than one strong superintendent has worn himself down tackling teachers' unions over less contentious issues than seniority rights. Although the fight might be tempting, particularly when the issue concerns the quality of instruction being offered to a whole lot of children, savvy superintendents choose their fights carefully. After all, any bitter fight between the superintendent and the district's teachers ensures a level of animosity that pretty much guarantees a lose-lose outcome for the district. Then too, the superintendent has to consider whether the fight can be won. What will be gained by forcing reluctant teachers to accept assignments they don't want?

Hurdles Erected by Other Schools and by Districts Themselves

Teachers are not the only ones ready to protest an assignment to a low-performing school. The high-performing schools that stand to lose some of their best teachers will protest too. Their PTAs will incite parents to demand that their children must retain their seasoned teachers. Some might even suggest that the replacement teachers, rotated from the low-performing schools, will bring down achievement levels in the schools that lost their pros. Parents of children in the easy-to-staff schools tend to have the ears of school board members, and consequently what on the surface seems to be a reasonable plan of action falls victim to the political pressures from the well-connected.

In some cases, a district's own policies inhibit its ability to recruit and retain quality teachers. Several urban districts, for example, enforce "work-here, live-here" rules. Buffalo, New York, is a prime example. The problems it has encountered recruiting and retaining quality teachers have garnered considerable national media attention. A reporter uncovered a 2001 survey of education students at Buffalo State College that revealed 71 percent of the aspiring teachers either would not apply for a job in Buffalo or would give preference to other districts because of their host city's insistence that teachers live within the city boundaries.[42] Student teachers in Philadelphia expressed the same attitude toward that city's residency requirement, listing it as one of three major barriers to working in the city schools. Teachers on the job said it was the primary reason they would consider leaving the district.[43] Clearly, districts ought to give more thought to removing the roadblocks they themselves erect.

What then can districts do to overcome these barriers? At a minimum, they have to start using three types of incentives more effectively. All three incentives have been around for a long time. Each works well in isolation from the others. But for hard-to-staff schools, districts will need to apply them as a package.

Incentive 1: Attractive Work Environments with Supportive Colleagues and Leaders

The first type of incentive concerns improving the work environment. This includes, for example, the work load. Districts should look for ways to reduce the student-teacher ratio in low-performing schools. Smaller classrooms and smaller schools create desirable work settings. Beyond that, to recruit and retain quality teachers in hard-to-staff schools, teachers have to be assured they will be given an opportunity to make a difference in the lives of their students. In addition, teachers want to work with a team of competent and collegial teachers under the leadership of a supportive principal. Nearly all of the research on exceptional schools that enroll high-achieving poor and minority students indicates that the presence of high-quality faculty and an exceptional principal are important ingredients of a good school. And finally, teachers in a hard-to-staff school also need to feel safe, respected, and appreciated. They should not be expected to work in unsafe facilities, to work extraordinary hours, or to buy school supplies out of their own pockets. They should be given extra incentives for working under conditions where their salaries are tied to student performance on a state exam.

Incentive 2: Control over the Classroom

Quality teachers expect to exercise considerable control over their curriculum and instructional approach, to be involved in school decisions, and to have access to the tools to do their trade. We have discussed the importance of classroom autonomy elsewhere (see Chapter 2).

Incentive 3: Differential Salaries

Finally, perhaps the most effective way to recruit and retain quality teachers is to pay them more for working in hard-to-staff schools than they could make teaching anywhere else. Yes, we're suggesting differential pay for quality teachers willing to join and then remain in a hard-to-staff school. Sure, most local teacher unions will oppose it, as will some teachers who choose to stay in easy-to-staff schools. And the community will say it is too expensive. Still, at some point, taxpayers and their representatives will be forced to face the dilemmas associated with recruiting and retaining quality teachers. The problem is no longer the superintendent's alone if the country is really serious about leaving no child behind.

Luring teachers into hard-to-staff schools with extra compensation is not an original idea. Maryland, for example, grants teachers cash incentives of $2,000 each if they agree to work in certain low-performing schools. Philadelphia does the same for teachers willing to work in nineteen of its hardest-to-staff schools.[44] Fairfax County Schools in Virginia pays teachers who have been certified in National Board for Professional Teaching Standards a bonus for working in schools with high concentrations of poor children.[45] Connecticut offers low-interest mortgages and assistance with down payments to teachers who work in high-poverty neighborhoods, while California offers educators $7,500 down-payment loans for agreeing to work in low-performing schools for five years.[46] In the past, that state also has offered certified teachers with four or more years of experience a state income tax credit ranging from $250 to $1,500.

However, because this credit has been available to any teacher, not just those heading for positions within hard-to-staff schools, it cannot be used to attract teachers in those schools.

But while it seems reasonable that money will work, no one knows how much money it might take. All we know for sure is that when a district pays its teachers higher salaries they are less likely to leave the profession.[47] Hanushek and his colleagues maintain that teachers are more easily attracted to a school by characteristics of their students than by salary incentives. Teachers in schools serving large numbers of academically disadvantaged black or Latino students, they remind us, are looking to go to better schools as career stepping-stones.[48] However, that does not mean teachers are immune to compensation incentives. It only means that it will take a lot more differential than we might have imagined. Hanushek and his coauthors argue that to reduce the probability of teachers leaving a district, "Schools serving a high proportion of students who are academically very disadvantaged and either black or Hispanic may have to pay an additional 20, 30, or even 50 percent more in salary than those schools serving a predominantly white or Asian, academically well-prepared student body."[49]

There is a cost for leaving no child behind, and it is not cheap.

RECOMMENDATIONS FOR RECRUITING GOOD TEACHERS IN HARD-TO-STAFF SCHOOLS

The above discussions lead us to make the following recommendations:

1. Use incentives to counteract seniority rules

Seniority rules channel teachers to preferred schools, while erecting road blocks into the hard-to-staff schools. As part of union contracts, these rules obviously cannot be discarded, especially not in competitive environments in which teachers can easily leave a district or the profession. However, the effects of seniority provisions can be blunted. The salience of seniority for teachers derives from the fact that it is a substitute for other kinds of career advancement. Teaching is a flat occupation offering few opportunities for promotion, either in the form of power, authority, and status, or in the form of financial compensation. So, teachers look forward to favored assignments as substitutes—for example, transfers into more desirable schools. Existing hierarchies of preferred schools, in other words, serve as career ladders.

This suggests that it might be possible to entice teachers with types of career rewards used in occupations with steeper career ladders, rewards such as promotions to positions of greater authority and responsibility, tasks posing a high level of technical challenge, positions bestowing high honor and prestige, and the like. Specialized schools provide many of these rewards. If teachers who work in hard-to-staff schools were rewarded with recognition, compensation, perks (such as extra vacation, good parking places, safety assurances), and other benefits, some of the stigma now associated with those schools could be reduced. We believe teachers in every district would volunteer for hard-to-staff schools given the right incentives.

2. Give teachers more control over their classrooms

At least some good teachers complain about being penned in by traditional curricula and by obsolete text materials. Often, today they are being driven by standardized tests, and are sometimes expected to teach to the test rather than guiding students in how to use their minds. Probably, there are lots of teachers who would try a hard-to-staff school if it promised them a chance to spread their wings and try different approaches, such as ones associated with Essential Schools, which were discussed in a previous chapter.

3. Create smaller schools and smaller classes

Districts throughout the country are trying to figure out ways to increase the likelihood that teachers in hard-to-staff schools can make a difference in the lives of their students. Charlotte-Mecklenburg, South Carolina, has long had a reputation for innovation. It decided the way to attract and hold competent teachers in its lowest-performing schools was by reducing the student-teacher ratio in such schools.[50] Moreover, in a previous chapter we noted that a number of urban districts have already converted, or are planning to convert some large urban schools into small schools-within-schools. We recommend that more urban districts should consider that approach as a way to attract more qualified teachers into poverty schools.

4. Pay a bonus for teaching in a hard-to-staff school

This tack will work best when two keys terms have been clearly defined, namely "teacher quality" and "hard-to-staff school." Teachers will accept differential salary only if they trust that local and state officials will not use subjective definitions. At a minimum, we can probably agree that a quality teacher has three years of experience and a state credential. The criteria also might include a state test of their verbal skills and specialized knowledge. We have already given our definition of the other term. We are persuaded by arguments put forward by Ronald Ferguson of Harvard University who maintains that teacher expertise, as measured by teacher education, licensing examination scores, and experience, explains 40 percent of the difference in student achievement in reading and mathematics.[51] We also buy his argument that every dollar spent on more highly qualified teachers produces greater increases in student achievement than a dollar spent on any other single program.

Boosting the salaries of teachers in hard-to-staff schools may be nearly impossible district by district. Some simply lack the resources. Others have boards of education dominated by the teacher unions. Many districts are so politically fragile that something as bold as paying teachers more to work in tough situations would be the undoing of its sponsor. One way around some of the barriers might be to give qualified teachers in hard-to-staff schools a federal bonus or a substantial tax credit. As part of its FY 2006 budget request, the Bush Administration asked for $64.6 million to pay for existing and new voucher programs. It also included $225 million for independent charter schools. Rather than pay parents to enable their children to flee public schools, why not use these federal dollars to strengthen poverty schools by attracting and retaining quality teachers? The exact amount of the tax credit could vary, depending on the largess of the Congress, the federal or state definition of "hard-to-staff school," and the criteria to be used to identify "quality" teachers. At the very least, the idea ought to warrant a trial experiment in a wide range of communities across the country.

5. Recruit more African-Americans and Latinos into teaching

A Tennessee study found that students who had a teacher of their own race for at least one of the four years tended on average to score 3–4 percent higher on standardized tests of reading and math than peers who had teachers of different races. This racial effect, though small, was stronger among poor children, children with inexperienced teachers, and children attending segregated schools—especially African-American children.[52]

6. Hire from nontraditional teacher-preparation programs

Lockwood suggests that school superintendents ought to consider pursuing additional teachers from nontraditional preparation programs. She found that alternative certification is a reform that shows potential for widening the diversity of the teacher workforce in order to make it more representative of the national student population.[53] According to the *New York Times*, more people are seeking jobs as teachers: "The most striking increase is in applications to programs that recruit people from other careers, provide minimal training, and send the new teachers into short-staffed schools, typically in poor urban neighborhoods."[54]

7. Integrate students into schools based on their parents' income

Schools serving more affluent students tend to attract and hold the better-qualified teachers. So why not balance the school's mix of students from poor and affluent families in schools where better teachers work? The proposal isn't going to be politically popular and it won't do a thing for a large district that serves an overwhelmingly poor clientele. But it just might work in a progressive community where parents and policymakers alike can agree that poverty is a better indicator of poor academic achievement than race. La Crosse, Wisconsin and Cambridge, Massachusetts school systems have tried this approach. The Wisconsin river town first moved to economic desegregation in 1992. Its superintendent says test scores are up and children from both poor and wealthy families are benefiting. Cambridge intends to bring the number of students enrolled in a free lunch program in any given school to within 5 percent of the citywide average. In some Cambridge schools in the past, up to 88 percent of the children were in the lunch program.[55]

CONCLUSIONS

We started this chapter documenting a surge of resegregation, which is producing additional hard-to-staff impoverished minority schools in unpreferred neighborhoods. We observed that no political will exists to desegregate schools. The black middle class has no stomach for school integration and probably would just as soon have "separate and equal" facilities if they could be assured of quality schools. Impoverished minority schools, unfortunately, are likely to remain with us. As things stand now, schools serving mostly poor and minority students will continue to receive fewer resources and have fewer well-trained teachers than schools serving majority white students. Blacks and Latinos will continue to attend schools where they are the majority; and blacks will continue to make up the majority of students in ghetto schools. School districts are unable to staff many, and maybe most, of their hard-to-staff schools with a stable and overwhelming percentage of quality teachers.

If desegregation is not an answer, what is? Our discussions should have made it clear that there are no easy answers. We described barriers that school districts are facing as they try to cope with the problem of staffing impoverished poor and minority schools. However, the situation is not hopeless. We suggested some approaches that districts should consider as they try to improve hard-to-staff schools. But, you may ask, what does all of this have to do what charter schools? Plenty! Look carefully again at the above recommendations. Only some might be "doable" within some districts, but every one of them is a perfect fit for charter schools. Perhaps charters were not designed for the purpose of attacking the problems of hard-to-staff schools, but they should have been. They provide strategic ways around rigid seniority rules, flat salary schedules, and standardized curriculum approaches and materials—all of which are keeping good teachers out of bad schools. A charter provides the flexibility needed for reaching out to nontraditional training programs, and it frees a school to provide the kinds of bonuses and other incentives likely to attract qualified teachers, including more minority teachers. In addition, unlike counterpart schools within a district, district-operated charters could raise funds to support their efforts.

Sure, as we conceded at the outset, there are now some independent charters doing some of these things. However, not only are they too few and scattered, but more important, districts cannot count them to be available when and where they are most needed. Only when a district operates its own charters can it use them strategically to address getting good teachers into hard-to-staff schools, as well as other district-wide problems, including those associated with at risk students, English learners, special education students, and others. Our proposal would expand the number of charter schools in all poverty neighborhoods within a district, which in some cases would include all poverty schools or even all schools in the district. But, perhaps the biggest advantage offered by district-operated charters is that, as part of a district, they would be in a position to build on other approaches to choice that many districts already have in place, including, for example, school-based management, small schools, specialized schools, and even open enrollment. District-operated charters would not be tied to the narrow model of charters now in vogue. They would be free to piggyback on the cumulative innovations that get cut short by still newer initiatives, even as they are beginning to show promise. District-operated charters, in short, would become models for integrating a variety of promising approaches to school choice.

However, district-operated charter schools will not work effectively without federal funding. There should be federal programs to fund school district-operated charters for low-income students with the goal of providing every district in the country an opportunity to create and operate charter schools for the benefit of impoverished minorities. Federal funds are needed to pay meaningful salary differentials to teachers who work in the hard-to-teach schools serving large percentages of poor and minority children. While the unions will never vote to allow the district to pay such teachers more out of local funds, the federal government is in a better position to pay them a stipend over and above their regular pay for tackling the toughest assignment in the district. Federal programs should also extend into communities so that charter schools can attack the dual challenges of economic integration and integrating the black, the Latino, and the Asian communities. Our sense is that while whites will not participate in school integration, they will be tolerant of efforts by minority communities to improve their own schools and will support the use of federal funds to help with that effort.

NOTES

1. James Conant, *Slums and Suburbs* (New York: McGraw-Hill, 1961).

2. Tamara Chuang and Cindy Arora, "Santa Ana Sees Crushing Hardship," *Orange County Register*, 6 September 2004, L–1.

3. Fermin Leal, "Santa Ana Classrooms Overflowing," *Orange County Register*, 15 September 2004, L–1.

4. Joel Rubin, "O.C.'s Whites a Majority No Longer," *Orange County Register*, 30 September 2004, B–1, B–6.

5. The statement "Seventy-one percent of Whites Now Live in Suburbs," comes from a report by the Lewis Mumford Center for Comparative Urban and Regional Research, "The New Ethnic Enclaves in America's Suburbs," 9 July 2001.

Available at www.albany.edu/mumford/reports. The quote is from Sheryll Cashin, *The Failures of Integration: How Race and Class Are Undermining the American Dream* (New York: Public Affairs, 2004), 92.

6. Data pertaining to the Long Beach school district were derived from the LBUSD website. Available at www.lbusd.k12.ca.us/research/demographics/dataquestDL.asp.

7. Mumford, "The New Ethnic Enclave," 2001.

8. Cashin, *The Failures of Integration*, 2004, 95–96.

9. Cashin, *The Failures of Integration*, 2004, 96.

10. Edward L. Glaeser and Jacob L. Vigdor, "Racial Segregation in the 2000 Census: Promising News" (Washington, DC: Brookings Institution Center on Urban and Metropolitan Policy, 7 April 2001).

11. Lewis Mumford Center for Comparative Urban and Regional Research, "Choosing Segregation: Racial Imbalance in American Public Schools, 1990–2000," 29 March 2002. Available at www.albany.edu/mumford/reports.

12. Cashin, *The Failures of Integration*, 2004, 28.

13. Cashin, *The Failures of Integration*, 2004, 135.

14. Cashin, *The Failures of Integration*, 2004, 146.

15. The Southeast Center for Teaching Quality, *Recruiting Teachers for Hard-to-Staff Schools: Solutions for the Southeast and the Nation* (Chapel Hill, NC: Author, January, 2002).

16. John E. Chubb, "The System," in *A Primer on America's Schools*, Terry M. Moe, ed. (Stanford, CA: Hoover Institution Press, 2001), 34.

17. Darryl Fears, "Schools' Racial Isolation Growing," *Washington Post*, 18 July 2001, A–3.

18. Eric A. Hanushek, John F. Kain, and Steven G. Rivkin, *Why Public Schools Lose Teachers* (Cambridge, MA: National Bureau of Economic Research, November 2001), 14.

19. *Patterns of Excellence: Policy Perspectives on Diversity in Teaching and School Leadership* (Atlanta: Southern Education Fund, 2002).

20. Kate N. Grossman, Becky Beaupre, and Rosalind Rossi, "Poorest Kids Often Wind Up with the Weakest Teachers," *Chicago Sun-Times*, 7 September 2001.

21. Piet Van Lier, "District to Ask for Levy," *Catalyst for Cleveland Schools* (January/February 2001), 6.

22. Sanctions attached to the No Child Left Behind Law apply only to schools that receive federal money for low-income students, though all schools are expected to meet the criteria. For further description and discussion of this law, see discussion in Chapter 6 of this book on school choice and the No Child Left Behind legislation.

23. Dale Mezzacappa, "Hundreds of Teachers In City Lacked Qualifications," *Philadelphia Inquirer*, 31 January 2002.

24. Stanford Research Institute, *The Status of the Teaching Profession, 2000: An Update to the Teaching and California's Future Task Force* (Santa Cruz: The Center for the Future of Teaching and Learning, 2000).

25. Rosalind Rossi, Becky Beaupre, and Kate N. Grossman, "5,243 Illinois Teachers Failed Key Exams," *Chicago Sun-Times*, 6 September 2001.

26. Pat Milhizer, "Rules for Teachers Could Get Tougher," *Chicago Sun-Times*, 29 January 2002.

27. Abby Goodnough, "School Chief Criticizes Order," *New York Times*, 16 October 2000, A–29.

28. M. H. Spiri, *School Leadership and Reform: Case Studies of Philadelphia Principals* (Philadelphia: Consortium for Policy Research in Education, May 2000).

29. Dana Markow, *The MetLife Survey of the American Teacher: Key Elements of Quality Schools* (New York: MetLife, Inc., 2001), 10–11.

30. *Minority Achievement in Maryland: The State of the State* (Baltimore: Maryland State Department of Education, September 1998).

31. S. Watson, *Keys to Improving the Philadelphia Public Schools* (Philadelphia: Consortium for Policy Research in Education, University of Pennsylvania, May 2001).

32. B. Useem, "In Middle Schools, Teacher Shortage Reaches Crisis Levels," The Philadelphia Fund. Available at www.philaedfund.org/notebook/Teacher%20Shortage.htm.

33. Stanford Research Institute, *The Status of the Teaching Profession, 2000*.

34. R. Rossi, B. Beaupre, and K. Grossman, *Chicago Sun-Times*, 6 September 2001.

35. Grossman and others, *Chicago Sun-Times*, 7 September 2001.

36. S. Pardington, "State Education Study Irks Union," *Contra Costa Times*, 23 October 2001.

37. Cynthia D. Prince, *Changing Policies to Close the Achievement Gap* (Lanham, MD: Scarecrow Press, 2004), 84.

38. Abby Goodnough, "Strain of Fourth-Grade Tests Drives Off Veteran Teachers," *New York Times*, 14 June 2001; Goodnough, *New York Times*, 16 October 2000.

39. Spiri, *School Leadership and Reform*, 2001.

40. A. Bradley, "Confronting a Tough Issue: Teacher Tenure," *Education Week*, 11 January 1999.

41. R. Gottlieb, "Teachers' Unions Face New Tests," *Hartford Courant*, 27 October 2001.

42. P. Simon, "Residency Rule Deters Teaching Hopefuls," *Buffalo News*, 8 January 2002.

43. Useem, "In Middle Schools, Teacher Shortage Reaches Crisis Levels," 2001.

44. D. Viadero, "Philadelphia Study: Teacher Transfers Add to Educational Inequities," *Education Week*, 18 April 2001. Available at www.edweek.com/ew/ew story.cfm?slug=31Mobility.h20.

45. Jay Mathews, "Virginia to Trim Teacher Bonuses," *Washington Post*, 20 November 2001.

46. M. Galley, "For Sale: Affordable Housing for Teachers," *Education Week*, 7 March 2001.

47. Richard J. Murnane and Randall Olsen, "The Effects of Salaries and Opportunity Costs on Length of Stay in Teaching: Evidence from Michigan," *Review of Economics and Statistics* 71, 2 (May 1989), 347–352; Richard J. Murnane and Randall Olsen, "The Effects of Salaries and Opportunity Costs on Length of Stay in Teaching: Evidence From North Carolina," *Journal of Human Resources* 25, 1 (Winter 1990), 106–124.

48. Hanushek, 2001, 2–3.

49. Hanushek, 2001, 19.

50. M. Sadowski, "Closing the Gap One School at a Time," *Harvard Education Letter* (September/October 2001).

51. Ronald Ferguson, "Paying for Public Education: New Evidence on How and Why Money Matters," *Harvard Journal of Legislation* 28 (Summer 1991).

52. Thomas S. Dee, as cited by Debra Viadero, "Teachers' Race Linked to Students' Scores," *Education Week*, 19 September 2001.

53. Anne T. Lockwood, *Who Prepares Your Teachers? The Debate over Alternative Certification* (Arlington, VA: American Association of School Administrators, February 2002).

54. Abby Goodnough, "More Applicants Answer the Call for Teaching Jobs," *New York Times*, 11 February 2002.

55. Steve LeBlanc, "Cambridge to Desegregate Schools Based on Economics Rather Than Race," Associated Press, 10 January 2002.

Conclusions

School choice is more than the options produced by a diverse bunch of schools. It is a vigorous social movement driven by twisted ideologies promising more than can possibly be delivered. Focus on the ideology, and the potential victims come into bold relief. Among them are parents still pondering their choices, and others already sending their kids to a charter school or a private school, thinking they will learn more than they would in the public schools. They might be pleased. But they might be disappointed. An incalculable number of marginal choice schools using questionable fiscal and educational practices are out there, and their numbers are growing each year. More important, even the choice schools earnestly doing their best are not producing the superior test results promised. But independent, autonomous choice schools are not going away. The count grows each year, and activists are busy pushing for still more.

Parents are not the only ones being duped. Everyone has been misled by careless half-truths being advanced on behalf of choice schools. Public school teachers and principals, and many local, state, and federal-level politicians are struggling to come to grips with charter and voucher schools. And they have questions. Is it really true that the public sector cannot provide real choices? Should we encourage the students to take vouchers and run? Should the district sponsor a charter school? How can a charter school justify taking money from school districts that most kids attend? Shouldn't local taxpayers have a say over all schools using their money? There are no easy answers to such questions, but we do believe that ultimately charter schools are worth salvaging, because the model—with some improvements—holds promise.

We conclude that independence has been a counterproductive dead end, because freedom granted to choice schools has produced few of the outstanding results advocates promised. Charter schools and voucher schools are being supported with the public's money and yet are not subject to many conventional oversight controls and regulations applicable to regular schools. Charter schools were supposed to use their freedom to become more innovative, which in turn would produce dramatically better student achievement compared to regular public schools. Okay, maybe no one promised "dramatic results," but how else can a national program of the scope and fervor behind vouchers and charters be justified? Anyway, forget the word, dramatic, for a moment. There is no consistent support for the claim that autonomous choice schools are outperforming comparable regular public schools.

An added benefit, advocates said, is that the competition from voucher schools and charter schools would force regular schools to produce better results. A large body of research says this is not happening in any systematic way. Instead, we have gotten fraud and malfeasance at charter schools justified under the banner of freedom, and neglect of the most pressing needs plaguing large school districts excused by free-market gibberish. Charter schools and school vouchers have promoted competition among schools that instead should be cooperating. Overburdened school districts are being faced with debilitating rivalry from schools that too frequently are merely duplicating conventional programs and approaches, and competing for some students while ignoring others.

So, we said, since choice schools are not meeting the expectations touted by their advocates, we have a proposal that we think makes better use of local money and the $320 million in federal funds set aside for choice schools. We believe charter schools should be established and operated only by local school districts. Interested districts should be able to obtain federal money to set up an intradistrict network of specialized schools capable of meeting their most pressing challenges. These challenges include teaching English learners, special education students, and at risk impoverished students in hard-to-staff schools. Other specialized schools may be needed for programs in math and science, or the visual and performing arts, or technology. This society cannot rely on random market forces to create schools where there is greatest need. If districts operated charters as specialized schools, district officials could place them where they are most needed to address their most pressing problems.

THE ASSESSMENT QUANDARY

Perhaps no issue connected with the school-choice movement is so important and yet so confounding as how to assess the performance of different types of schools. There are two imponderable challenges here.

One is categorizing schools in a meaningful way. The other is assessing differences between so-called "types" of schools. We do not believe these issues can be resolved.

Ambiguity of Terms

Consider first the ambiguity inherent in the key terms. The recurrent blasts of hot air can cause us to forget that choice schools cannot be portrayed in simple generalities. Charter and voucher schools are only abstractions, figures of speech. Schools going by those names are all over the board. The array of approaches they are taking and the range in their quality and fiscal health precludes simple generalizations. Charter schools simply cannot be characterized as categorically better or worse than public schools. The same goes for private schools. We should all be wary of anyone who talks like that. And yet, this perplexing diversity is often disguised under neat-sounding statistics, leaving parents and policy makers with no clue about what a particular school might do for a child.

Fallacies of Statistical Studies

Just where can one get solid, credible information about charter schools or voucher programs? Not from the statistical studies of test scores we have seen, and certainly not from the acolytes' warped upbeat reports. Choice schools selectively attract certain kinds of students, who after all are in the school by choice. Because many schools will be doing worse than the average, it is hazardous for parents to pick a particular school from overblown conclusions based on statistical studies. Just remember that average scores obscure more than they reveal, because they mask typically undisclosed variation not captured even in traditional measures of standard deviation (which are seldom mentioned anyway). Think of it like this. If the average scores for a group of charter or voucher schools in the region are higher than the overall public school average, it means that at least some of them are doing better than regular schools. That is a good thing. But of course, maybe only a few charter or voucher schools are pulling their group average way up. And, in any case, because there is variation around any average, you can be certain that some charters or voucher schools are doing worse than the average public school, maybe much worse. Not so good.

What all of this means is that anyone being enticed by a good average score for charter schools in a region, or even for a district, is taking a big chance that a child will be scholastically worse off in a charter school than in the typical public school. And, even if the average is limited to students in a given school, some children will be doing better and some will be doing worse than the school average; it is still a crapshoot for a particular child. Of course, the same statements apply to public schools as well, and to be fair, public school districts are also guilty of putting out misleading averages without mentioning the downside. But that doesn't distract from the fact that even when their averages are good, many choice schools are scholastically worse, often much worse, than the typical public school—not to mention the best public schools.

We have come to believe (with respect to achievement test results anyway) that on the whole, choice schools are no better or worse than regular schools. But being only similar, or even a little better, cannot be very comforting to advocates who took taxpayers' dollars in exchange for a promise that choice schools would produce superior results. Being only similar must be even less comforting to the politicians who bought the argument. It also makes it difficult to rationalize expending the effort and money now going into independent charter schools. Perhaps now it is time to reconsider the fact that many districts have some regular schools that might work better if they had charters. A charter would free them of some regulations and enable them to hire and retain qualified teachers, allow them to offer smaller classes, and otherwise give them more discretion to meet the particular demands of students and their parents. If parents demanded more of their regular schools, instead of sending their kids away, public school districts might improve.

The Testing Dilemma

Choice promoters probably got their movement off on the wrong foot by promising to demonstrate dramatic improvements in academic achievement in exchange for freedom from regular-school governance and the rules and regulations that accompany it. Initially, the choice proponents had things going their way. Parents unhappy with traditional public schools found the alternatives attractive. Consequently, the only evaluation of the choice schools was whether they could attract students and hold them once enrolled. As long as they had waiting lists of students, met state fire and safety codes, and stayed fiscally solvent, these choice schools were considered educationally successful. But then the rules changed dramatically when charter schools and schools that accepted federal vouchers were caught up in the No Child Left Behind legislation. Suddenly, they too had to test their students and show adequate yearly progress. And the choice schools had to use the same tests that the states developed for all the other public schools in the states. Now for the first time, policy makers, legislators, and parents alike could make comparisons across schools, something that hadn't been possible before. The hoax of the superiority of choice schools was about to be exposed.

Now, choice advocates are attempting to wiggle out of the promise they made about boosting achievement by using the same excuses they complained public schools always use. You know: the fallacies of tests, too many troubled, nonwhite pupils, bad statistical analyses, and the like. We described a way to make more sense out of test scores—namely, by focusing on the variance and changes in the rankings of schools (or students) that started at the top, middle, and bottom of the distribution. Too often a few good schools can pull the average up or down, often at the expense of students in other parts of the distribution. Everyone deserves to know that, but no one bothers to tell us.

It is unfortunate that test scores are such a deceptively simple way to assess schools. For, while they have their place, tests now seem to be swamping other forms of assessment, with some dire consequences. They tap only a small part of the knowledge universe, and they do not accurately measure a student's ability to apply the information. It is especially disconcerting that some schools are eliminating electives and that so little attention is being given to other critical or enriching subjects, such as history, current events, and the arts. Moreover, tests may not fit the special missions of some schools, such as schools serving emotionally disturbed children or drop outs. Some schools are focusing on culture, language, good behavior, or values and are not even trying to improve test scores in the usual sense. We described the Coalition of Essential Schools, for example, which goes about teaching kids to think in unconventional ways not driven by test scores. Many at risk schools in all three sectors also have to worry about things in addition to average test scores. In pushing for and then accepting test scores as the benchmark of success or failure, spokespersons for choice steered the movement into a quagmire of confusion.

If it's all about test scores, states can lower standards to make their scores look better, and teachers can figure out what is on the test and how to teach to it. Beyond all of that, as we have said, when individual scores get aggregated to the soaring heights of schools, programs, and states, they become meaningless. Comparing the standardized test scores of Johnny and Billie in a classroom at Adams Elementary makes statistical sense. Comparing the test scores of charter schools with regular schools throughout Arizona is nonsense, if not fraudulent. Rather than perpetuating the nation's warped obsession with tests, researchers should be cautioning the public about the pitfalls and calling for alternative forms of assessment. But until they arrive, we are stuck with standardized tests to measure academic achievement.

School Choice and the No Child Left Behind Legislation

The No Child Left Behind (NCLB) act of 2001 requires all students to pass tests in their subjects by 2014. At the same time, it institutionalizes the right of parents with a child in a school with faltering test scores to choose another regular school or charter school. NCLB stipulates that every school must make "adequate yearly progress," as measured by a specified percentage of students in each student subgroup passing tests in English and math. Subgroups include special-education students and English learners, and all subgroups must meet their goals. High schools must graduate a minimum percentage of students.

How It Works. If a school falls short in the same subject for two consecutive years, parents must be notified in a timely manner that they can request to transfer to a higher-performing school, including a charter school, with transportation paid by the failing school. If the school does not improve by year 2, it must provide private tutoring. In year 3, it must take "corrective action" (for example, replace the staff, add curriculum, or hire an outside expert). In year 4, it must plan for restructuring the following year. In year 5, the school must restructure in one of five ways: become a charter school, replace all or most staff (including the principal), hire an "outside entity" to manage the school, submit to a state takeover, or carry out other major restructuring. Sanctions apply only to schools that receive federal money for low-income students, though all schools are expected to meet criteria.

Positive Effects. In some respects the law is having a favorable impact. To avoid the federal dog house, school districts all over the country are scrambling to find better ways to teach students how to do better on the tests. Testing is forcing teachers to focus on students who have been held back by personal handicaps and failed policies. Parents are being informed about school performance (although sometimes too late to take action), and at least parents have hope that things will improve for their children. Now, at least someone seems to care about low-performing schools, and people who count are asking the right questions.

Many schools appear to be trying. They are hiring consultants, switching teachers between grades and subjects, providing longer days, after-school tutoring, and summer school, hiring "instructional leaders" as principals, breaking down large schools into smaller ones, and eliminating electives to make more time for math, language, and reading instruction. In some cases, principals and other administrators are substituting for classroom teachers to give them time to work individually with children. Since the legislation applies to charters, it gives parents with children in charter schools a basis of comparison—a protection that does not apply to parents with children in private schools. That is all to the good, and supporters of the law say it might be enough to produce positive results, especially as schools eventually discover effective solutions.

The Downside of NCLB. However, teachers frequently complain that test results are not being realistically adjusted to account for the enormous differences in students' circumstances. In addition, in schools with high student turnover, different individuals are being tested from year to year. And, don't be taken in by some of the empty promises. For one thing, the option of selecting another regular or charter school is too often unavailable, because most of the better schools are already filled to capacity. Moreover, transferring to an existing charter school is no panacea. Remember that many existing charter schools are no better, and some (especially the ones with available seats) are worse, than other nearby schools. Nor is there any guarantee that sponsors will use test scores to close down low-performing charters. Anyway, converting a school to an independent charter can be a long and cumbersome process, which may or may not be a solution, depending on what the school does with its charter. What about firing all the teachers? That step is certain to rile the unions and entail divisive negotiations. The threat of a state takeover of low-performing schools seems idle, at least for now, because most states are not interested in or equipped for this responsibility. The hope that "outside entities" will step up to turn around failing schools is another vacuous alternative, considering that there are so few of these entities; some of them are already facing severe criticism.

Other Criticisms. So, it comes down either to restructuring or expanding the number of schools from which parents can choose. Our proposal to encourage school districts to start and operate their own charter schools in poverty neighborhoods would do the latter. However, both restructuring and starting more charter schools for low-income children will take more money. How are faltering schools supposed to restructure if they have to dip into existing funds to provide new programs, transportation, tutoring, summer school, and the other options mentioned? Similarly, creating more small schools and charter schools will require more resources. Without more money, many educators are finding it hard to take the NCLB mandates seriously. Barbara Kerr, president of the California Teachers Association, calls it the "No Child Left Untested" Law, which she and other critics call a joke without additional funding.[1] However, it is worth mentioning that some dollars are being funneled into lagging poverty schools, and the prospect is that more are coming. In April 2005, the NEA sued to prohibit the Department of Education from withholding money when a state must spend more than Washington sends.

Perhaps the most ominous criticism of NCLB is being advanced by Gerald W. Bracey, who maintains that the ulterior motive behind the legislation was to create still another excuse for overhauling and privatizing the public schools.[2] He sees mandatory testing as a free-market scheme to once again document the widespread failures of public education. The goals of this act, says Bracey, were set unrealistically high, and then underfunded, to ensure that a large number of schools will fail, and thus add more fuel to a half century of criticism that has been used to justify vouchers and charters. Some of his arguments are echoed by Berliner and Biddle.[3]

While this position deserves to be taken seriously, we should point out that Bracey, as well as Berliner and Biddle, and other revisionists are pushing the theme that, on the whole, America's schools are pretty good right now—certainly not as bad as the critics maintain. We are concerned that (although it is not their intent) their cogent defense of schools can be interpreted to mean that schools do not need fixing. As we have argued throughout these pages, many schools do need to be overhauled, especially schools attended by poor minorities. So, while we are not in favor of sly methods designed exclusively for the purpose of attacking schools, we are hopeful that universal testing will at least have two positive benefits. Not only will testing show that particular populations of students are being seriously shortchanged, but it will also prod schools to do something about it for a change. Therefore, our already expressed reservations about testing aside, we are ready to concede that it may be better to test neglected children than to ignore them—not because tests are flawless, but because they can illuminate problems that school districts will then be compelled to fix.

In any case, notwithstanding the criticisms, NCLB has become a fact of life that everyone will have learn to live with. We can only hope that the public will be able to weigh the advantages and disadvantages so that this law will not become another hoax.

A Broken Contract

Where are we now? We say that the bargain didn't make sense at the start, and it makes even less sense now—after a decade-and-a-half of sputtering blather and disappointing results. So, give it up! What bargain? The deal was to give choice schools unbridled autonomy so they could show up low-performing public schools. They haven't been able to demonstrate that for all the reasons we have explained, and they won't be able to do it. So, take back the independence. No, don't scrap charter schools or even school vouchers necessarily. Just put them back under the control of public school districts where they can be useful. This would take some doing, we know. But then choice schools could make contributions to the public schools where help is desperately needed, and without being under an unrealistic testing cloud. They could actually specialize in doing things that make a difference, as opposed to some of the routine and haphazard approaches that are now being passed off as innovation. If schools could demonstrate that they are tackling significant problems, they would not have to make unrealistic claims about test-score superiority, and they might be excused for being only average. That is no excuse for persistent low performance, of course. But being average isn't bad when a school is up against tough odds.

THE THORNY MOTIVATION QUESTION

Parents are thinking about more than academic achievement when they select a choice school. To many people, the word choice is a euphemism for demanding a public subsidy. Many parents want to use tax dollars to support their religion or to get away from other people's children. One letter writer in a local paper put it bluntly, "It is not the government's money being spent on education but our own. Those of us who believe that the public school system is not doing its job have a right both to avoid it and to refuse to support it with our tax money." We are delighted to learn that a citizen can retrieve his tax dollars. Following this logic, any citizen could stop contributing taxes to build highways and use that money to fix up the old homestead driveway. And, best of all, that citizen would not have to chip in to pay for expenses connected with building more roads for people who don't have them. Everyone else would have to do that.

However, we certainly do not believe that every parent looking for options wants a handout or is being driven by racial prejudice. Some simply want a small school, or one with teachers who will listen to them. Others are willing to go anywhere just to get their children away from harmful drug- and violence-ridden schools, or the hundreds of hard-to-staff schools forced to put unprepared teachers in classrooms serving the neediest children. Deciding whether a school meets such requirements is probably easier than assessing its scholastic merits. Yet, ironically, even though choice schools often measure up well on these and similar qualities, choice proponents seldom mention them—probably because they are locked on to standardized test scores that give them political credibility. Consequently, we don't hear much about the outstanding teachers that often gravitate to small choice schools looking for an opportunity to spread their wings and try things they aren't encouraged to do in larger regular schools.

COMPETITION IS NOT WORKING

Instead, choice backers like to talk about competition. They proudly tell us that choice schools aggressively compete with regular schools, grabbing students and their allocated tax dollars. This of course probably leaves the public school on the losing end worse off. But not to worry, say choice advocates. Competition from outside a district will be a wake-up call that, through some mysterious force, will compel lagging schools to turn around. Notice that competition drains district resources, but we have to pretend that it is the individual schools that will be hurt. Some researchers even claim to have documented the powers of competition. Hoxby says it only takes a few choice schools to turn around a big district, like Detroit for example (see Chapter 2). But don't ask her how that could happen, because she doesn't really know. She speculates a lot. But the reality is that the explanations haven't concerned her enough to test them out. So, she drones on about the statistical significance of simple correlations. It never occurred to her, and some others touting the merits of competition, that if public schools are improving, it is coming on the heels of a decade of reforms encased in lots of threatening rhetoric about what will happen to school districts that don't shape up. Charters and vouchers are not occurring in a vacuum after all. Usually, districts that sponsor school choice programs also are trying out other initiatives.

We think that improvement probably has more to do with a district's overall attack than the presence of a few charter schools or vouchers. Again, choice proponents have only hurt themselves with the rapturous applause. By jumping to take credit where it may not be due, they lose credibility. We suppose that charter schools and vouchers do deserve some thanks for waking up lethargic school districts. But let's not go overboard here. Choice schools are a small part of wide-ranging reform movements sweeping through many school districts.

BUREAUCRACY IN PERSPECTIVE

The so-called school bureaucracy always comes up in discussions of school choice. But what is it? The word bureaucracy is a fiction, not a research construct. It doesn't really exist, certainly not in any one form. Even choice proponents see it in different ways. First, in one breath they tell us the educational bureaucracy is so impervious to reform that parents will never find choices unless they abandon regular public schools. In the second breath they are proclaiming that a small handful of choice schools are forcing school districts to turn around. Which is it? Is the bureaucracy ossified or is it malleable?

Of course the question is nonsense. There is no single bureaucracy. School districts, a critical part of the bureaucracy, take many forms. Some have been responsive and innovative. No doubt others are being choked by stacks of state and local education codes. Their plight is exactly why we were hopeful about charter schools when they appeared over a decade ago, and why we have devoted so much time following their evolution. But choking and overwhelmed or not, these school districts will not be revolutionized by a few thousand foundering schools—schools designed to help a select few children escape public schools. That idea always seemed to us implausible. Even if, under ideal conditions, competition could nudge some schools, there is no convincing argument that the unpredictable outcome of competition beats the straightforward approach of targeting resources to make specific changes happen.

The distressing irony is that the charter-school system turns out to be no better than the public school bureaucracy critics are so fond of bashing. Maybe it's worse. For, as we have seen, many charter schools have been involved in corruption, hundreds of others have failed because of sloppy planning and second-rate leadership, and others are struggling to stay afloat. Too many are valiantly coping with inadequate facilities, unable to offer credulous students even the minimum enrichment courses, extracurricular programs, and basic services provided by most public school districts. Charters have been billed as fierce competitors, but then whine when districts don't rush to bail them out. And, then there is the haunting absence of evidence that they boost learning in any predictable way. Sure, there are many good charter schools; some are exemplary. But there are many good public schools. It is time to rethink the whole concept of independence from the mythical bureaucracy.

The simple fact is that the public cannot rely on indecisive competition from autonomous charters and vouchers to reform the bureaucracy, nor to bail out public education. The answers have to come from within the public sector. We, like many others, once thought that changing school districts is a hopeless dream. But the outlook is improving. A host of reforms over the past decade has produced shock waves to which many school districts are responding. Responding slowly perhaps, but there are now countless good schools in the public sector from which parents can choose. Many were discussed at length in this book—thousands of magnet schools; hundreds of schools providing alternative, vocational, and special education; countless schools using school-based management; a growing number of large schools going small; and innovative school networks like a small number of model Pilot Schools in Boston and over a thousand schools associated with the Coalition of Essential Schools. And, there are many, many more reforms out there providing good choices within the public sector. Every year, government agencies and foundations identify exemplary blue-ribbon public schools. There is even hope for impoverished schools, if this society wakes up to the severity of the problem and begins supporting federally funded, district-operated charter schools capable of recruiting good teachers.

Oh, sure, all of these approaches have faults—very serious ones in some cases. But, as we said at the outset, if choice aficionados were really concerned about the welfare of children, they would stop spewing their bubbly appeals for piecemeal free-market approaches that can only undermine public schools, and devote more energy to the task of fixing the promising developments already out there in the public schools that most children attend. Infusing charter schools with the experience and promise of small schools initiatives, school-based management, magnets, and specialized alternative schools will produce an imposing reform.

THE HEAVY COSTS OF INDEPENDENCE

While approximately thirteen states require charter schools to operate within local school districts, the truth is that the vast majority of the charter schools (88 percent) are located in other states that require or allow them to become fully or partially legally independent from districts. Moreover, even some schools operating within districts have managed to achieve far-reaching levels of freedom. But the doctrine of unbridled autonomy, which is somehow supposed to produce meaningful reform, is proving to be deadend. On the one hand, there is no evidence that independence causes schools to be better in any respect. On this point, we have reviewed a number of sources throughout this book that suggest many schools do not use their independence, and when they do, their innovations often resemble what can be found in at least some districts. Some schools are hiding under the cloak of innovation to create risky and hollow programs. On the other hand, charters are paying a high cost for this unrestrained freedom. On their own, often with only minimal funding and marginal facilities, they typically are in no position to offer the services and special programs available in most district schools, such as heath professionals, speech therapists, and language specialists, or even school lunch programs. They typically do not provide enrichment activities in the arts and music, and many do not offer a full range of extracurricular programs and activities, ranging from clubs to athletics. Moreover, they cannot call on districts for technical assistance in areas like planning, scheduling, and computer hardware, or for administrative support with routine chores, such as filling out reports and enrolling students. And, there is little evidence that charter schools have had much influence on district schools, at least in part because of their isolation from, and competition with, other district schools. We are not saying that most charters are afflicted with all of these shortcomings. But the pervasiveness of the most serious disorders, ranging from fraud to mismanagement, is itself enough to create serious misgivings about the would-be advantages of independence.

On the contrary, instead of promoting the creative potential of charter schools, independence has stifled it. Instead of acting as models of innovation and beacons of reform, many charter schools are struggling to stay afloat, and at least some are facing the prospect of bankruptcy. Instead of benefiting from charter schools as they expected, many students are being shortchanged with watered down versions of comprehensive school programs, sitting in substandard buildings and facilities, being taught by inexperienced and sometimes poorly trained teachers, who though sometimes blessed with a creative flair, are themselves isolated from better prepared and more experienced colleagues.

Nevertheless, we have not given up on charter schools. What we object to is the unrealistic rhetoric driving this frenzied movement and the absurd idea that choice schools need to be independent. Charter schools, we believe, would be stronger as part of districts, and conversely as members of districts, they would be in a position to strategically serve and influence other district schools. District-operated charters offer several advantages not available to independent charters.

ADVANTAGES OF DISTRICT-OPERATED CHARTER SCHOOLS

Chapter 5 addressed at length this question: How can charter schools be used more effectively to improve racially and economically segregated schools? We live in a society divided into culturally isolated enclaves, snugly nested behind social and physical barriers erected to keep impoverished minorities at a safe distance from middle-income neighborhoods and upper-class elites. Even as we look the other way, media outlets are spreading the distressing news that, after decades of self-deceptive desegregation programs, communities and schools are more segregated than ever before. School districts can look forward only to still more hard-to-staff impoverished schools overflowing with low-achieving children, schools staffed by relatively inexperienced, uncredentialed teachers who have been inadvertently sucked into the void left by competent teachers fleeing to the more desirable schools.

What can school districts do? Certainly, it has become imperative for this society to come up with better ways to place good teachers in low-performing, hard-to-staff schools. That will not be easy, and it is not only because school bureaucracies don't care. It is, in large part, because paralyzing union policies prevent school districts from either paying bonuses or controlling teacher transfers. We maintain that charter schools that have been started and operated by school districts themselves, supported with federal funds, and designed for impoverished students, would provide a way around some of these problems. District-operated charters would provide district officials with the flexibility needed to control salaries and transfers. The concept of differentiated staffing, based on career ladders that are tied to graduated salaries, has been around for half a century. The time has come to use it to staff low-achieving schools.

Autonomous schools can't do it. Districts are in the best position to assess when and where such charters would be most helpful, and they have authority to convert or start up a critical mass of such schools in strategic locations without relying on unpredictable, random market forces. As district schools, these charters would be eligible for technical help and other district resources. The federal government should reallocate some of the money now earmarked for programs that only encourage parents looking for choices to flee public schools, and target this money to school districts struggling to improve public schools. If a charter school can provide a small stable environment with good, dedicated teachers, low-achieving minorities will certainly be better off than they are now, and they will eventually show progress in a variety of ways.

Of course, district-operated charter schools will be more effective in some districts than in others, but they can play a positive role in all districts. Many districts are sincerely struggling to improve schools that serve at risk children, but find that their hands are tied. These are places with good superintendents, backed up by strong boards committed to the education of all the children under their jurisdictions. For such districts, charter-school legislation becomes a tool for moving the bureaucracy in ways that benefit those most in need of its services.

What about the districts that are not concerned about helping children who are at risk? We don't know how many districts fall into this category, but obviously, there are some. A few defiant districts have been placed under court order to improve, often without much success. Some others simply have other priorities. We know that charters cannot turn these districts around overnight. In fact, there is a distinct danger that such districts will co-opt charter schools, subvert their intent, and dilute or undermine the potentials we have described. Nevertheless, even in districts that do not care about the condition of schools serving poor minorities, charters can be helpful. They will help because co-optation is a two-way street. That is, there are always pockets of administrators, teachers, and parents eager to gain control of district-operated charters and use them as wedges to push for district-wide changes.

IMPROVING UPON THE CHARTER SCHOOL MODEL

So, let's look past the empty promises and turn our attention to the choice schools themselves. The charter-school model does lay out some exemplary features. Okay, it has not produced heroic schools, but they need not be heroic. They need only provide sound approaches to school improvement. So, what are their good points? Well, charters are small and decentralized; the best ones have attracted exceptional, if sometimes inexperienced teachers, and a relatively few are even specialized. That sounds good. But wait a minute! These features—small, decentralized, specialized, recruiting good teachers—aren't they already embedded in reforms that have been around a long time? Are they really unique to the charter model? Decentralized schools have been operating for decades. Come to think of it, so have small schools, magnets, and specialized schools.

Maybe the real power of the charter model is that it combines many promising reforms. An integrated, comprehensive model: now that is no small feat. But it is disappointing that we seldom hear choice devotees talking about the pioneering reforms that have enriched the charter-school model. It is also unfortunate, and that isn't just because we believe in giving credit where it is due. The blatant disregard for other reforms, such as smallness, decentralization, and specialization, is unfortunate because the rich experience associated with them has so much to offer charter schools. These other reforms are, after all, pinnacles of the charter-school model, and therefore, they contain elements and insights that should improve charter schools if incorporated in the charter model. Once again, the advocates' zeal has gotten in the way. Charters have been promoted as a unique, stand-alone invention without peers. Read the tons of books and articles on choice and see if there is any acknowledgement of the other parallel reforms, reforms not only similar to charter schools, but also that sometimes have produced better results. Charters are pioneers mainly in the sense that they have tried, not always successfully to be sure, to put it all together. If they are to be made stronger, it will only occur by drawing more sustenance from their roots.

Weighing Components of the Charter School Model

We have tried to put charters and vouchers in a larger context of other, closely related approaches to choice, approaches that embody features bound to strengthen any choice model. Each approach has something to offer—open enrollment, magnets, school-based management, small schools, and the others discussed throughout the book. Indeed, charter schools are so intertwined with precursor paradigms that it is almost impossible to separate their effects from the charter model. Take size, for example. Charter schools tend to be small. But so do stand-alone small schools without charters. Ironically, the latter have consistently produced better results than charters. So, shall we attribute the outcomes being reported for charter schools to the charter, or to its *size*? If it is size, then forget all the prattle about charter schools. Redirect charter school resources to the task of creating more small public schools. But release them from some of the stifling rules and give teachers real authority over their classrooms.

The same reasoning applies to schools using school-based management. How much of what charters are doing is due to their independence from districts and how much can be attributed to decentralization, which certainly does not require charter status? Create more decentralized schools within traditional school districts. And this time, give them real authority. And, let's not forget teacher recruitment. How do you disentangle the effects of charter school programs from the kinds of teachers they attract? Often they are relatively inexperienced and uncredentialed. But sometimes they are also dedicated and creative, innovative people. Every district has a share of venturesome, creative or just plain highly competent teachers who are ready to jump at an opportunity to develop their own teaching styles. They sometimes seem to end up in charter schools. But it isn't necessary to create charters or vouchers to welcome creative teachers. Just give them a supportive environment within public school districts, with some control over their classrooms, and let them go. Choice fans, and their doting Department of Education admirers, should be directing their efforts and resources toward expanding these approaches alongside charter schools.

Features of Other Models Worth Incorporating into the Charter School Model

But while it is often difficult to sort out the relative influence of the several reform strategies that charters have adopted, extracting from each model still other components that charters have not yet adopted is a simpler task. Our analysis revealed several features of these other reforms that could significantly improve charter schools. We will mention again only a few of the most important ones. Of course, the main one, as we are fond of repeating, is to place charter schools within school districts. There is no need, and no excuse, for creating a marginal state for them independent of regular public schools. Most classroom-based charter schools do not appear to be doing anything different from regular public schools. Moreover, the cases where they are doing something innovative are not helping the public school districts; instead the charter schools are taking public funds away from them. Not only are charter schools isolated into themselves, but they compete with the very school districts that could benefit from what they are trying to do. So, we say, put charters back into public districts where they can make a difference.

Our second recommendation is more sweeping. We believe all choice schools should be required to assist school districts with the special demands being made of them, which are outstripping the capacity of regular schools. This proposal has two components. One is focused goals compatible with a district's needs. What choice schools offer now depends on the whims and preferences of their creators, whereas we maintain their goals and contributions should be explicitly directed to meeting the challenges facing school districts today. This proposal doesn't make these schools subservient to district administrators, because once approved, they could be given autonomy—as exemplified in Boston's Pilot Schools and hundreds of specialized schools, magnets, and site-managed schools across the country. The other component is membership in a network of schools. The network feature has fewer precedents, but there are some forerunners. For example, Boston's Pilot Schools have formed a mutual aid network, and, of course, The Coalition of Essential Schools operates as a huge national network. But neither of those examples simultaneously requires schools in the network to establish specializations.

That observation, however, brings up another recommendation culled from the other models. Successful SBM schools focus on a concrete set of standards that clearly identify the knowledge and skills students are expected to acquire. Schools participating in the Coalition of Essential Schools are also urged to identify skills that students are expected to acquire. A student's progress is then dependent on ability to publicly demonstrate those skills. For the most part, charter schools as a group are more preoccupied with flexing their autonomy than with establishing concrete objectives. Consequently, the movement has been directionless in this respect. As a condition for a charter, a school should be required to include proof of consensus on focused scholastic goals and describe ways to demonstrate progress.

The fourth recommendation is based on the impressive level of professional development provided for schools associated with the Coalition of Essential Schools and for some magnet schools. While many charter schools have solid professional development programs, they are not a central feature of the model. But extensive professional development should be a requirement.

Our fifth recommendation is that all choice schools need more funding. The task of starting up an unconventional school can be staggering. While charter schools get some of the money allocated to students, most do not capture overhead needed for buildings and the like. If charter schools were to be run by districts, they also should be able to raise funds and then submit to audits. Beyond fund-raising, district-operated charter schools should be eligible for specially formulated grants from the federal government to support existing programs, and for the broader purpose of developing more robust models.

Toward an Integrated Approach to School Choice

This brings us to our final recommendation, which is undeniably the most far-reaching. We recommend that the multitude choice reforms now operating as separate programs, and supported from distinct funding sources, should be combined into one comprehensive choice model. This society is incurring incalculable opportunity costs because of the excessive attention being given to charters and vouchers, as though they are the only approaches to choice worth considering. These two programs have become flash points blinding the country to other and perhaps more effective approaches that would provide better choices within the public school system. In particular, we are recommending that the morass of reforms in play should be merged into one model. Many existing reforms are relatively effective, and some are promising. However, no one option is sufficient. In combination, on the other hand, they would produce the most effective choice model imaginable. In a previous chapter, we touched briefly on the advantages of creating an integrated model from open enrollment, small schools, school-based management, and the Coalition of Essential Schools, each of which represents a different aspect of the social system that should be included. But the scope of our proposal goes well beyond them. Just consider a few programs from the scores available right now:

- Charter schools
- School voucher programs
- Specialized schools
- Magnet schools
- Alternative schools
- Decentralization managed through school-site councils
- Smaller high schools initiatives (now funded at $330 million at the federal level plus more from private parties)
- The Coalition of Essential Schools
- Before- and after-school interventions
- Money set-asides for tutoring and literacy programs (now funded at $50 million)
- Curricula enrichment (now funded at $10 million)
- Nongraded instruction
- Individualized instruction
- Knowledge Is Power Program for low-income children
- Merit pay and team teaching
- Myriad local responses to the ubiquitous "No Child Left Behind" legislation

A truly robust model of choice could be created by combining the most promising aspects of each approach into a cohesive and unified model. The shame is that, although the federal government has a heavy hand in most of these initiatives, each operates independently at the school level. The government could create unified grants that incorporate a variety of funding sources, so that each district is not saddled with the chore of administering various grants separately. If these separate programs were combined through a synchronized plan for reforming schools from top to bottom, schools would demonstrate dramatic improvements. Beyond existing programs, some of the nine trillion dollars that has been spent on the war on poverty could be effectively used by schools for dropout prevention and work-study programs, and for district-operated charter schools.

Given the momentum and enthusiasm for charter schools and voucher programs, these two choice approaches are ideal vehicles for mobilizing a coordinated attack on the crushing challenges menacing the nation's schools. They could serve as models for how to tackle massive reform. Dozens of professional associations and organizations—ranging from networks for specialized schools and magnet schools to national and regional research associations, to vocational and performing arts program administrators, to teachers' unions—could work with state and federal legislatures and government agencies to see that more coordination and concentrated funding among the multitude existing education reform programs.

A LOOK AT THE FUTURE

Years after charter schools were first introduced, we are left to ponder what they might have become had they been conceived and introduced by prominent insiders within the education community rather than by steadfast critics of public education. It seems to us that charter schools are exactly what school superintendents and their boards were looking for, with their flexible staffing, relaxed rules, opportunities to raise money, and some federal funding. Instead, educators viewed them at best as irritants, and at worst as threats to the very foundation of public education. To understand what happened, we need look no further than California, where in 1993 an initiative had been introduced that would give parents a $2,600 voucher enabling them to send their children to private and public schools of their choice. Growing numbers of immigrants were swamping previously all-white schools, and critics were on overtime, blasting away at state regulations and an overstuffed bureaucracy that they imagined was suffocating public education. Voucher opponents wanted the state legislature to do something to head off this roaring free-market movement. Up stepped Gary Hart, a former schoolteacher turned state legislator, who introduced legislation that would make California the second state in the nation that had authorized charter schools.

The ploy worked. The voucher initiative went down in defeat, in no small part because charter schools offered to give parents a choice without going the private school route. However, the downside was that charter schools became tainted as a voucher-like alternative, the lesser of two evils. Moreover, it was a hollow victory for avid charter-school believers who saw them as a positive alternative to the existing structure of public schools. The law was after all a compromise between, on the one hand, quelling private school zealots, and on the other, not upsetting the educational establishment too much. Consequently, the original California legislation allowed no more than 100 charter schools, and there is still a cap today (although it is larger). Moreover, in California, charter schools could be authorized only by school boards, which would have final say in approving all applications. And, then, of course, there was no money set aside for them, which clinched it: they would be highly dependent on school districts for any resources they might decide to cough up. To top off their plight, the California Department of Education initiated a program that would give money for another program, a new initiative called Demonstration Restructuring in Public Education. Districts looking to reform their schools had a clear choice: go for a charter school that they would have to somehow fund themselves, or pick one of their regular schools and walk away with a major state grant. No wonder there were only forty-eight charter school applications the first year.

This early association with the voucher movement in bellwether California left an indelible mark on charter schools. Charter school legislation slowly extended across the states, being billed as a voucher-like alternative to entrenched public school bureaucracies. As it spread, the very word "charter" evoked fear and loathing among educational interest groups. Just as public school teachers, administrators, and school boards had united against vouchers, so they all stood shoulder to shoulder against its poorly understood cousin. If they had understood it better, they might have embraced it. We were impressed with the first wave of schools. As noted in other chapters, Corwin and his colleague, Marcella R. Dianda, were among the first researchers to study both the California law and the early adopters in that state, and by 1995 they had observed some charter schools that were doing innovative things which could be useful to school districts if and when they ever decided to support these schools.

In February 1995, Schneider delivered a keynote address to the annual meeting of the executive directors and presidents of the school administrator associations from across the nation, which was hosted by the American Association of School Administrators (AASA). He talked about the rapid spread of charter schools across the country. He, of course, was well aware that this audience was dead set against them. He chose that topic because he was convinced that public-school administrators could use charters to their own advantage. The message was simple: fighting charter legislation would only drive charters out of the public school arena into the hands of public-school critics; so quit fighting charters and co-opt them. Charters would work best under the auspices of local school boards rather than under the control of unknown and unregulated citizens and private companies. Schneider reasoned that a law like California's, which allowed only school boards to authorize them, is better than one like Arizona's, which bypasses the public schools and empowers just about anyone to create and operate a charter school. If you fight charter-school legislation and lose, he warned, you will have more Arizona laws. But if you co-opt the movement now, you can have charters that your own superintendents can create, take credit for, and use for their own reform goals. The audience did not like the speech, but some recognized that they needed to hear it. A short time later, Schneider and Dianda wrote an article advising school superintendents to use charter schools to reform failing and troubled public schools.[4] The AASA subsequently officially supported the concept that school boards should create their own charter schools.

That all happened a decade ago. What is taking so long for districts to adopt charter schools? What has turned educators against them is the fact that they have been so staunchly supported by voucher proponents and antipublic school fanatics who have linked charters to their free-market cause. It wasn't always so. Early charter school advocate, Ted Kolderie, along with his Minnesota colleagues, worked for change within the existing system.[5] But it was not long before free-market advocates took over the charter-school movement. Chester E. Finn, Jr., one of the loudest and most persistent critics of the public school establishment, early on embraced charter schools as a potential alternative to all that he deemed wrong with the public K–12 system. In his words, "Despite bushels of effort, barrels of good intentions, and billions of dollars, most reform efforts have yielded meager dividends."[6] And then, he found charter schools. Finally, a reform Finn could get enthusiastic about. He saw charter schools as a hybrid, with some similarities to regular schools, and possessing some attributes of private schools, but possessing differences from both. He said they would "reinvent public education." Writing with two others, Finn explained Charters this way:

We think of charters as "reinventing public education." Traditionally, Americans have defined a public school as any school run by the government, managed by a superintendent and school board, staffed by public employees, and operated within a public-sector bureaucracy. "Public school" in this familiar sense is not very different from "public library," "public park," or "public housing project."

Now consider a different definition: a public school is any school that is open to the public, paid for by the public, and accountable to public authorities for its results. So long as it satisfies those three criteria, it is a pubic school. It need not be run by government. Indeed, it does not matter—for purposes of its "publicness"—who runs it, how it is staffed, or what its students do between 9 and 10 a.m. on Tuesdays.

Charter schools are part of a bigger idea: reinvented public education in which elected and appointed officials play a strategic rather than a functional role. Charter schools mean public support of schooling without governmental provision of schools.[7]

Finn's rhetoric enrages the educational establishment, but it pales to their dislike for the party line gushing from the Center for Education Reform, another nonstop public-school basher. As we mentioned elsewhere, when the AFT published data questioning the performance of charter schools, the Center for Education Reform swung into action. Its president wrote editorials and letters to newspapers nationwide questioning the

AFT's credibility and defending charters. Her organization then issued a press release that reaffirmed the allegiance of six national organizations to charter schools.[8]

Charter schools have now become the darlings of politicians on both sides of the aisle. Why not? Charter schools offer reform on the cheap. They have given state and federal legislators a chance to throw around all the buzz words: reform, restructuring, flexibility, parental choice, innovative curriculum, small class sizes, parental involvement, less bureaucracy, greater freedom from rules and regulations. And, best of all, they have not needed to spend a whole lot of taxpayers' dollars. At the state level, most legislators simply said charters would be paid for by transferring the dollars with the student. That doesn't cost anybody much of anything. Members of congress have come through with some start-up money, but in the scope of things, it is a drop in the bucket, and it gets them lots of goodwill.

This atmosphere of blistering rhetoric, political opportunity, bargain-basement costs, and the voucher-like image of charter schools, explains why those school superintendents whom Schneider tried to reach in 1995 turned a deaf and hostile ear. Administrators who did venture to support the idea of operating their own charters frequently found themselves outsiders in their own districts, uninvited to meetings of district principals, left off district mailings, and generally ignored by the central office when assistance was requested. Schneider concluded in a presentation made in 2000 that superintendents were not rushing to take advantage of charter-school laws to convert some of their schools into charter schools.[9] Only three states out of the twenty-seven with charter-school laws had more than fifteen preexisting charter schools. Only in Georgia did nearly all charters convert from existing public schools, because that is the only option the state law allows. California started out only allowing charters to be authorized by local school boards, and so it isn't surprising that many of its earliest charters were converted, preexisting public schools. In Arizona, which allows almost anybody to form a charter, only 10 percent of the charter schools were converted from existing public schools. In addition, it is important to note that many if not most converted schools are very autonomous within their districts and have not necessarily been started by individuals closely affiliated with school district administrators. In fact, many converted schools have a hostile relationship with the district. They are not what we mean when we refer to district-planned and district-operated choice schools.

But the small number of converted public schools doesn't mean that the idea of a local superintendent creating charters out of his regular schools is a bad idea. Had the antipublic school forces not grabbed up charter schools for themselves and enlisted them in their fight against the establishment, it is entirely possible that school districts would have eagerly embraced the movement on their own. It certainly doesn't make it easy for a superintendent to convince a board or a teachers' union to consider converting a school to a charter when the first thing that comes to their mind is "vouchers." But maybe the tide is turning. Around the country, school systems are slowly starting to experiment with the possibilities of converting some of their schools to charter schools operated under the purview of the school board. Some superintendents, and many principals and teachers are intrigued with the flexibility that charter legislation offers. They also are responding to the pressures from parents for different kinds of schools, services, and programs.

In many districts, charters are beginning to fill a much-needed niche. For example, in 2003, a well-regarded and high-performing high school in Los Angeles announced that it wanted to become a charter. Granada Hills High School had one of the best academic records in the district, but it was bothered by cuts in district funding and hampered by rules that limited its own fund-raising abilities. Frankly, it thought it could do better on its own for its 3,800 students. Initially, Los Angeles Unified Schools Superintendent Roy Romer was hesitant to endorse the conversion, thinking it might start a trend. But a year later, he had no objections when the high school sought and obtained a five-year extension to its charter.[10] Other superintendents have been a little more cagey. Some have created schools with many attributes of charter schools, but still governed as regular schools. In Prince William County Schools in Virginia, for example, two specialty schools were designated for children whose parents demanded high involvement in their education. So high, in fact, that part of the requirement to get into these schools is a parental contract that spells out the number of hours each week that the parents will spend baking cookies, chaperoning field trips, running workshops, or helping out in the office. In addition, the children wear uniforms and adhere to strict behavioral standards. The two schools are so popular that the county school system must hold a lottery to select their students.[11]

And, in 1996, former New York City Schools Chancellor Rudy Crew removed ten chronically low-performing schools from the administrative control of their subdistricts and created a new geographically noncontiguous one just for them. His takeover of his own district schools, akin to a state takeover, was rather unprecedented. We would go so far as to suggest it was akin to creating ten similar charter schools within his district. Eventually, fifty-eight elementary and middle schools were removed from the New York City Schools' community subdistricts and placed in Crew's Chancellor's District, where they operated from 1996–2003. All were among the city's lowest-performing schools. Once in the Chancellor's District, a new, highly structured improvement plan was imposed on them, along with more staff. Class size was reduced, instructional time was increased, the school day was lengthened, and the school calendar was extended by one week. After-school programs were implemented and students had access to tutoring in small-group settings. The time devoted to literacy instruction in the elementary schools was three times more intensive than spent on math. Teachers had access onsite to four staff developers as well as an onsite teacher center staffed by a teacher specialist who offered coaching and professional development. Assessments were designed to provide regular feedback to classroom teachers. All this cost more money, of course, and these schools got it. As a result, it was possible to pay certified teachers a 15 percent pay raise for additional work. Teachers who didn't work out were quickly transferred elsewhere and replaced with quality instructors. Independent analysis of the effort showed that these schools were successful in raising student literacy; in fact, even when controlling for the effects of teacher resources and per-student expenditures, the Chancellor's District's schools still performed significantly better in reading than the comparison schools.[12]

Crew eventually left New York Public Schools; a new mayor got elected; and with the turnover, new policies replaced existing ones. The Chancellor's District was dissolved and the schools within it returned to the regular district. The point is, for awhile, a public school superintendent had been able to demonstrate that schools, operating within the structure of an existing school system, could function as charter schools, and had the freedom to experiment and to break new ground.

Others will try. They should be encouraged. They should know that charter schools are not just another form of vouchers. They are, in fact, a school administrator's best antidote against vouchers. However, no one will ever fully appreciate what charter schools can become as long as the hoaxes being pawned off by school-choice hucksters are allowed to go unchallenged. Not while choice proponents get away with their misleading claims based on trivial and wildly inconsistent testing results. Not while we are all being duped by a host of false and misleading promises of reform, spearheaded by frail schools barely able to offer basic programs of instruction. Not with convoluted arguments about the healthy effects of aimless rivalry. Not while anyone believes that school bureaucracies are incapable of reform. And certainly not while the newspaper editorial writers are flooding the country with propaganda insisting that the charter-school model is without precedent and that effective choice schools can flourish only outside the traditional public sector.

The challenge before us now is to turn the tables on the hoaxsters and direct the tide of enthusiasm for charters and vouchers into an occasion for systematically restructuring the division of labor among schools in both the public and private sectors. The spirit of choice can be used to promote cooperation among schools in the public sector—and perhaps as well, between the public and private sectors. Let's hope this nation will eventually transform charter school and voucher programs into fully integrated models that incorporate the best of existing reforms. Ultimately, let us look forward to the day when charter and voucher schools will function within the public sector as district-planned and district-operated schools, having predetermined missions capable of meeting the actual needs of our children.

NOTES

1. Duke Helfand, " 'House Parties' Draw Attention to Education," *Los Angeles Times,* September 26, 2004, B–1, B–14.

2. Gerald W. Bracey, "The 12th Bracey Report on the Condition of Public Education," *Phi Delta Kappan,* 84, 2002. See also Bracey's book, *The War against America's Public Schools: Privatizing Schools, Commercializing Education* (New York: Allyn & Bacon, 2002).

3. David C. Berliner and Bruce J. Biddle, *The Manufactured Crisis: Myths, Fraud, and the Attack on America's Public Schools* (Reading MA: Addison-Wesley, 1995).

4. J. Schneider and M. Dianda, "Coping with Charters," *The School Administrator* 52, 7 (August 1995), 20–23.

5. Ted Kolderie, *Beyond Choice to New Public Schools: Withdrawing the Exclusive Franchise in Public Education* (Washington, DC: Progressive Policy Institute, 1990).

6. C. E. Finn, Jr., B. V. Manno, and G. Vanourek, *Charter Schools in Action: Renewing Public Education* (Princeton: Princeton University Press, 2000), 14.

7. Finn, Manno, and Vanourek, *Charter Schools in Action,* 15–16.

8. "Charter Leaders Dismiss AFT Report: Teachers' Union Deliberately Skews Data against Charters," 16 July 2004. Unpublished news release. Center for Education Reform. www.edreform.com. The six organizations that signed onto the release attacking the AFT study were the Black Educators for Educational Options; the Center for Education Reform; the Education Leaders Council; the National Association of Charter School Authorizers; the Charter Friends National Network; and the Thomas B. Fordham Foundation, the organization headed up by Chester E. Finn, Jr.

9. J. Schneider, "Learning from Public Schools That Became Charter Schools," presentation to the American Association of School Administrators' National Conference on Education, San Francisco, 3 March 2000.

10. Joetta L. Sack, "With Little Debate, L.A. High School Gets New Charter," *Education Week,* 19 May 2004, 5.

11. C. A. Samuels, "Parents' Mandatory Volunteering," *Washington Post,* 22 October 2004, B–1, B–4.

12. P. Phoenix, D. Siegel, A. Zaltsman, and N. Fruchter, *Virtual District: A Retrospective Evaluation of the Chancellor's District, 1996–2003* (New York: Institute for Education and Social Policy, Steinhardt School of Education, New York University, June 2004), 27.

Selected Bibliography

RESEARCH AND ANALYSES OF CHOICE PROGRAMS

Alexander, Karl L., and Larry J. Griffin. "School District Effects on Academic Achievement: Reconsideration." *American Sociological Review* 41 (1976): 144–152.

Alexander, Karl L., and A. M. Pallas. "School Sector and Cognitive Performance: When Is a Little a Little?" *Sociology of Education* (April 1985): 115–128.

American Federation of Teachers. *Do Charter Schools Measure Up? The Charter School Experiment after Ten Years*. Washington, DC: The American Federation of Teachers, 2002.

Anderson, Lee, Nancy Adelman, Kara Finnigan, Lynyonne Cotton, Mary Beth Donnelly, and Tiffany Price. *A Decade of Public Charter Schools: Evaluation of the Public Charter Schools Program, 2000–2001*. Evaluation Report. Stanford, CA: SRI International, 2002.

Armor, David L., and Brett M. Peiser. "Interdistrict Choice in Massachusetts." In Paul E. Peterson and Bryan C. Hassel, eds. *Learning from School Choice*. Washington, DC: Brookings Institution, 1998.

Arsen, David, D. Plank, and G. Sykes. *School Choice Policies in Michigan: The Rules Matter*. East Lansing: Michigan State University, 1999.

Becker, Henry J., Kathryn Nakagawa, and Ronald G. Corwin. "Parent Involvement Contracts in California's Charter Schools: Strategy for Educational Improvement or Method of Exculsion?" *Teachers College Record* 98 (Spring 1997): 511–536.

Bulkley, Katrina. "Educational Performance and Charter School Authorizers: The Accountability Bind." *Educational Policy Analysis Archives* 9 (1 October 2001): 1–35.

Camilli, Gregory. "Texas Gains on NAEP: Points of Light?" *Education Policy Analysis Archives* 8 (21 August 2000). Available at http://epaa.asu.edu/epaa/v8n42.html.

Cobb, C., and G. Glass. "Ethnic Segregation in Arizona Charter Schools." *Education Policy Analysis Archives* 7 (1999) [Electronic journal]. Available at http://epaa.asu.edu/epaa/v7n1/.

Coleman, James S., T. Hoffer, and S. Kilgore. *High School Achievement: Public, Catholic and Private Schools Compared.* New York: Basic Books, 1982.

Cookson, Peter W., and Kristina Berger. *Expect Miracles: Charter Schools and the Politics of Hope and Despair.* Boulder, CO: Westview Press, 2002.

Corwin, Ronald G., and Henry J. Becker. "Parent Involvement: How Do Parents Participate?" In Ronald G. Corwin and John F. Flaherty, eds. *Freedom and Innovation in California's Charter Schools.* Los Alamitos, CA: Southwest Regional Laboratory/WestEd, 1995.

Corwin, Ronald G., Lisa Carlos, Bart Lagomarsino, and Roger Scott. *From Paper to Practice: Challenges Facing a California Charter School.* San Francisco: WestEd, 1996.

Corwin, Ronald G., and Marcella R. Dianda. "What Can We Really Expect from Large-Scale Voucher Programs?" *Phi Delta Kappan* 75 (September 1993): 68–74.

Corwin, Ronald G., and John F. Flaherty, eds. *Freedom and Innovation in California's Charter Schools.* Los Alamitos, CA: Southwest Regional Laboratory/WestEd, 1995.

Corwin, Ronald G., and Krishnan Namboodiri. "Have Test Scores and Individuals Been Overemphasized in the Research on Schools?" In Ronald G. Corwin, ed. *Research in the Sociology of Education and Socialization* 8. Greenwich, CT: JAI Press, 1989: 141–176.

Dianda, Marcella R., and Ronald G. Corwin. *Vision and Reality: A First-Year Look at California's Charter Schools.* Los Alamitos, CA: Southwest Regional Laboratory, 1994.

Dianda, Marcella R., and Ronald G. Corwin. *What a Voucher Could Buy: A Survey of California's Private Schools.* Los Alamitos, CA: Southwest Regional Laboratory, February 1993.

Fiore, Lessley, and M. Harwell. *Integration of Other Research Findings with Charter Schools and Students with Disabilities: A National Study.* Washington, DC: Office of Educational Research and Improvement, U.S. Department of Education, 2000.

Fuhrman, S. H., and R. F. Elmore. *Ruling Out Rules: Evolution and Deregulation in State Educational Policy.* New Brunswick, NJ: The Eagleton Institute of Politics, Rutgers University, 1995.

Good, Thomas L., and Jennifer S. Braden. *Charting a New Course: Fact and Fiction About Charter Schools.* Alexandria, VA: National School Boards Association, 2000.

Heise, Michael, and James E. Ryan. "The Political Economy of School Choice." *Yale Law Journal* 111, 8 (2002). Available at www.questia.com/PM.qst?a=o&d=5000773591.

Henig, J. R., M. Moser, T. T. Holyoke, and N. Laciereno-Paquet. *Making a Choice, Making a Difference? An Evaluation of Charter Schools in the District of Columbia.* Washington, DC: Center for Washington Area Studies, George Washington University, 1999.

Henig, Jeffrey R. *Rethinking School Choice: Limits of the Market Metaphor*. Princeton, NJ: Princeton University Press, 1994.

Hill, Paul, R. Lake, and others. *A Study of Charter School Accountability*. Seattle, WA: Center on Reinventing Public Education, University of Washington, 2001.

Hill, Paul, L. Pierce, and J. Guthrie. *Reinventing Public Education: How Contracting Can Transform America's Schools*. Chicago: University of Chicago Press, 1997.

Horn, J., and G. Miron. *Evaluation of the Michigan Charter School Initiative*. Kalamazoo, MI: Western Michigan University, July 2000.

Hoxby, Caroline M. *Achievement in Charter Schools and Regular Public Schools in the United States: Understanding the Differences*. Cambridge, MA: Harvard University and National Bureau of Economic Research, December 2004.

Izu, Jo Ann, Lisa Carlos, Kyo Yamashiro, Lawrence Pincus, Naida Tushnet, and Priscilla Wohlstetter. *Los Angeles Unified School District Charter School Evaluation*. San Francisco: WestEd, 1998.

Lockwood, Anne T. *The Charter School Decade*. Scarecrow Press, 2004.

The Manhattan Institute. *What Do We Know About Vouchers and Charter Schools? Separating the Rhetoric from the Reality*. Research Brief. Santa Monica, CA: RAND, 2000.

Manno, Brunno, Chester E. Finn, Jr., Louann A. Bierlein, and Gregg Vanourek. "How Charter Schools Are Different: Lessons and Implications from a National Study." *Phi Delta Kappan* 79 (1998). Available at www.pdkintl.org/kappan/karticle.htm.

Maranto, Robert, Scott Milliman, Frederick Hess, and April Gresham, eds. *School Choice in the Real World: Lessons from Arizona Charter Schools*. Boulder, CO: Westview Press, 1999.

Miron, Gary, and Christopher Nelson. *Student Academic Achievement in Charter Schools: What We Know and Why We Know So Little*. Occasional Paper No. 41, National Center for the Study of Privatization in Education. New York: Teachers College, Columbia University, December 2001.

Mulholland, L. *Arizona Charter School Progress Evaluation*. Phoenix, AZ: Morrison Institute for Public Policy, Arizona State University, 1999.

Namboodiri, Krishnan, Ronald G. Corwin, and Linda Dorsten. "Analyzing Distributions in School Effects Research: An Empirical Illustration." *Sociology of Education* 66 (October 1993): 278–294.

National Center for Education Statistics. *Trends in the Use of School Choice: 1993 to 1999*. Washington, DC: U.S. Department of Education, 2000.

National Center for Educational Statistics. *Private Schools in the United States: A Statistical Profile*. Washington, DC: U.S. Department of Education, 1993–1994 through 1999–2000. http://nces.ed.gov/pubs/ps/97459008.asp.

National Center for Educational Statistics websites: http://nces.ed.gov/surveys and http://nces.ed.gov/pubsearch/majorpubs and http://nces.ed.gov/pubsearch/pubsinfo.asp?.

Rhim, G.L.M., and M. J. McLaughlin. "Charter Schools and Special Education: Balancing Disparate Visions." Paper presented at the 2nd Annual National Charter School Conference, Denver, CO, March 1999.

Schneider, Joe. "Five Prevailing Charter Types." *The School Administrator* (August 1999). Web Edition. Available at www.asa.org/publications/sa/1999_08/schneider.htm.

Simon, Christopher A., and Nicholas P. Lovrich. "Private School Enrollment and Public School Performance: Assessing the Effects of Competition upon Public School Student Achievement in Washington State." *Policy Studies Journal* 24, 4 (1996). Available at www.questia.com/PM.qst?.

Stout, Robert T., and Gregg A. Garn. "Nothing New: Curricula in Arizona Charter Schools." In Robert Maranto, Scott Milliman, Frederick Hess, and April Gresham, eds. *School Choice in the Real World: Lessons from Arizona Charter Schools.* Boulder, CO: Westview Press, 1999: 159–172.

Teske, Paul M., Jack Schneider, and Sara Buckley. *Does Charter School Competition Improve Traditional Public Schools?* Center for Civic Innovation, June 2000. Available at www.manhattan-institute.org/html/cr_10.htm.

Texas Education Agency. *Texas Open-Enrollment Charter Schools Fifth-Year Evaluation: Executive Summary.* Austin, TX: School of Urban and Public Affairs, University of Texas at Arlington, July 2002.

Wells, Amy Stuart. "Charter School Reform in California: Does It Meet Expectations?" *Phi Delta Kappan* 80 (1998). Available at www.pdkintl.org/kappan/karticle.htm.

Zimmer, Ron, Richard Buddin, Derrick Chau, and others. *Charter School Operations and Performance: Evidence from California.* Santa Monica, CA: Rand Corp., 2003.

PROS AND CONS OF SCHOOL CHOICE

Allen, Jeanne, and Melanie Loony. *Charter School Closures: The Opportunity for Accountability.* Washington, DC: Center for Educational Reform, October 2002.

American Federation of Teachers. "Private School Vouchers: The Track Record." Center on Privatization (March 2001). Available at www.aft.org/pubsreports.

Apple, Michael, and Gerald W. Bracey. *Vouchers.* Milwaukee, WI: Center for Education Research, Analysis, and Innovation, University of Wisconsin, 24 January 2001.

Berliner, David C., and Bruce J. Biddle. *The Manufactured Crisis: Myths, Fraud, and the Attack on America's Public Schools.* Reading: Addison-Wesley, 1995.

Bogden, James. "Cyber Schools." *National Association of State Boards of Education Journal* (Autumn 2003): 33–37.

Bracey, Gerald W. *The War Against America's Schools: Privatizing Schools, Commercializing Education.* New York: Allyn & Bacon, 2002.

California Legislative Analyst's Office. *Executive Summary: Assessing California's Charter Schools.* Sacramento, CA: Author, January 2004.

California Teachers Association. "Freedom Invites Abuse in Some Schools." *California Educator* 8 (October 2003).

Chubb, John E., and Terry M. Moe. *Politics, Markets, and America's Schools.* Washington, DC: Brookings Institution, 1990.

Coons, J. E., and S. D. Sugarman. *Education by Choice: The Case for Family Control.* Berkeley, CA: Berkeley University Press, 1978.

Corwin, Ronald G. *Private Schools and Parental Choice.* Los Alamitos, CA: Southwest Regional Laboratory, 1993.

Danner, John, and J. C. Bowman. "The Promise and Peril of Charter Schools." [Electronic journal]. Available at www.educationreview.homestead.com/ 2003charterschools.html.

Finn, Chester E., Jr., Bruno V. Manno, and Gregg Vanourek. *Renewing Public Education.* Princeton, NJ: Princeton University Press, 2000.

Friedman, Milton. *Capitalism and Freedom.* Chapter VI, "The Role of Government in Education." Chicago: University of Chicago Press, 1962.

Greene, Jay P. "The Surprising Consensus on School Choice." *Public Interest* 144 (Summer 2001). Available at www.thepublicinterest.com.

Greene, Jay P., Marcus A. Winters, and Greg Forster. "Apples to Apples: An Evaluation of Charter Schools Serving General Student Populations." CCI Working Paper. New York: The Manhattan Institute for Policy Research, July 2003.

Hirschman, Albert O. *Exit, Voice, and Loyalty: Responses to Decline in Firms, Organizations, and States.* Cambridge, MA: Harvard University Press, 1970.

Hoxby, Caroline M. "How School Choice Affects the Achievement of *Public* School Students." Paper prepared for Koret Task Force meeting on 20–21 September. Stanford, CA: Hoover Institution, 2001.

Johnson, Tammy, Libero Della Piana, and Phyllida Burlingame. *Vouchers: A Trap, Not a Choice.* Oakland, CA: Applied Research Center, October 2000.

Kolderie, Ted. *Beyond Choice to New Public Schools: Withdrawing the Exclusive Franchise in Public Education.* Washington, DC: Progressive Policy Institute, 1990.

Lake, R. J., and M. D. Millot. *Autonomy, Accountability, and the Values of Public Education.* Seattle, WA: Institute for Public Policy and Management, University of Washington/RAND, 1996.

Levin, Henry M. "The Theory of Choice Applied to Education." In W. Clune and J. Witte, eds. *Choice and Control in American Education, Vol. II: The Practice of Choice, Decentralization, and School Restructuring.* New York: Falmer Press, 1990: 285–318.

Meier, Kenneth J., and Kevin B. Smith. "School Choice: Panacea or Pandora's Box?" *Phi Delta Kappan* 77 (1995). Available at www.pdkintl.org/kappan/ karticle.htm.

Merrifield, John. *The School Choice Wars.* Lanham, MD: Scarecrow Press, 2001.

Minar, Barbara. "Vouchers and the False Promise of Academic Achievement." *Rethinking Schools Online* (February 2002). Available at www.rethinking schools.org/special_reports/voucher_report/index.shtml.

Nathan, J. *Charter Schools: Creating Hope and Opportunity for American Education.* San Francisco: Josey-Bass, 1996.

National Education Association. "Charter Schools: A Look at Accountability" (April 1998). Available at www.nea.org/charter/accnt98.html.

Newmark, C. M. "Another Look at Whether Private Schools Influence Public School Quality: Comment." *Public Choice* 82 (1995): 365–373.

Patterson, Jennifer C. "The Truth About School Choice." *Curriculum Administrator* 37 (January 2001). Available at www.questia.com/PM.qst?.

Pearson, Judith. *Myths of Educational Choice.* Westport, CT: Praeger Publishers, 1993.

Peterson, Paul E., and William G. Howell. "Latest Results from the New York City Voucher Experiment." Paper presented to the Association of Public Policy and Management, Washington, DC, November 2003.

Richard, Alan. "States' Work on Charters Still Unfolding." *Education Week* (20 March 2002). [Electronic journal]. Available at www.pacharterschools.com/nation_news/jan_mar-02.html.

Rothstein, Richard. "Charter Conundrum." *The American Prospect* 9: 1 July–1 August 1998. Available at www.prospect.org/print/V9/39/rothstein-r.html.

Smith, Kevin B., and Kenneth J. Meier. *The Case against School Choice: Politics, Markets, and Fools.* Armonk, NY: M. E. Sharpe, 1995.

Witte, J. F. *The Market Approach to Education: An Analysis of America's First Voucher Program.* Princeton, NJ: Princeton University Press, 1999.

Witte, J. F. "Who Benefits from the Milwaukee Choice Program?" In Bruce Fuller and Richard F. Elmore, eds. *Who Chooses? Who Loses? Culture, Institutions, and the Unequal Effects of School Choice.* New York: Teachers College Press, 1996: 118–137.

ALTERNATIVE FORMS OF SCHOOL CHOICE

Alves, Michael J., Ralph Edwards, and Charles V. Willie. *Student Diversity, Choice and School Improvement.* Westport, CT: Bergin & Garvey, 2002.

Center for Collaborative Education. "How Are the Boston Pilot Schools Faring? An Analysis of Students, Demographics, Engagement, and Performance." Boston Pilot Schools Network website, 2002. Available at www.ccebos.org/pilotschools/schools.html.

Chandler, Louis. *Traditional Schools, Progressive Schools: Do Parents Have a Choice?* Washington, DC: The Thomas B. Fordham Institute, 1999.

Coalition of Essential Schools website, "About CES" and "About the Small Schools Project." Available at www.essentialschools.org.

Education Commission of the States. "School-Based Management." *The Progress of Education Reform 1999–2001* 2, 5 (April–May 2001).

Hannaway, Jane, and Martin Carnoy, eds. *Decentralization and School Improvement: Can We Fulfill the Promise?* San Francisco: Jossey-Bass Publishers, 1993.

Holloway, John H. "The Promise and Pitfalls Site-Based Management." *Educational Leadership* 57, 7 (April 2000). Available at www.ascd.org/cms/objectlib/ascdframeset/index.cfm.

Leithwood, K., and T. Menzies. "Forms and Effects of School-Based Management: A Review." *Educational Policy* 12, 3 (1998): 325–346.

Magnet Schools of America website, "About MSA." Available at www.magnet.edu/about.htm.

McPartland, James, and others. "Improving Climate and Achievement in a Troubled Urban High School through the Talent Development Model." *Journal of Education for Students Placed at Risk* 3, 4 (1998): 337–361.

Nexus Interview with Ted Sizer. "How Schools Fail Kids and How They Could Be Better" (June 2002). Available at www.essentialschools.org.

SCHOOL SIZE

Ayers, W., G. Bracey, and G. Smith. *The Ultimate Education Reform? Make Schools Smaller.* Milwaukee, WI: Center for Education Research, Analysis, and Innovation, University of Wisconsin-Milwaukee, 2000.

Conant, James B. *A Nation at Risk: The Imperative for Educational Reform.* Washington, DC: National Commission on Excellence in Education, 1983.

Cotton, K. *New Small Learning Communities: Findings from Recent Literature.* Portland, OR: Northwest Regional Educational Laboratory, December 2001.

Darling-Hammond, Linda, J. Ancess, and Ort S. Wichterle. "Reinventing High School: Outcomes of the Coalition Campus Schools Project." *American Educational Research Journal* 39, 3 (Fall 2002): 639–673.

Howley, C. M., and R. Bickel. *School Size, Poverty, and Student Achievement.* Washington, DC: The Rural School and Community Trust, 2002.

Irmsher, Karen. *School Size.* ERIC Digest No. 113. Eugene, OR: ERIC Clearinghouse on Educational Management, 1997.

Lee, V. E., and J. B. Smith. "High School Size: Which Works Best and for Whom?" *Educational Evaluation and Policy Analysis* 19 (1997): 205–227.

Meier, D. W. "The Big Benefits of Smallness." *Educational Leadership* 54, 1 (1996): 12–15.

Mitchell, S. "Jack and the Giant School." *The New Rules* 2, 1 (Summer 2000). [Electronic journal]. Available at www.newrules.org/journal/nrsum00schools.htm.

Raywid, M. A. *Current Literature on Small Schools.* Charleston, WV: ERIC Clearinghouse on Rural Education and Small Schools, 1999.

Shorr, A. A., and J. E. Hon. "They Said It Couldn't Be Done: Implementing a Career Academy Program for a Diverse High School Population." *Journal of Education for Students Placed at Risk* 4 (1999): 379–391.

Steifel, L., P. Iatarola, N. Fruchter, and R. Berne. "High School Size: Effects on Budgets and Performance in New York City." *Educational Evaluation and Policy Analysis* 22, 1 (Spring 2000).

U.S. Department of Education. *An Overview of Smaller Learning Communities in High Schools.* Office of Elementary and Secondary Education and Office of Vocational and Adult Education. Washington, DC: Author, November 2001.

Wasley, P. A., M. Fine, R. M. Gladden, and others. *Small Schools, Great Strides: A Study of New Small Schools in Chicago.* New York: Bank Street College Education, 20 June 2000.

Whitaker, K. S. "Implementation Processes, Structures, and Barriers to High School Restructuring: A Case Study." *Journal of School Leadership* 8 (1998): 504–532.

BUREAUCRACY AND ORGANIZATIONAL NETWORKS

Blau, Peter. *Bureaucracy in Modern Society*. New York: Random House, 1956.

Blau, Peter M. "Decentralization in Bureaucracies." In M. N. Zald, ed. *Power in Organizations*. Nashville, TN: Vanderbilt University Press, 1970.

Corwin, Ronald G. *Education in Crisis*. New York: John Wiley & Sons, 1975.

Corwin, Ronald G. "Patterns of Organizational Control and Teacher Militancy: Theoretical Continuities in the Idea of Loose Coupling." In Ronald G. Corwin, ed. *Research in the Sociology of Education and Socialization* 2. Greenwich, CT: JAI Press, 1981: 261–291.

Namboodiri, Krishnan, and Ronald G. Corwin. *The Logic and Method of Macro Sociology: An Input-Output Approach to Organizational Networks*. Westport, CT: Praeger, 1993.

DISTRICT-OPERATED CHARTER SCHOOLS IN A SEGREGATED SOCIETY

Cashin, Sheryll. *The Failures of Integration: How Race and Class Are Undermining the American Dream*. New York: Public Affairs, 2004.

Deschenes, Sarah, David Tyack, and Larry Cuban. "Mismatch: Historical Perspectives on Schools and Students Who Don't Fit Them." *Teachers College Record* 103, 4 (November 2001).

Fears, Darryl. "Schools' Racial Isolation Growing." *Washington Post*, 18 July 2001, A–3.

Grossman, Kate N., Becky Beaupre, and Rosalind Rossi. "Poorest Kids Often Wind Up with the Weakest Teachers." *Chicago Sun-Times*, 7 September 2001.

Hanushek, Eric A., John F. Kain, and Steven G. Rivkin. *Why Public Schools Lose Teachers*. Cambridge, MA: National Bureau of Economic Research, November 2001.

Lewis Mumford Center for Comparative Urban and Regional Research. "Choosing Segregation: Racial Imbalance in American Public Schools, 1990–2000," 29 March 2002. Available at www.albany.edu/mumford/reports.

Lewis Mumford Center for Comparative Urban and Regional Research. "The New Ethnic Enclaves in America's Suburbs," 9 July 2001. Available at www.albany.edu/mumford/reports.

Lockwood, Anne T. *Who Prepares Your Teachers? The Debate over Alternative Certification*. Arlington, VA: American Association of School Administrators, February 2002.

Orfield, Gary. *Schools More Separate: Consequences of a Decade of Resegregation*. Cambridge, MA: The Civil Rights Project, Harvard University, July 2001.

The Southeast Center for Teaching Quality. *Recruiting Teachers for Hard-to-Staff Schools: Solutions for the Southeast and the Nation*. Chapel Hill, NC: Author, January 2002.

Index

About the Authors

RONALD G. CORWIN is a Professor Emeritus of Sociology at Ohio State University, where he taught during most of his career. He has also taught at Teachers College, Columbia University, and served as director of basic research in the U.S. Department of Education. He has been a vice president of the American Educational Research Association and has held elected positions in the American Sociological Research Association. Author or co-author of fifteen books and two dozen contributed chapters, he also edited a series of books on educational research. His work has appeared in the *American Sociological Review* and other sociological journals, including *Sociology of Education,* for which he served as an associate editor.

Colleagues in the discipline voted him one of the five individuals who have made the greatest contributions to the growth and development of the sociology of education and one of the top contributors to the field of educational administration. For over a decade, Professor Corwin has been following the school choice movement, and previously has published a dozen monographs and articles on the topic.

E. JOSEPH SCHNEIDER serves as Distinguished Senior Fellow, National Policy Board for Educational Administration, Washington, DC, and for the past ten years he was the Deputy Executive Director of the American Association of School Administrators (AASA). He has also served as President of Leadership Development Resources, an educational consulting company based in Arlington, VA. From 2000 to 2004 he was Executive Secretary of the National Policy Board for Educational Administration, a coalition of ten national education associations. For fifteen years he was the CEO of a Washington-based education association that represents university-based research centers and nonprofit educational agencies.

Schneider is author or co-author of twelve books, including *Exploding the Myth: Another Round in the Education Reform Debate, Ensuring the Reality of School Reform,* and *Educational Administrator's Communication Handbook* (forthcoming). He is also author of seventeen papers, including "A Cautionary Word About Charters."